IMAGES of America

NEW LONDON COUNTY TROLLEYS

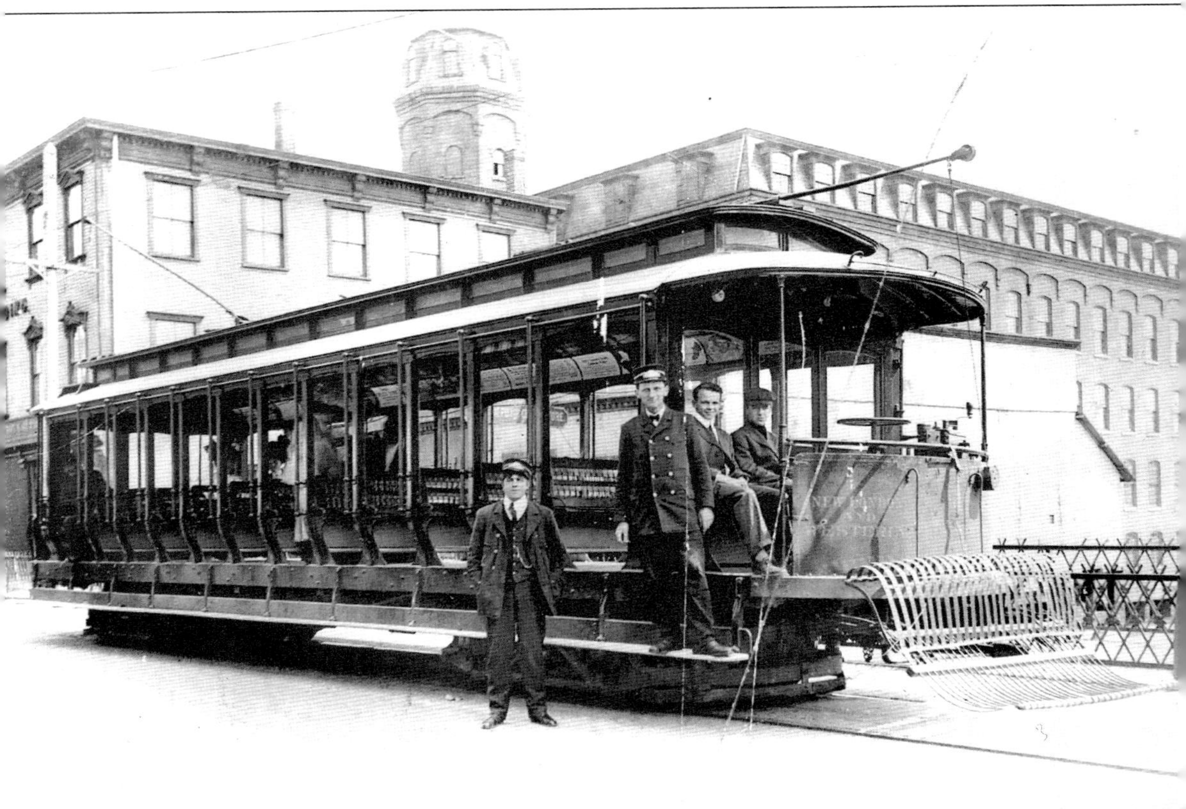

Streetcar systems helped form the face of many eastern Connecticut towns and cities. This picture shows Groton and Stonington Street Railway car No. 19 in front of the Ponemah Mills building in the Taftville section of Norwich. This building can still be seen today and is an impressive example of 1890s architecture. The Jewett Car Company built this open car in 1904.

IMAGES
of America

NEW LONDON COUNTY TROLLEYS

Connecticut Motor Coach Museum

ARCADIA PUBLISHING

Copyright © 2004 by Connecticut Motor Coach Museum
ISBN 978-0-7385-3580-7

Published by Arcadia Publishing
Charleston, South Carolina

Printed in the United States of America

Library of Congress Control Number: 2004101538

For all general information, please contact Arcadia Publishing:
Telephone 843-853-2070
Fax 843-853-0044
E-mail sales@arcadiapublishing.com
For customer service and orders:
Toll-Free 1-888-313-2665

Visit us on the Internet at www.arcadiapublishing.com

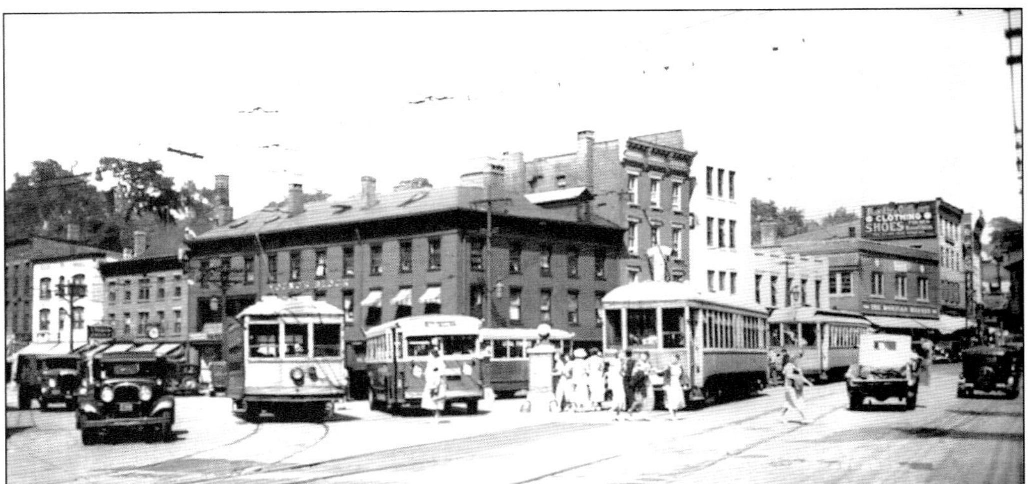

In this 1936 photograph of Franklin Square in Norwich, transportation by trolley car, bus, and car can clearly be seen.

Contents

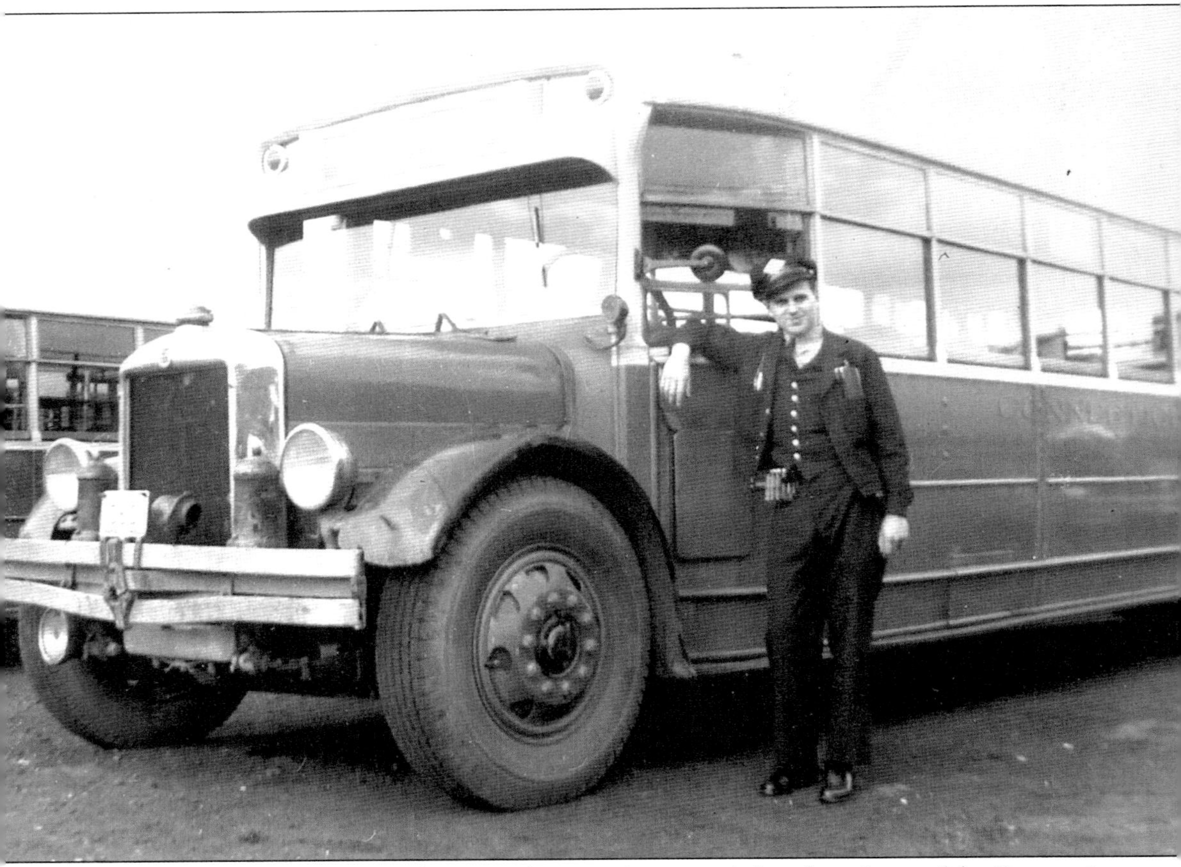

Horace Bromley is shown in this 1940 photograph as a newly hired employee of the Connecticut Company with a Model Z240 Yellow Coach.

This book is dedicated to Horace D. Bromley (1918–1990), who faithfully photographed the operation of the Connecticut Company in the Norwich area. All of the photographs in this book are from the Bromley Collection.

Bromley was born in Norwich and lived there until 1940, when he took a job with the Connecticut Company in Hartford as a streetcar operator and later as a bus driver. When he retired in 1984, after 44 years of service, he was the last bus driver on the roster to run streetcars.

Without Horace Bromley's dedication to streetcar history, the photographs shown in this book would not exist today.

The proceeds from the sale of this book will go directly to the Connecticut Motor Coach Museum in East Windsor to maintain their collection of historic motor coaches.

—Alan J. Walker
President

Connecticut Motor Coach Museum
P.O. Box 297
East Windsor, CT 06088
(860) 623-4732

Introduction

The first Europeans in eastern Connecticut settled New London in 1646, followed by Norwich in 1660, Preston in 1687, Putnam in 1693, and Plainfield in 1699. Puritans made up most of the population, and they lived close to their houses of worship. Every morning, the farmers walked to their fields and returned home at night. Rarely did anyone travel outside the village.

By the 1860s, many farms were abandoned as the land was worn out, and the owners moved on to Ohio, Indiana, and Illinois. Those who were left turned to the quickly developing textile industry in eastern Connecticut for work. There was little need for people to travel very far from home, as most now lived in company housing located right at the mill complex. People, including the mill managers who also lived in company housing, walked to work. At this time, stagecoach service was almost the only way to travel, unless one wanted to ride a horse. There was no system of public transportation.

The Norwich Horse Railroad was incorporated in 1864 and became the first public transportation system in New London County. New London followed with the New London Horse Railroad in 1886 and the Montville Horse Railroad in 1889. These lines were eventually electrified, with Norwich as the first in 1889.

The Peoples Tramway, started in 1893, was the first line in the Putnam area. In 1904, all the lines in Norwich, New London, Willimantic, and Putnam were merged into the Consolidated Railway Company, which had formally been called the Worcester and Connecticut Eastern Railway. The Consolidated Railway Company served as a holding company for most street railway properties owned or leased by the New Haven Railroad.

On May 31, 1907, the Consolidated Railway Company was merged into the New York, New Haven & Hartford Railroad Company (NYNH&H). On that same day, the Thomaston Tramway, located in Western Connecticut, changed its name to the Connecticut Company. The Connecticut Company then entered into an agreement with the NYNH&H to operate all its owned and leased street railway lines in Connecticut. On February 28, 1910, all the street railway properties of the NYNH&H in the state of Connecticut were conveyed to the Connecticut Company.

Lack of good roads and the high cost of automobiles helped keep the streetcar lines relatively prosperous from 1900 through World War I. During that time, wages in the mills began to rise above the subsistence level, and for the first time since the Puritans settled in eastern Connecticut, families actually had extra money to spend. They could travel by streetcar to Norwich and New

London to shop in stores not available in the small villages. Some people actually spent 70¢ to ride from New London or Norwich all the way to Worcester, Massachusetts.

With this extra money, people were looking for things to do on the weekends. The trolley companies were also looking for a way to increase the profit on their cars by getting weekend riders. Trolley parks were built as a destination at the end of many lines, in places such as Franklin and Dayville. These parks featured things such as picnic groves, ballparks, and dance halls.

In 1914, an investigation was opened by the Interstate Commerce Commission into the business dealings of the New Haven Railroad. Some company officers were indicted for conspiracy to violate antitrust laws. The company had already been forced to dispose of extensive street railway holdings in Massachusetts and had received an offer from the Shoreline Electric Railway to lease all of its eastern Connecticut streetcar lines. On July 7, 1913, the New London, Norwich, and Putnam divisions were leased to the Shoreline Electric Railway for 99 years. The lease included almost 90 miles of track, 134 cars, and five carbarns, all for an annual rental of $247,500.

The eastern lines now joined the Shoreline Electric Railway, which operated a line from Stony Creek in Branford to New London, with a branch to Essex. It also connected with the New Haven division of the Connecticut Company at Stony Creek. The lease agreement for the eastern lines included an option to buy the property within 10 years for $4,650,000. The eastern lines were actually quite valuable to the Shoreline Electric Railway because they enabled the company to connect with lines in Worcester and Rhode Island. It was actually possible to travel from New York City all the way to Boston through either Worcester or Providence.

The schedules and routes of the lines in New London County remained the same under the ownership of the Shoreline Electric Railway as they had been under the Connecticut Company. The only real change was the green paint applied to the formerly yellow cars. During this period, the basic fare was 5¢, with additional charges for traveling between divisions. By the end of 1919, however, the fortunes of the Shoreline Electric Railway began to decline. This was caused by two severe accidents during the year and a labor strike in July 1919. Wages had climbed considerably, from 30¢ per hour in 1915 to 42¢ per hour in 1918; a 40 percent increase in three years. Fares did not keep up with the cost of wages, and the Shoreline Electric Railway was forced to declare bankruptcy late in 1919. The Shoreline receiver asked the court to void the lease with the Connecticut Company. This became effective April 1, 1920, when control of the New London, Norwich, and Putnam lines was transferred back to the Connecticut Company.

By 1920, the trolley business was not doing as well as the New Haven Railroad had anticipated. Operating expenses had increased considerably, especially the cost of electricity to operate the lines in eastern Connecticut. The generating station at Dyer Dam, north of Norwich, had seen better days. The plant was no longer able to generate electricity using its water turbines, as the equipment had deteriorated, and the only source of power was the steam plant that was much more costly to operate than the water turbine. The company was forced to purchase electricity from the Eastern Connecticut Power Company, a predecessor of the Connecticut Light and Power Company. Very costly repairs were made to put the water turbine back on line to avoid paying high commercial electric rates.

All this caused the management to look very closely at the cost of operating the lightly patronized lines north of Tafts Junction. The first line to have service discontinued, the Moosup line from Central Village, had one car that met all cars from Norwich and Putnam. The line was abandoned in November 1925. The next service to be discontinued was the entire Putnam division from Norwich to Putnam in December of the same year.

By 1934, the Connecticut Company was losing more than $1,000,000 a year statewide. Only the Hartford division showed a profit. The New Haven division broke even, while all the other divisions lost money. By then, the New Haven Railroad had entered bankruptcy and could no longer carry the debt of its subsidiary, the Connecticut Company.

This was the beginning of the end of streetcar service in most of Connecticut. The cost of operating a bus was actually more than a streetcar, but the cost of maintaining the track, overhead wire, and power distribution systems was not required with buses. The business decision was made to discontinue all streetcar operations except for the Hartford and New Haven divisions. All the local New London lines stopped service in 1932, and the entire Norwich-New London division was converted to motor coach by the end of 1936.

All the surplus cars were disposed of in 1937. Some wooden cars, apart from the wheels, were sold to local residents for use as summer cottages. A few newer steel cars were moved to New Haven on flatcars. The rest of the fleet was scrapped in Norwich.

One car that operated in eastern Connecticut still exists. Car No. 65, built by the Wason Manufacturing Company in 1905, operated on the Putnam and Norwich divisions until sometime in the 1920s. At that time, it was transferred to the Hartford division, where it operated until the end of service in July 1941. It was than acquired by the Connecticut Trolley Museum, which was incorporated in 1940 to help preserve street railway history in Connecticut. Car No. 65 was moved to the museum grounds in East Windsor in 1941, where it remains to this day. The car is occasionally operated for the public. It is one of the few physical reminders of the street railway era in eastern Connecticut.

The entire Norwich-New London motor coach operation was sold to a private operator in 1961. The private operator, Thames Valley Transit, went out of the bus business in 1968. Service today is provided by a public agency, Southeastern Area Transit (SEAT).

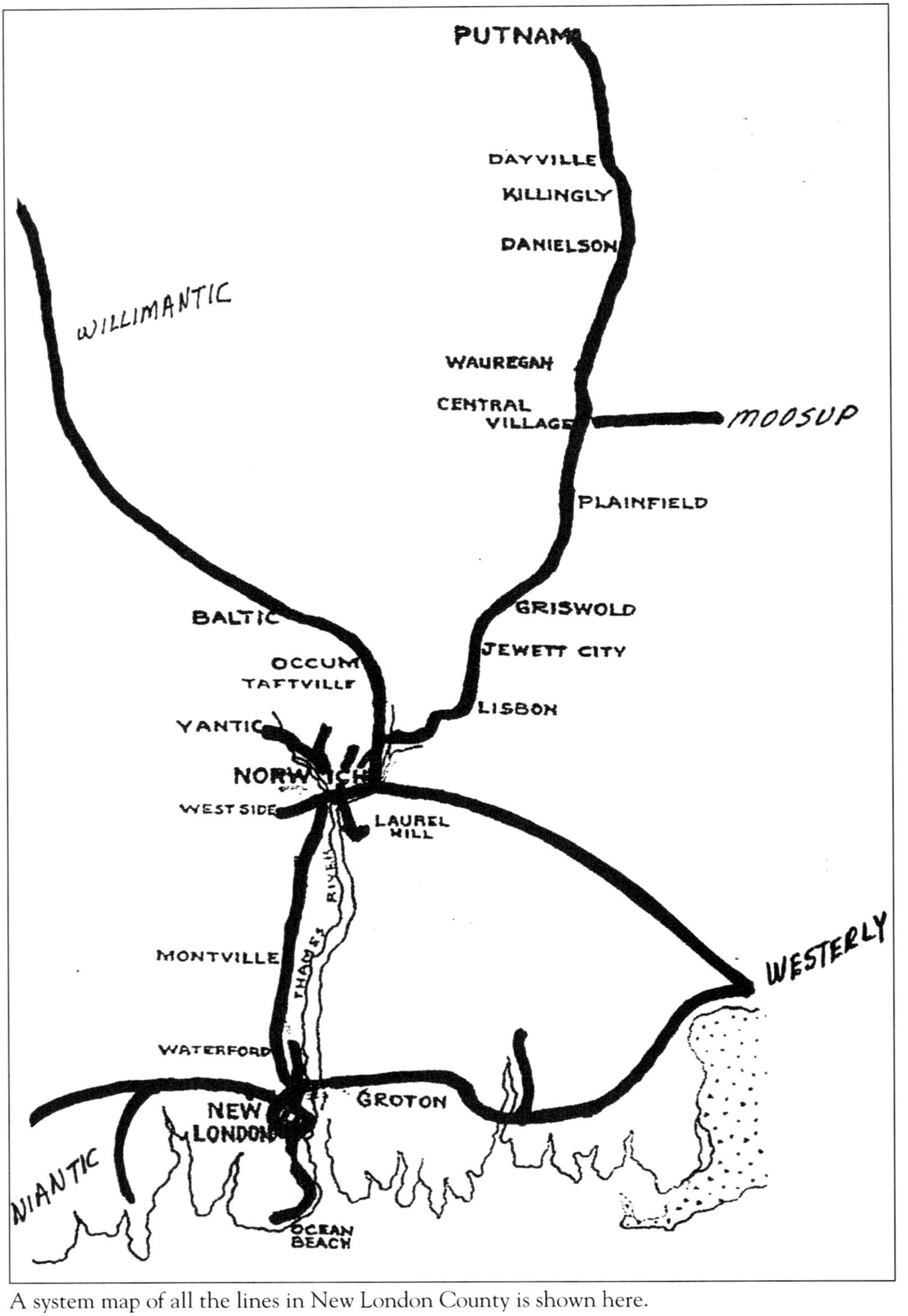

A system map of all the lines in New London County is shown here.

One

New London Lines

The New London Horse Railroad was chartered in 1888 to build lines in the city of New London. In June 1893, its name was changed to the New London Street Railway, and lines were built to Ocean Beach, Jefferson Avenue, Post Hill, and Broad Street.

The Montville Horse Railroad was chartered in 1889 and renamed the Montville Street Railway in 1895. Their charter allowed them to build a line on the west side of the Thames River to connect New London and Norwich.

In September 1904, the New London Street Railway was sold to the Consolidated Railway Company, a subsidiary of the powerful New York, New Haven & Hartford Railroad, who also acquired the Montville Street Railway. Just like the Norwich lines, the operation of streetcars in New London was no longer economically feasible for the Connecticut Company after the 1920s. New London service on the Ocean Beach, Post Hill, Jefferson Avenue, and Broad Street lines was converted to bus on April 11, 1932. The former Montville Street Railway line from New London to Norwich continued to run until March 1934, when it too was converted to bus.

The Connecticut Company sold the bus operation to Thames Valley Transit in 1961. In 1968, Thames Valley was succeeded by a public transit agency, Southeastern Area Transit. New London lines operated out of a carbarn on Montauk Avenue from the early horsecar days until the end of streetcar service in 1934.

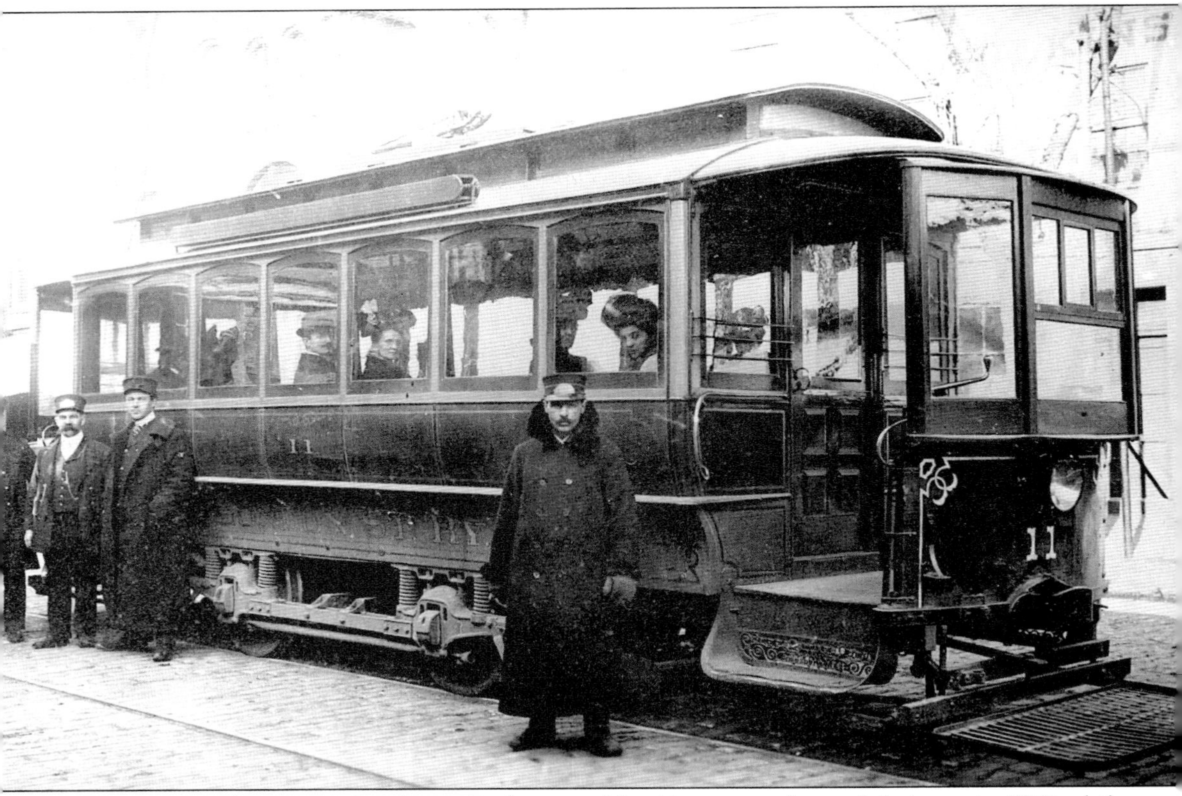

The crew of New London Street Railway car No. 11 poses in front of their car in 1893 while stopped at the Parade in New London. The car was built in 1892 for the New London Street Railway by the Briggs Carriage Company of Amesbury, Massachusetts. This was one of the first streetcars purchased by this company.

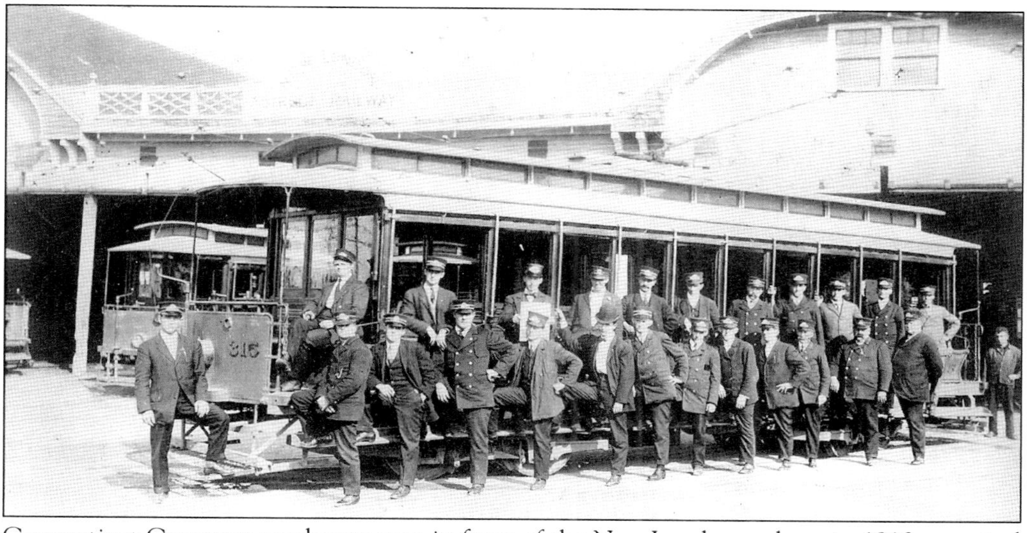

Connecticut Company employees pose in front of the New London carbarn in 1910, a typical scene of the era.

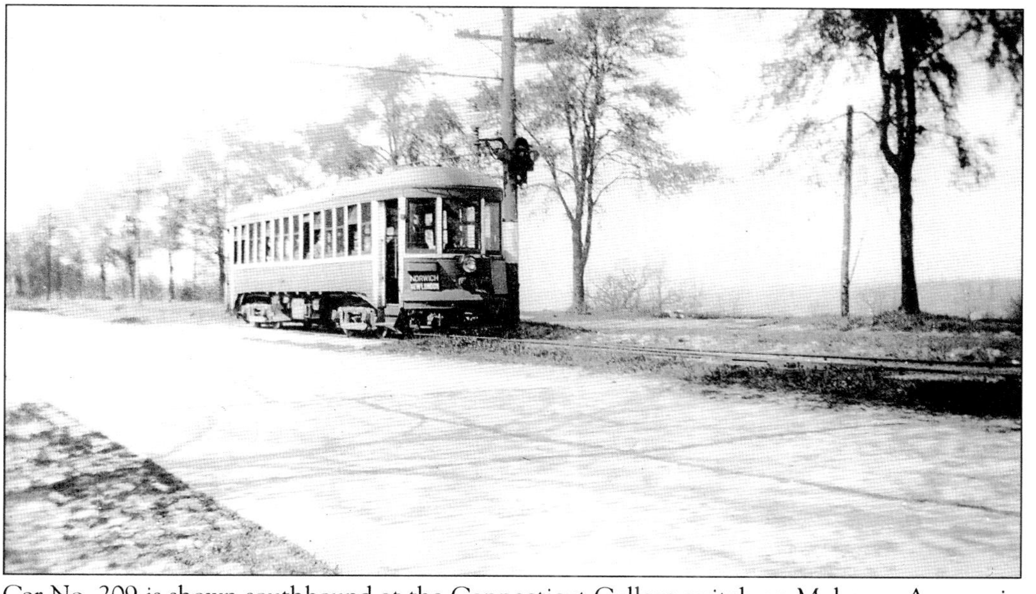

Car No. 209 is shown southbound at the Connecticut College switch on Mohegan Avenue in this May 1933 view.

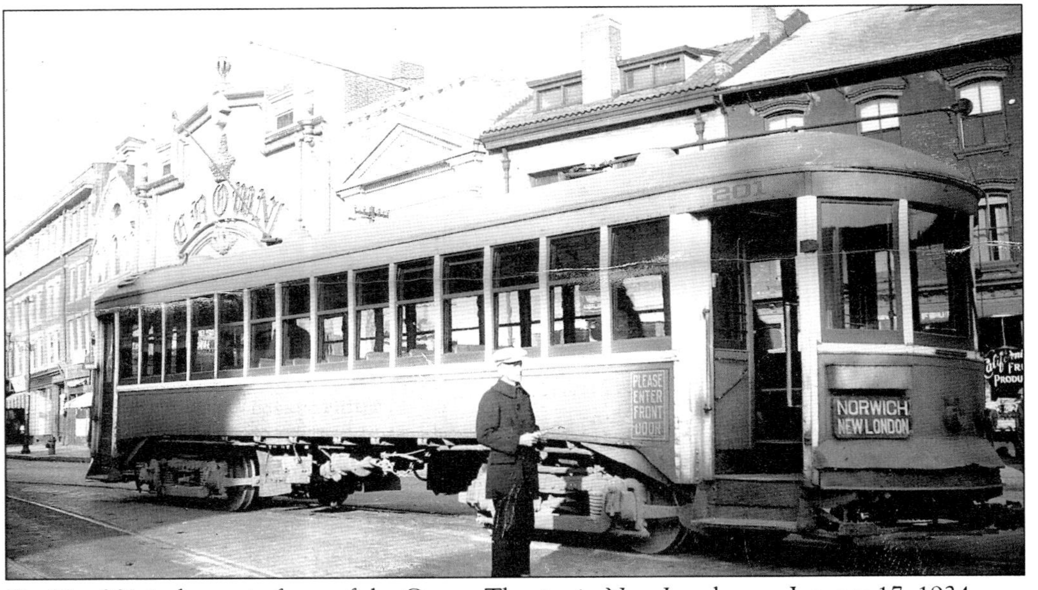

Car No. 201 is shown in front of the Crown Theater in New London on January 17, 1934.

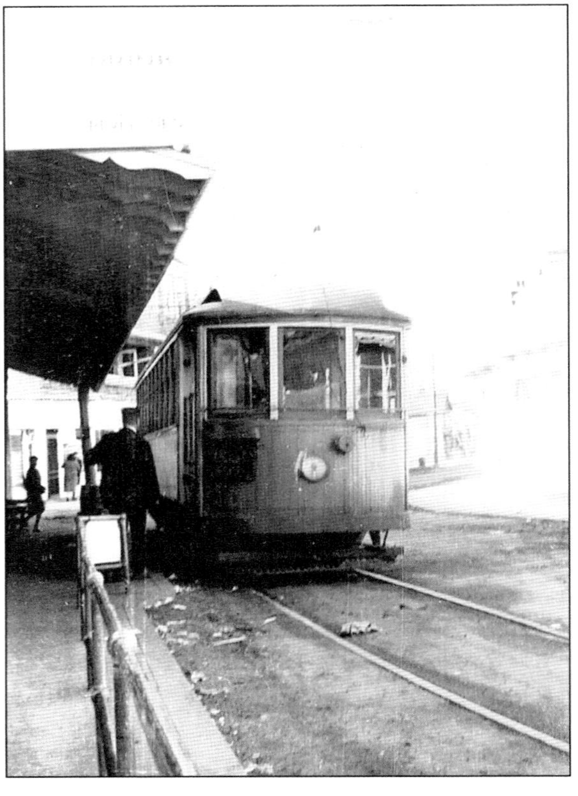

This car is waiting for passengers at the Ocean Beach terminal.

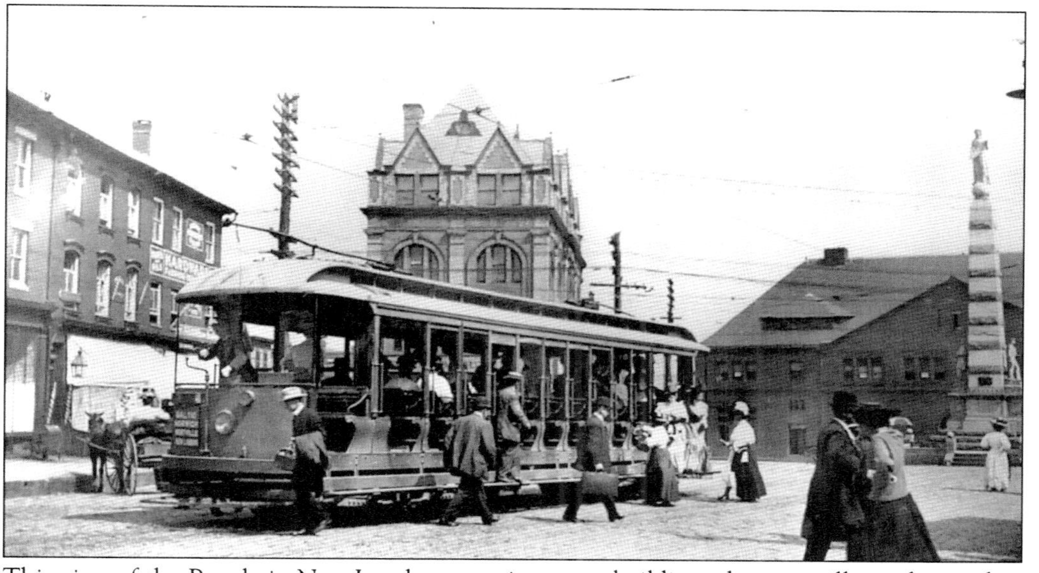

This view of the Parade in New London contains many buildings that are still standing today, including the railroad station, which is still used by Amtrak and commuter trains. The 13-bench open car, a favorite of riders in the summer, will leave shortly for Norwich and Baltic.

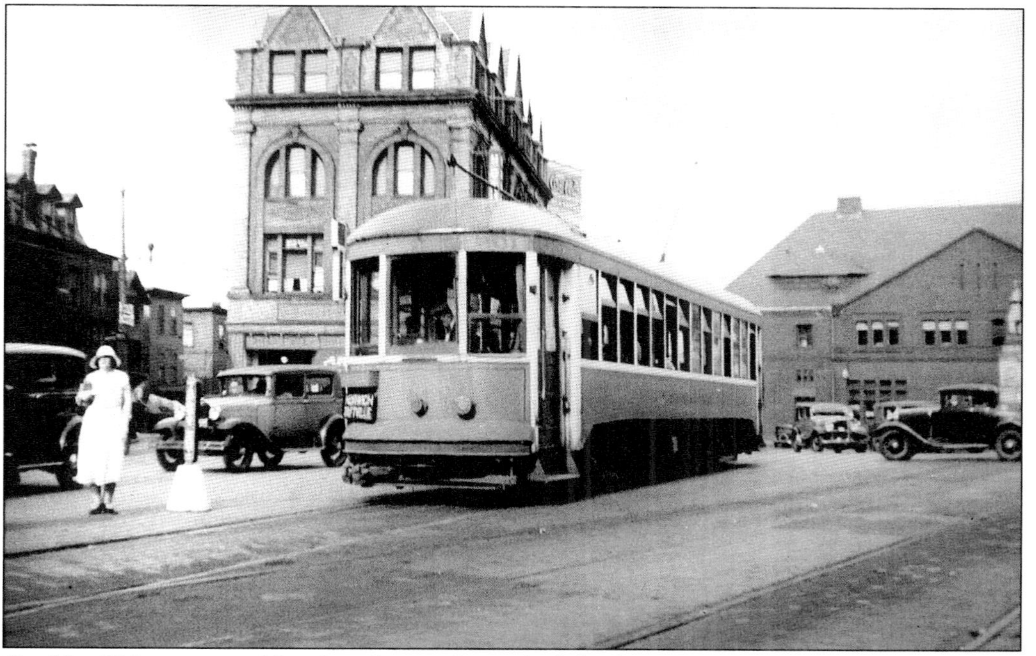

Car No. 201 is seen in New London at the end of the line in 1933. Operations on this line ceased in 1934.

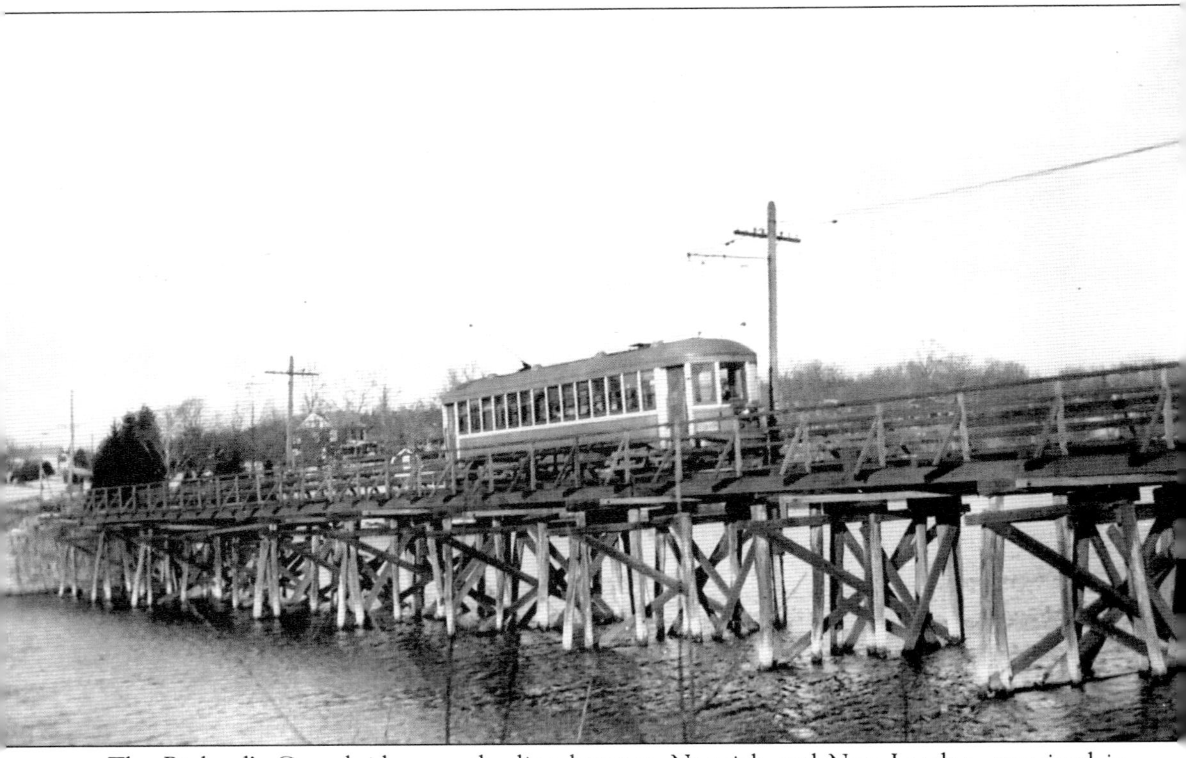

The Richard's Cove bridge, on the line between Norwich and New London, remained in operation until March 18, 1934, when the line switched to service by bus. All other lines in this area had been converted to bus in 1932.

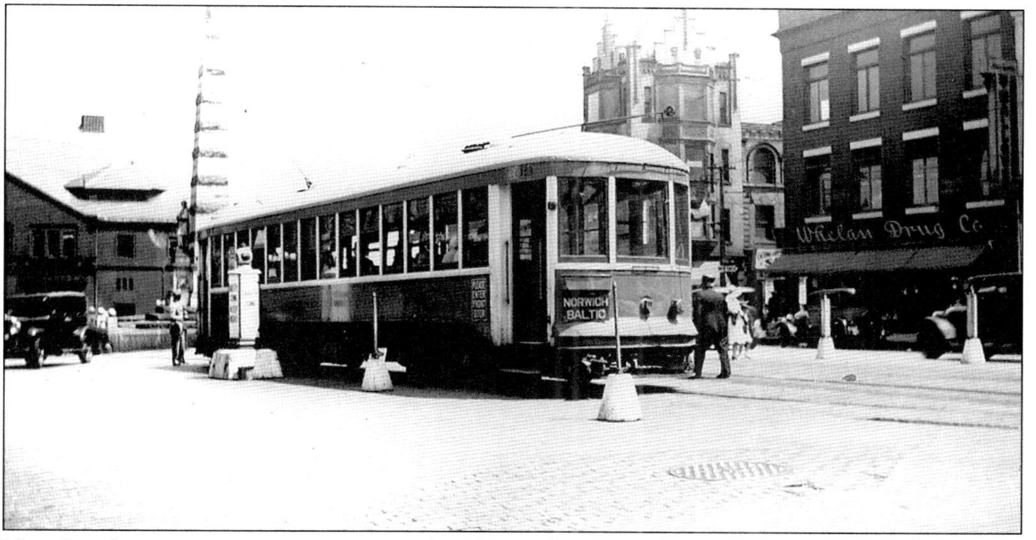

New London saw streetcar service until 1934, as shown in this picture featuring several well-known structures.

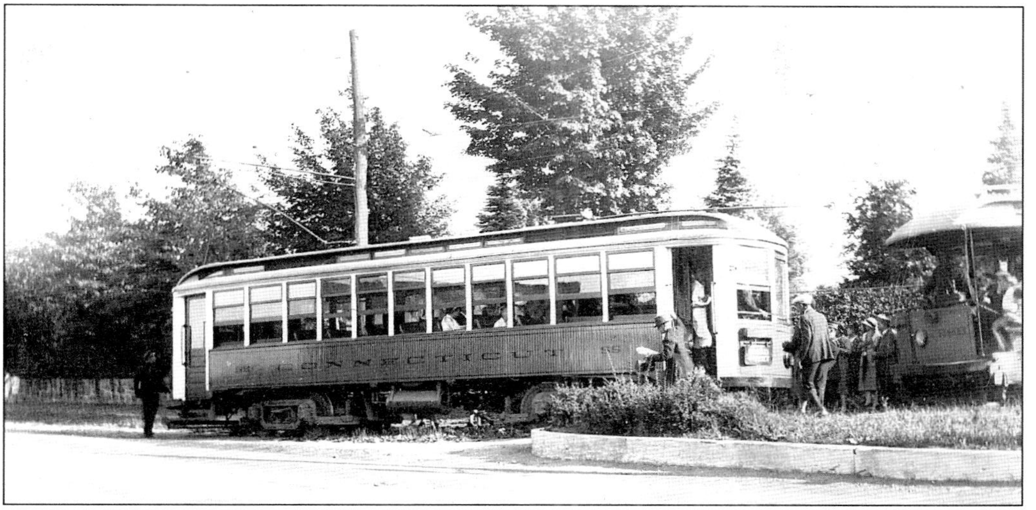

Car No. 155, shown here in New London in August 1930, was built by the Wason Manufacturing Company in 1901. It originally served with the Putnam division.

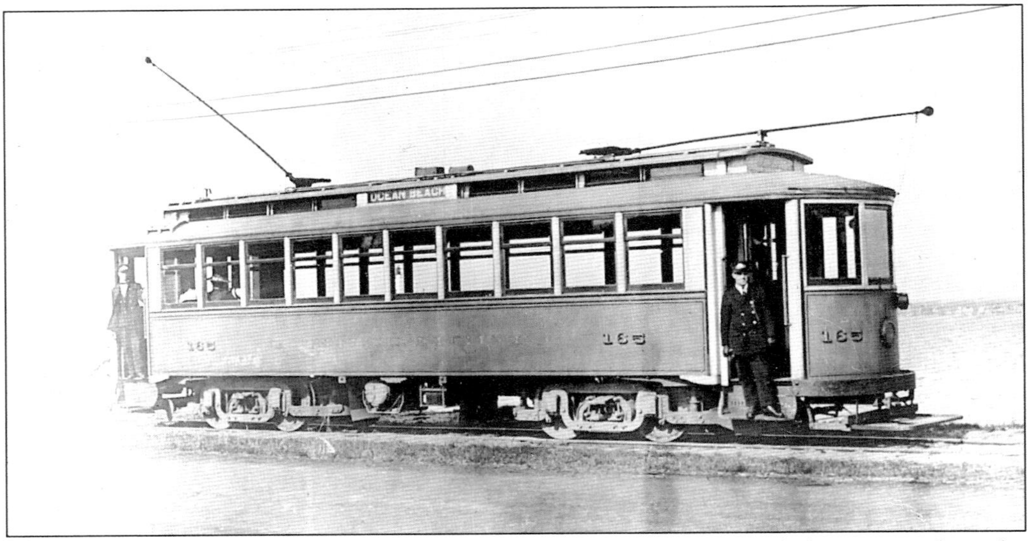

Many of the trolley lines had amusement parks at one end. This provided an escape from the city for many, was a good use of equipment, and provided revenue for the streetcar company. Car No. 165, shown in this photograph, is on the Ocean Beach line in New London.

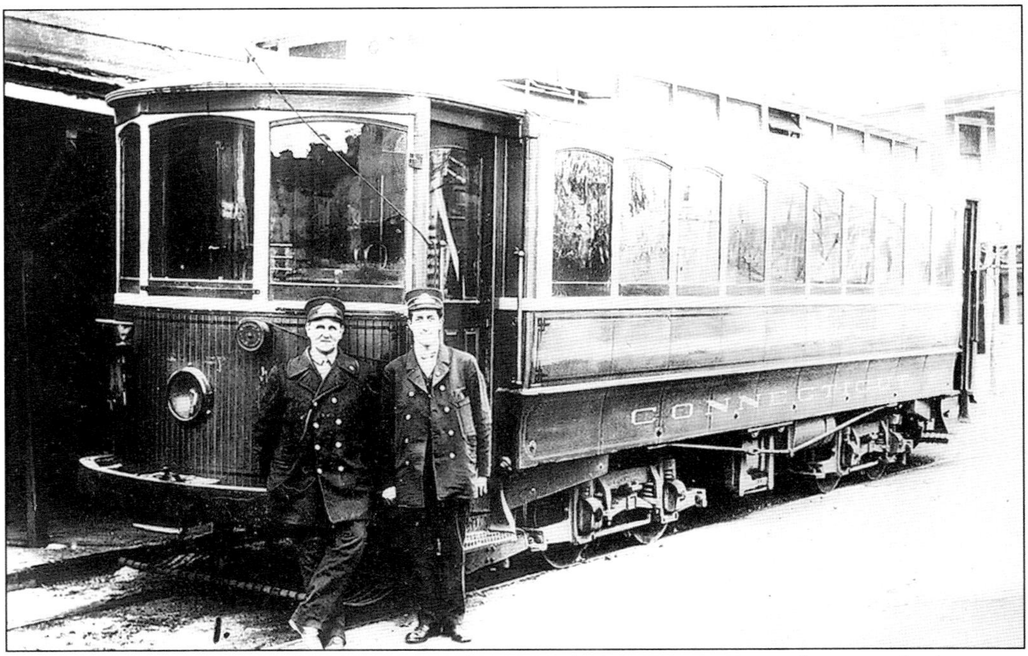

At the end of the line at the Ocean Beach terminal, this crew waits to depart with their car. The car, which originally operated in Bridgeport, was built by the J. G. Brill Company of Philadelphia, Pennsylvania, in 1900. It was destroyed in the 1916 fire at the Thamesville barn.

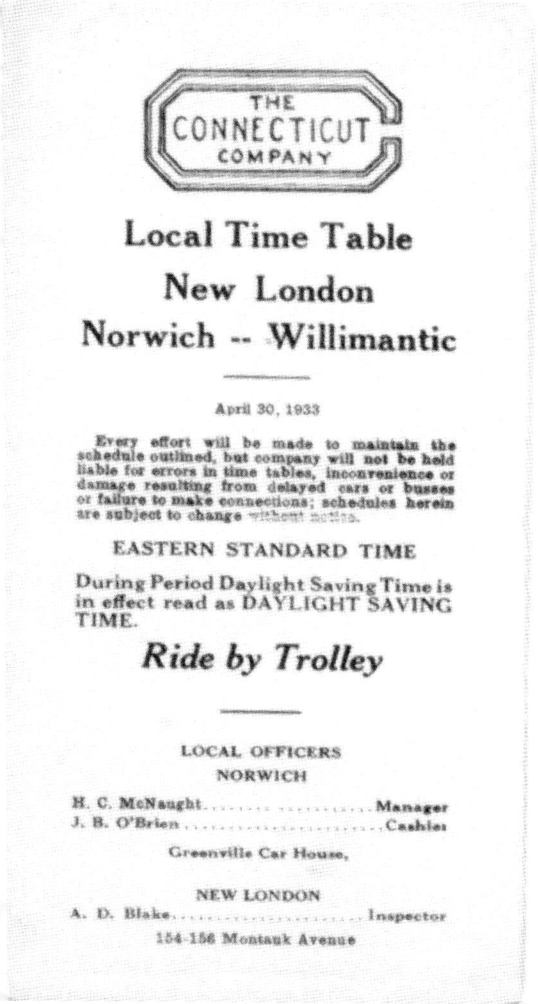

THE CONNECTICUT COMPANY

Local Time Table

New London

Norwich -- Willimantic

April 30, 1933

Every effort will be made to maintain the schedule outlined, but company will not be held liable for errors in time tables, inconvenience or damage resulting from delayed cars or busses or failure to make connections; schedules herein are subject to change without notice.

EASTERN STANDARD TIME

During Period Daylight Saving Time is in effect read as DAYLIGHT SAVING TIME.

Ride by Trolley

LOCAL OFFICERS

NORWICH

H. C. McNaught.................... Manager

J. B. O'Brien.......................... Cashier

Greenville Car House,

NEW LONDON

A. D. Blake.......................... Inspector

154-156 Montauk Avenue

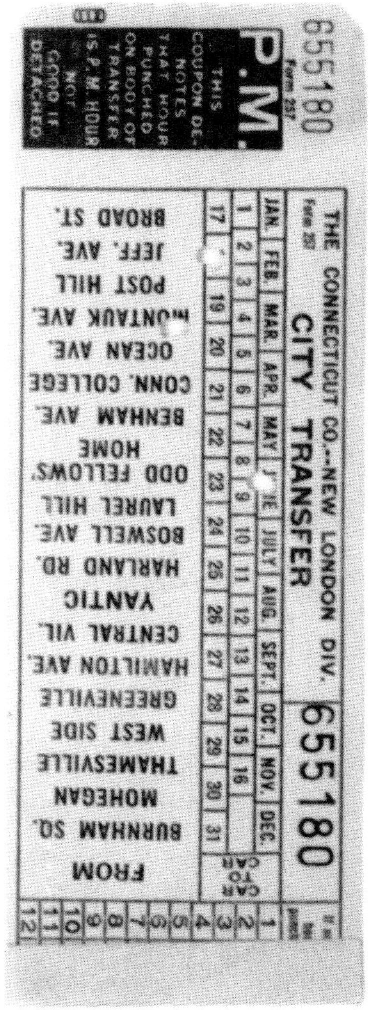

This New London division transfer was used when the passenger had to ride on more than one line to reach his destination. Note the transfer is punched, indicating this was used on June 18 starting at Montauk Avenue.

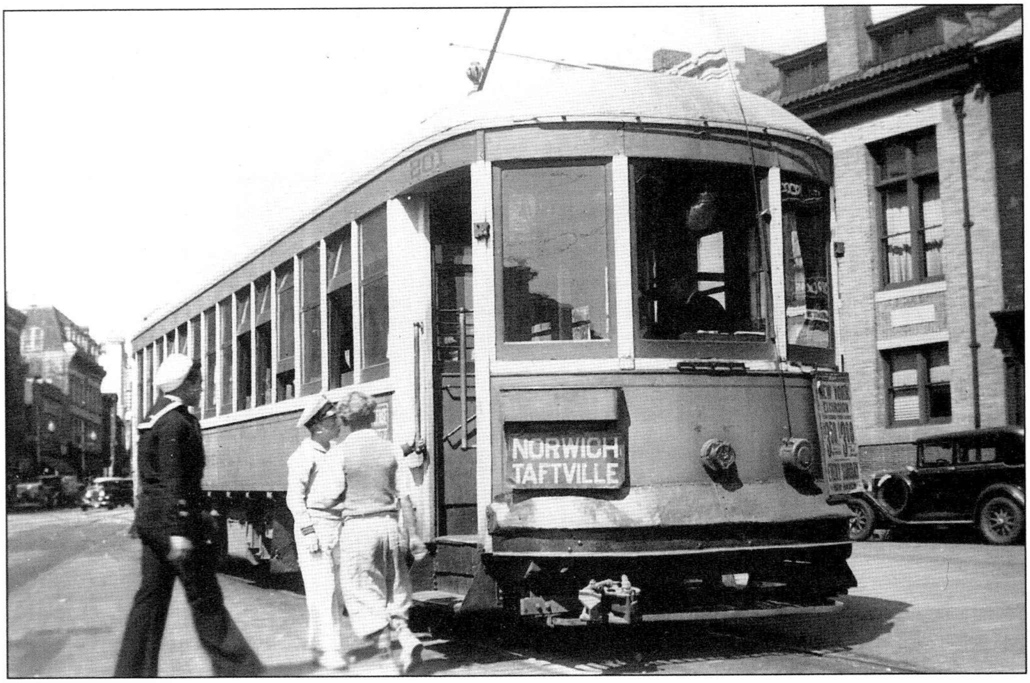

Car No. 201 is loading passengers, including some sailors who happen to be in town, to go from New London to Norwich.

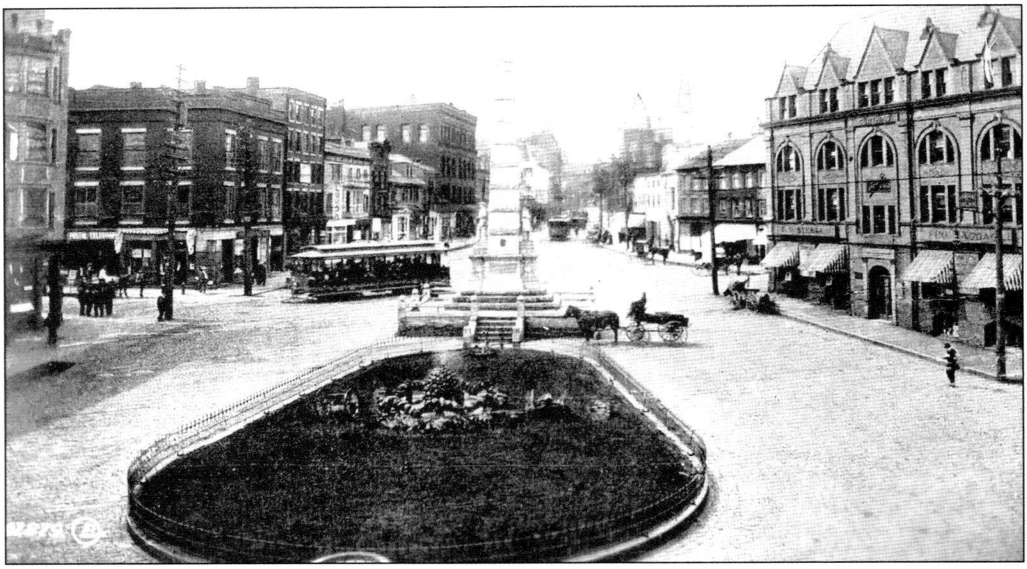

This New London and East Lyme Street Railway car, shown here on Bank Street in New London, would make the 12-mile trip to Niantic in about an hour. During the busy summer months, there was a car leaving New London for Niantic every 30 minutes.

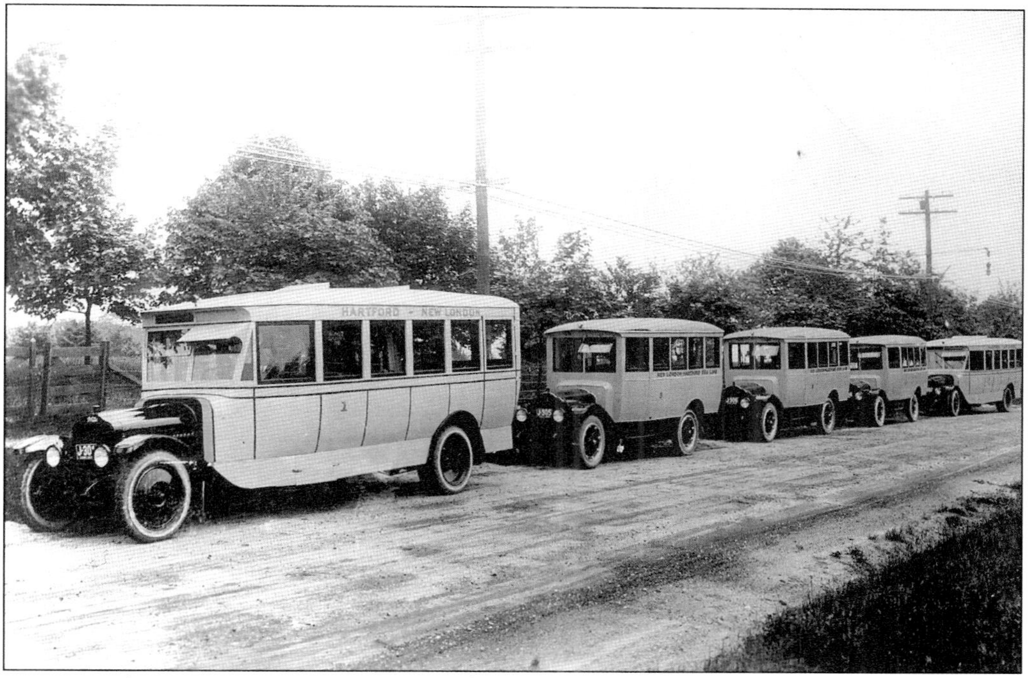

Motor coaches came early to New London, as seen in this 1921 view taken on Ocean Avenue. These are some of the first buses purchased by the Connecticut Company.

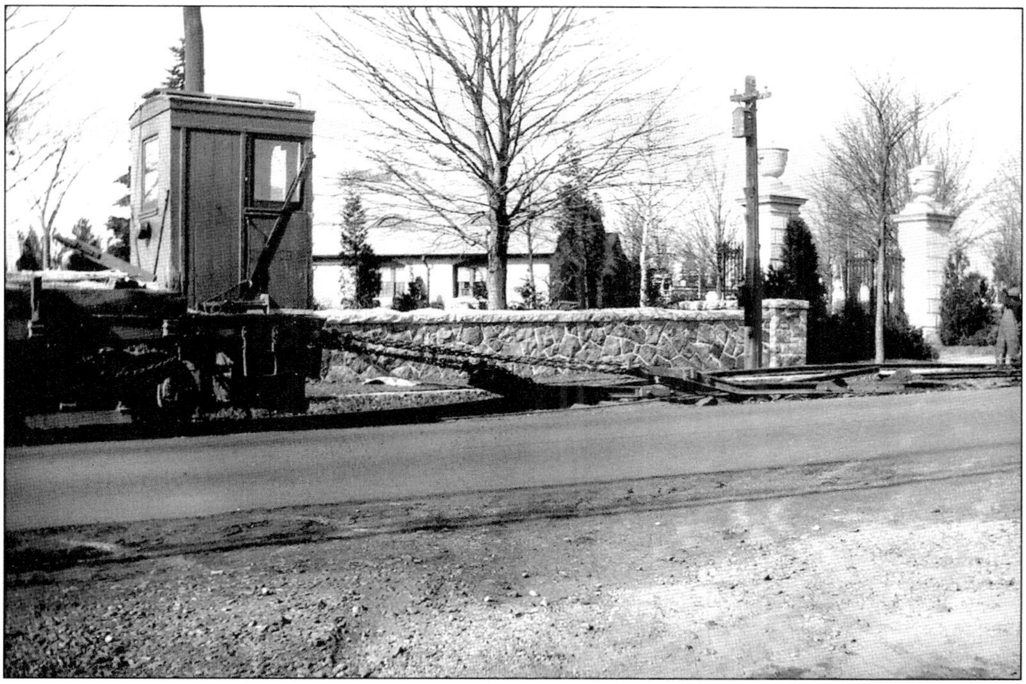

Work car No. 0335 is shown tearing up the track on Ocean Avenue in New London in 1932.

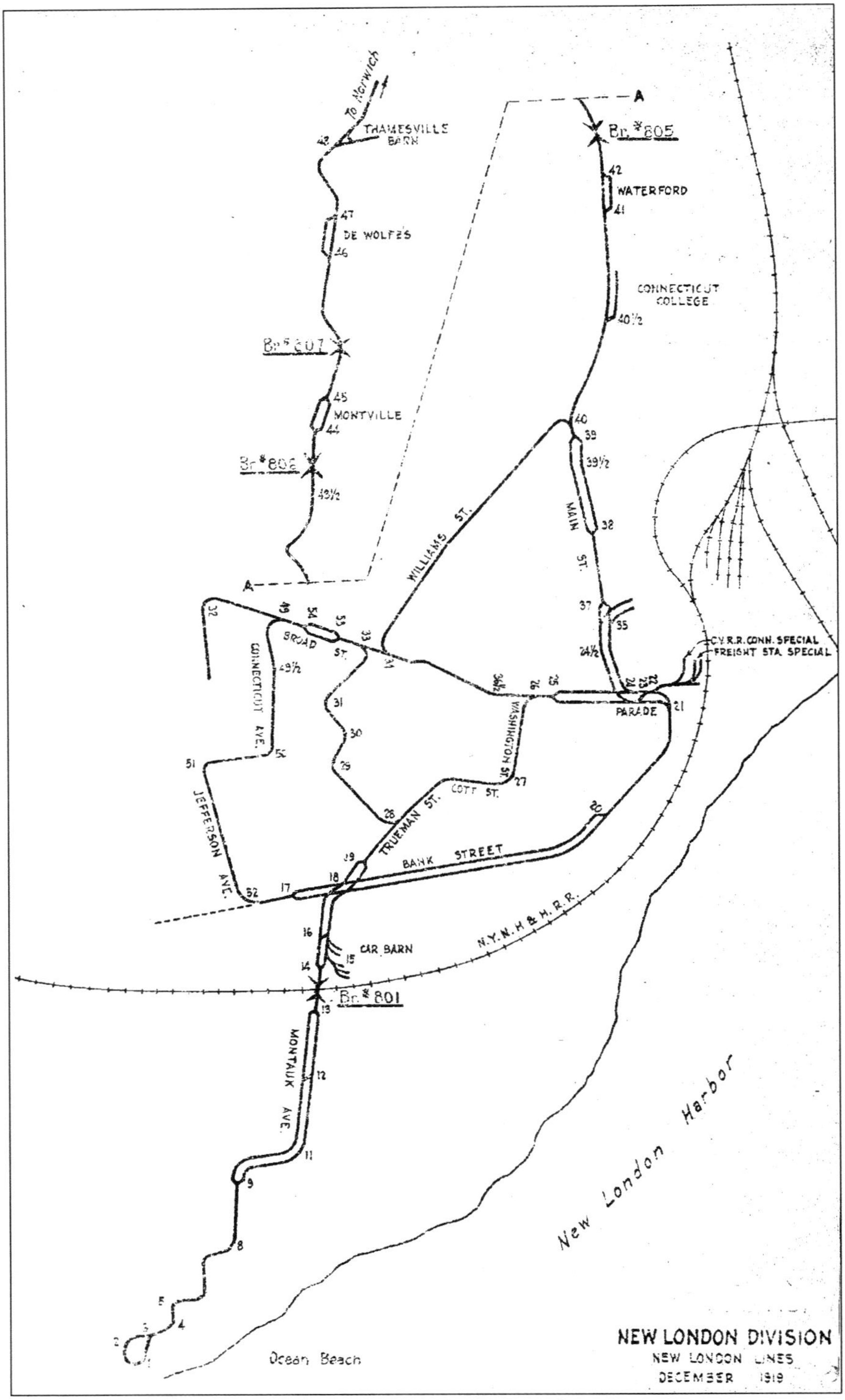

Downtown New London lines are pictured in December 1919.

Two

NORWICH LINES

In 1864, the Norwich Horse Railroad was incorporated and received a charter from the General Court, the predecessor to the General Assembly, to build a line from the center of Norwich to Greenville, then a separate town. It took the original investors years to raise the necessary capital, so construction did not actually start until 1870. The cars started to operate the same year. The line had nine horsecar drivers who worked on four miles of track. The business made only enough to cover operating expenses and was not sufficient to cover construction costs, so the line soon went bankrupt. In 1882, a new company was formed, the Norwich Street Railway Company, which purchased the assets of the former horsecar line.

In 1889, the Norwich Street Railway was given permission to electrify its lines from the public utilities commission. The Ponemah Mills Company, in the Taftville section of Norwich, had considerable waterpower available and was already generating enough electricity to power its mill buildings and still have excess electricity to sell. This relieved the street railway company of the expense of having to build its own power station. Following completion of the overhead wire construction, electric streetcars began to run in Norwich in 1892.

The Ponemah Mills Company also operated its own in-plant electric railway. This line ran from c. 1894 until 1965. The two pieces of equipment used in that operation are now at the Connecticut Trolley Museum in East Windsor.

By 1900, the Norwich trolley lines extended from Franklin Square nine miles to Baltic and five miles to Yantic, providing transportation for the employees of the large textile mills located there. Lines also ran to West Main Street, Boswell Avenue, and Laurel Hill, more residential sections of the city.

In September 1904, the Norwich Street Railway was sold to the Consolidated Railway Company, a subsidiary of the powerful New York, New Haven & Hartford Railroad for the astronomical sum, at that time, of $110 a share.

The Norwich lines, along with the other city lines in New London County, operated almost unchanged from World War I through the 1930s. In 1935, the parent of the Connecticut Company filed for bankruptcy and could no longer fund the deficits of its subsidiary. On May 19, 1936, the federal bankruptcy court in New Haven granted the Connecticut Company permission to spend $283,000 to purchase vehicles to convert the Norwich division to buses; by then, all the other lines had been converted to motor coach or abandoned.

The Norwich-New London operation of the Connecticut Company was sold to a private operator in 1961. The private operator, Thames Valley Transit, went out of the bus business in 1968 and was succeeded by a public agency, Southeastern Area Transit (SEAT). Most of the bus routes still follow the original routes of the streetcar days.

Norwich had two carbarns, one in the Greenville section—the primary facility for the Norwich-New London operations—and a smaller barn in the Thamesville section.

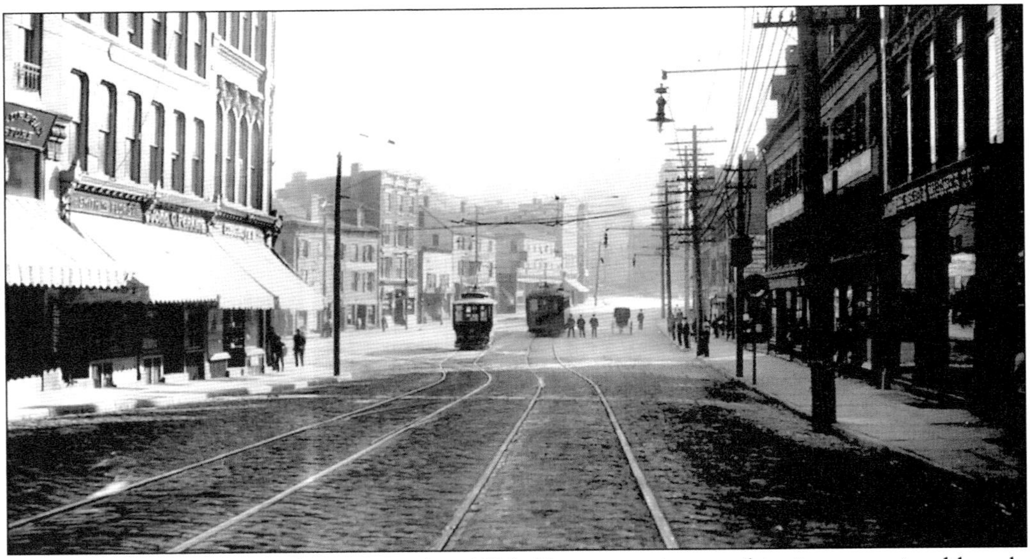

Franklin Square in Norwich is pictured *c.* 1895. Transportation, at this time, remained largely by horse and carriage or on foot. The lack of horse or foot traffic in this view suggests that the picture was taken on a Sunday.

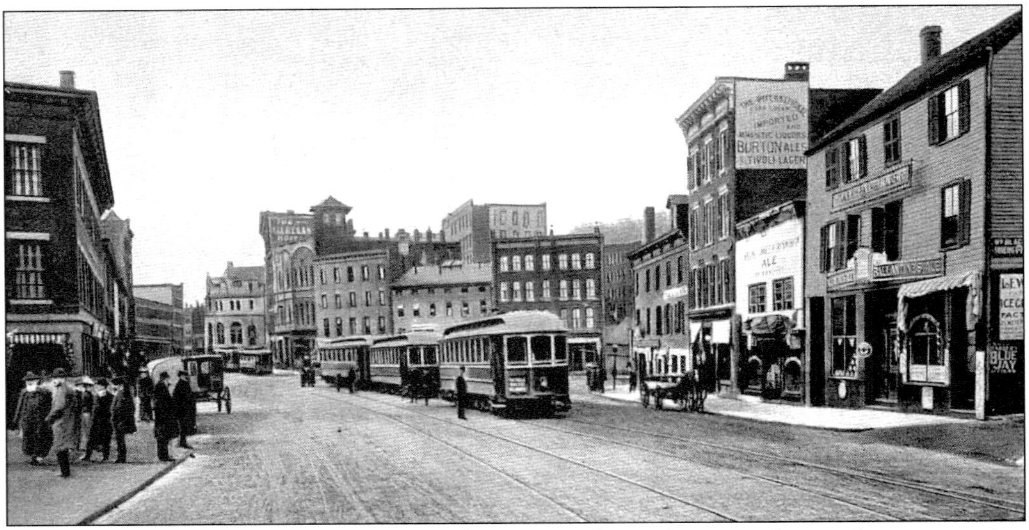

This postcard view of downtown Norwich *c.* 1909 shows the main forms of transportation available: trolley cars, horse, and foot.

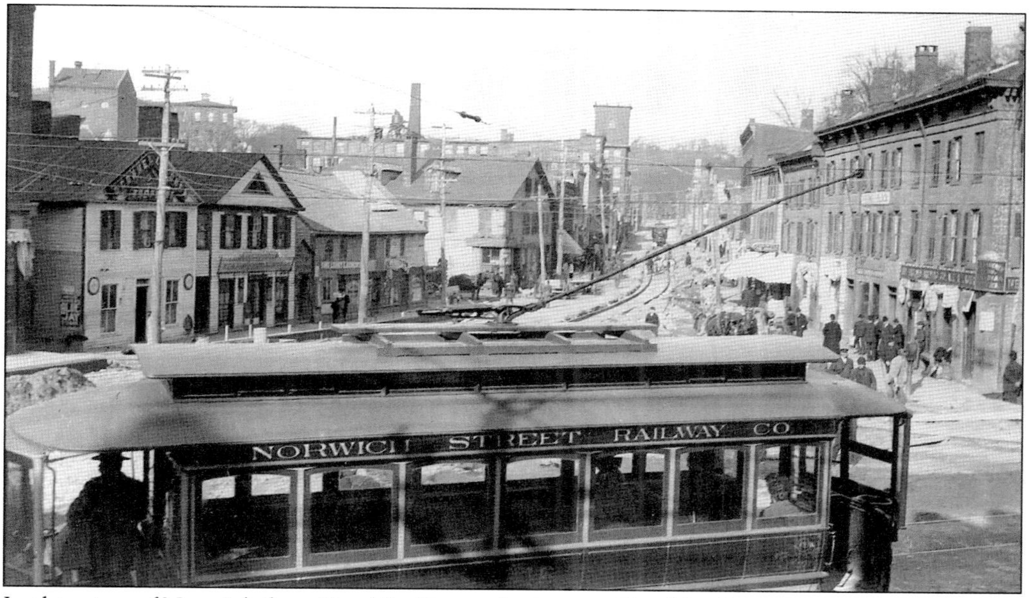

In this view of Norwich from Franklin Square looking up Franklin Street, streetcars run on one line while another line is constructed to expand service in this area.

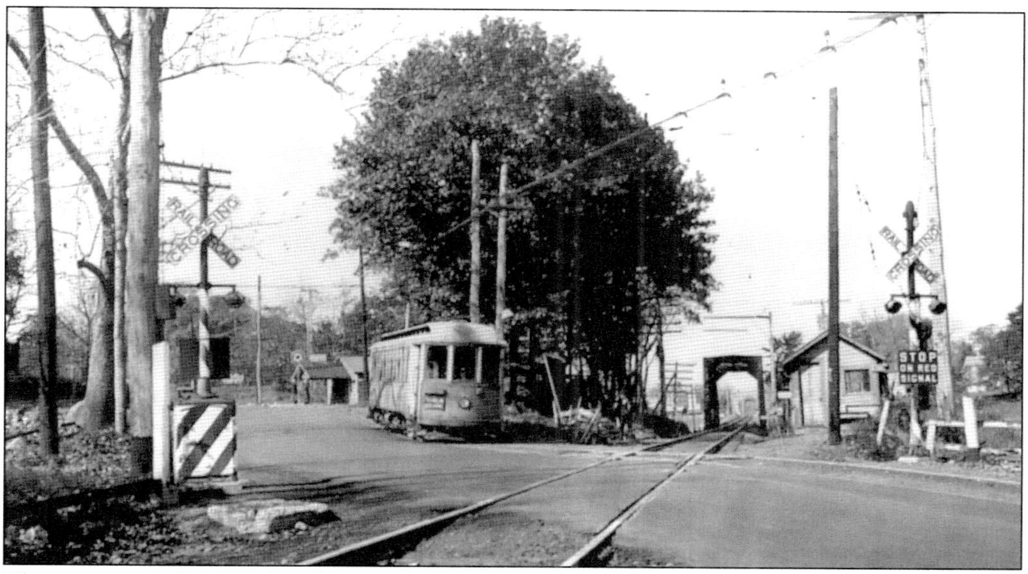

This picture, taken in October 1936, shows car No. 152 at the Central Vermont Railway crossing in the Yantic section of Norwich. Streetcar service on the Yantic line ceased on December 13, 1936.

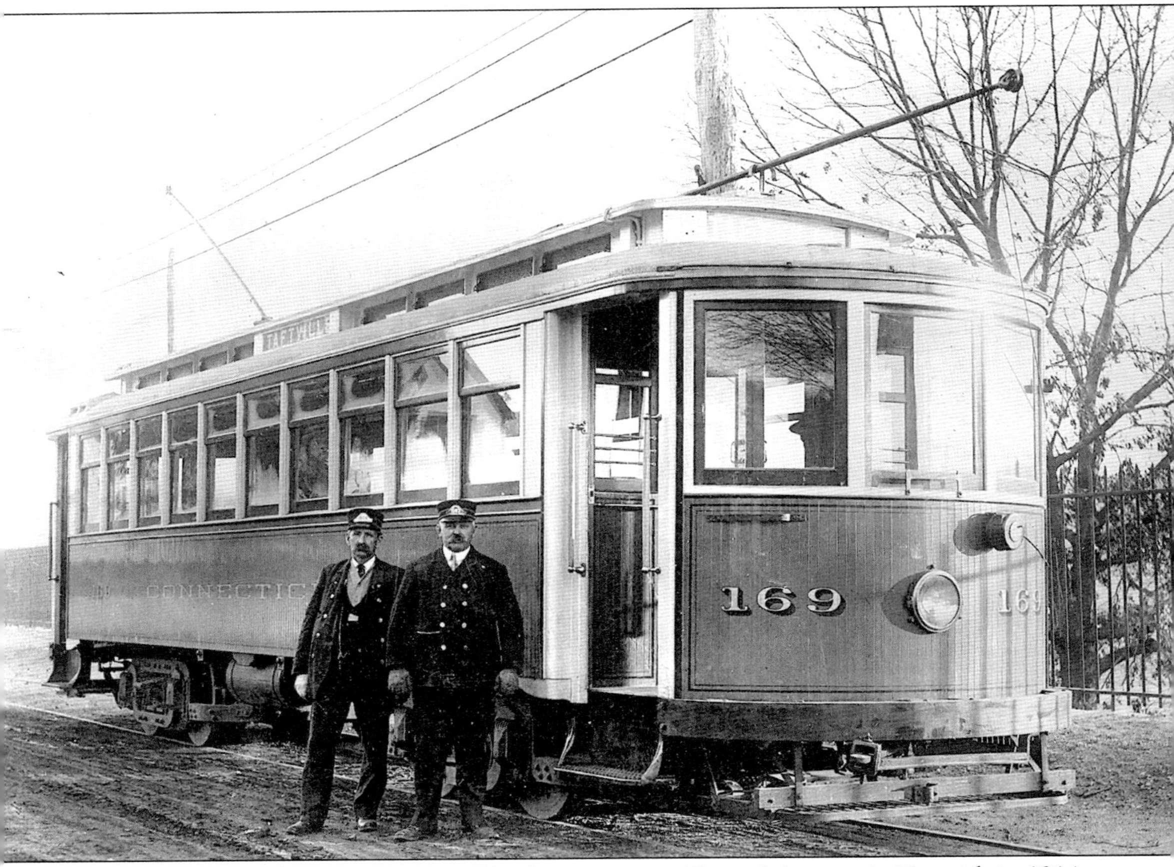

Car No. 169 and its operators pose for this picture on Central Avenue in Norwich in 1914.

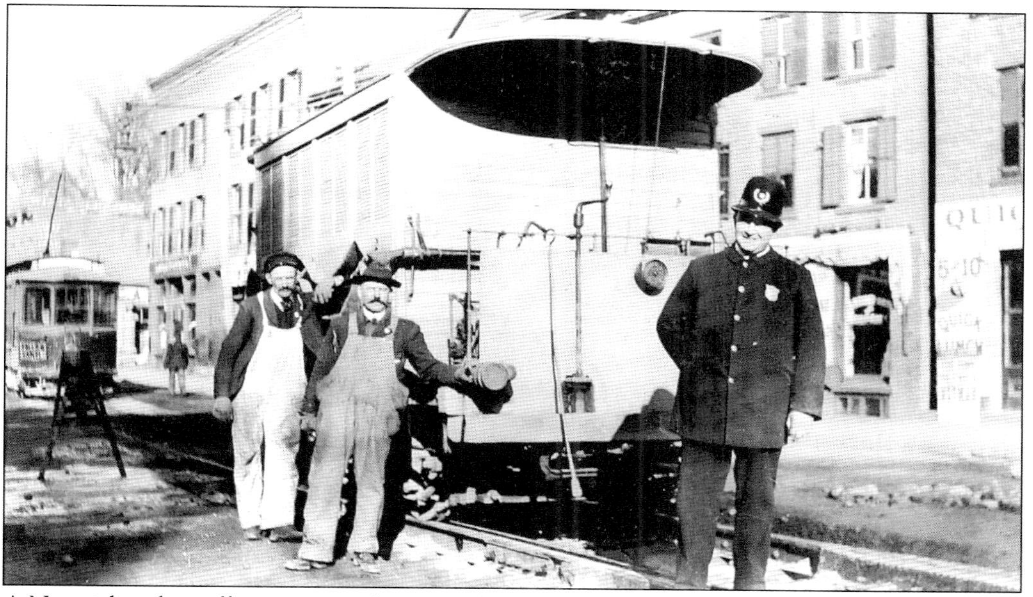

A Norwich police officer poses with Norwich Street Railway maintenance men Eddie Maloney and Elmer Mulkin in this 1896 view.

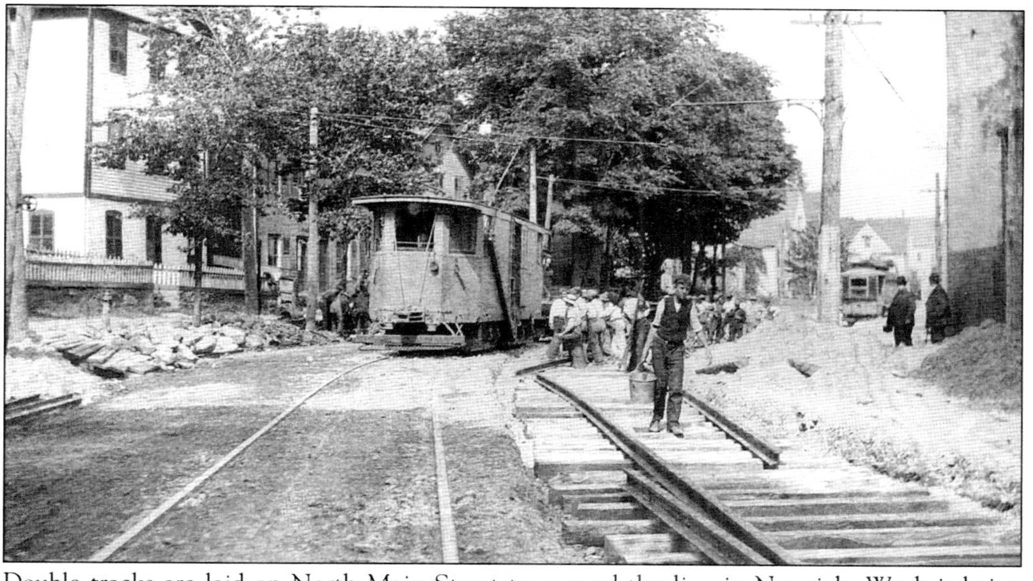

Double tracks are laid on North Main Street to expand the line in Norwich. Work is being done with available equipment, including a snowplow with its plow blades taken off. Many lines used plows as work cars and locomotives during the summer.

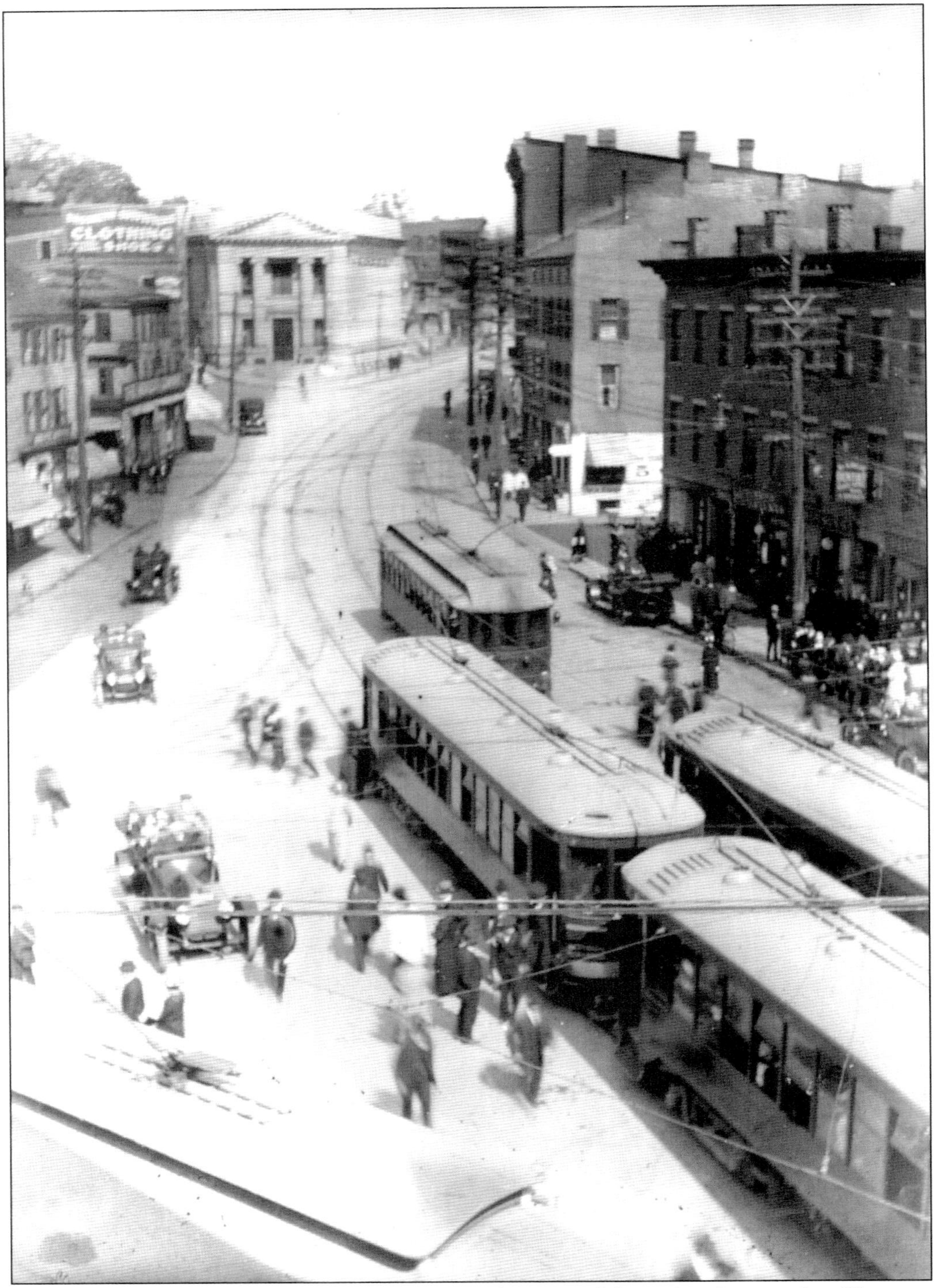

This bird's-eye view of Norwich was taken *c.* 1920. The automobiles in this photograph will become more popular and, within about 20 years, cause the closing of most of the streetcar lines.

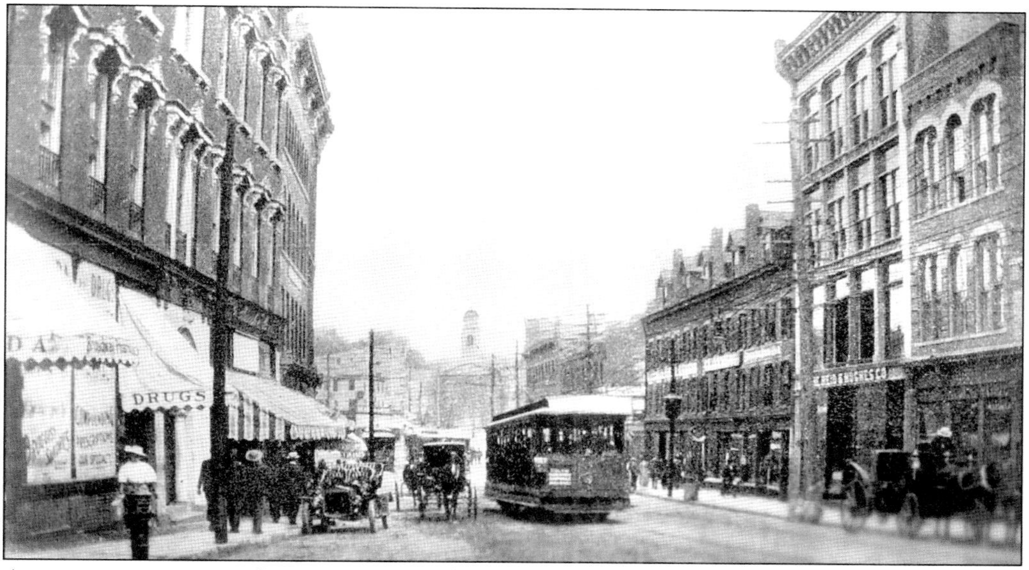

An open car is seen in downtown Norwich in this *c.* 1910 photograph.

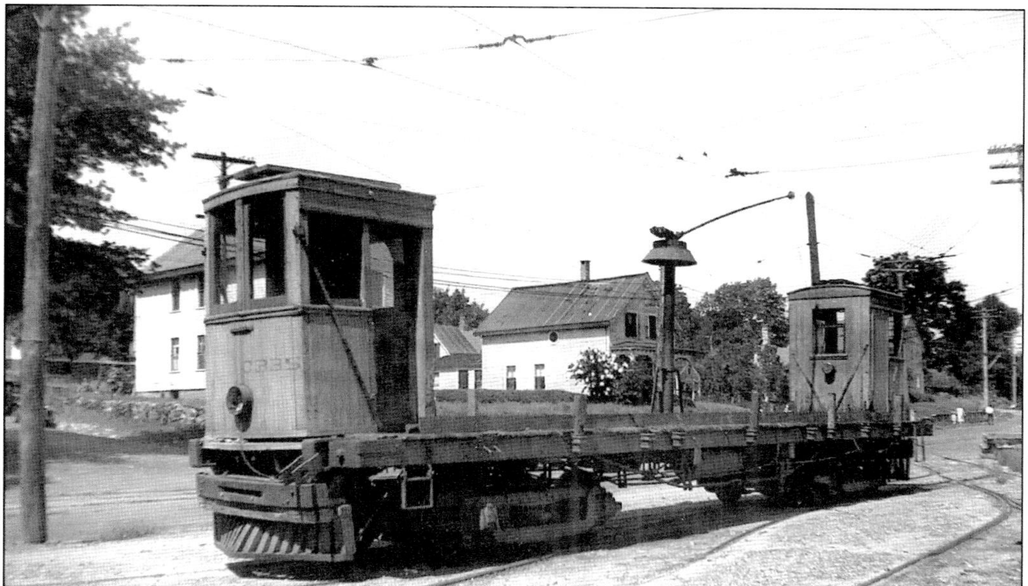

All transit operations need support equipment, and the trolley lines were no exception. While many of the pieces of support equipment were made from older passenger cars that were obsolete, this flatcar, shown in Norwich, was built in this configuration specifically for track maintenance and other repair work needed along the line.

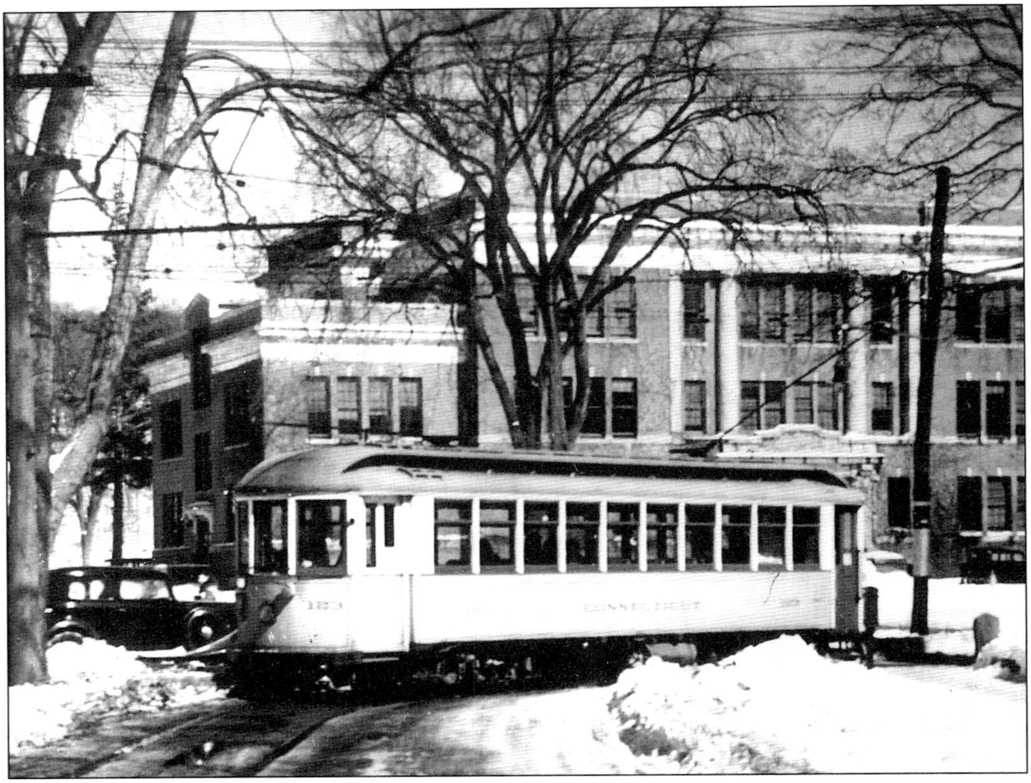

Snow did not stop car No. 123. This car was built by the Osgood Bradley Company in 1910.

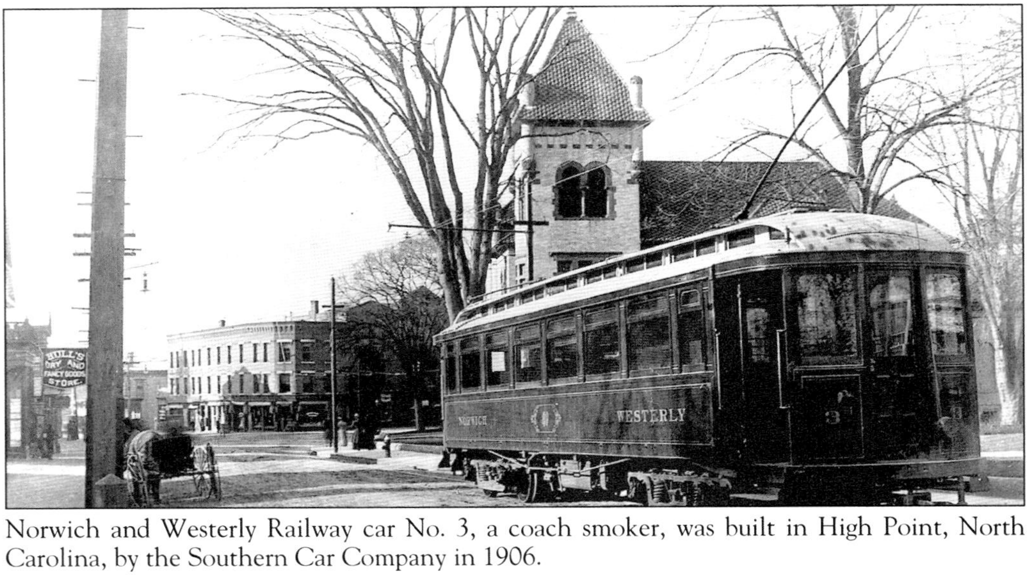

Norwich and Westerly Railway car No. 3, a coach smoker, was built in High Point, North Carolina, by the Southern Car Company in 1906.

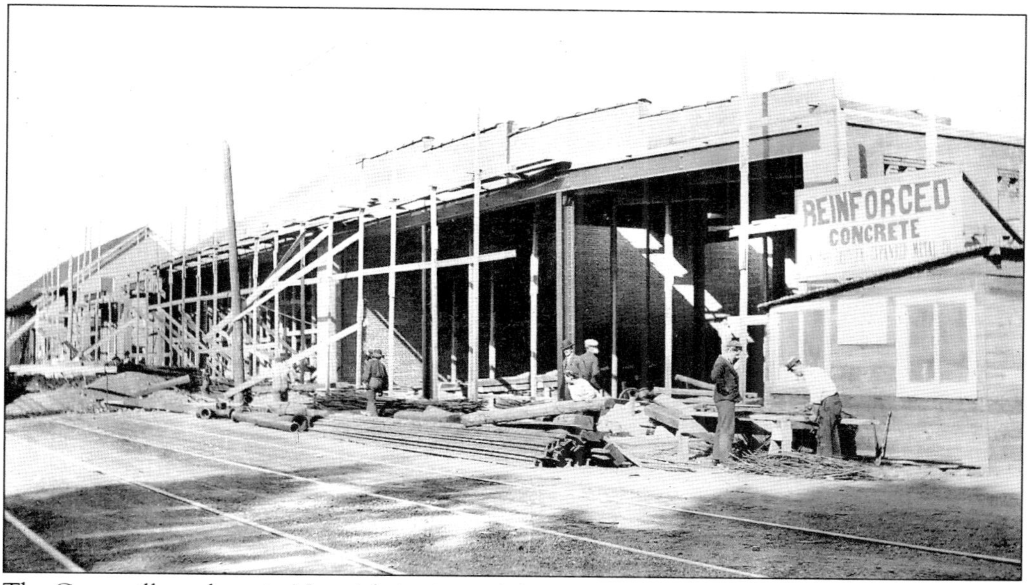

The Greenville carbarn in Norwich is pictured during construction in 1905.

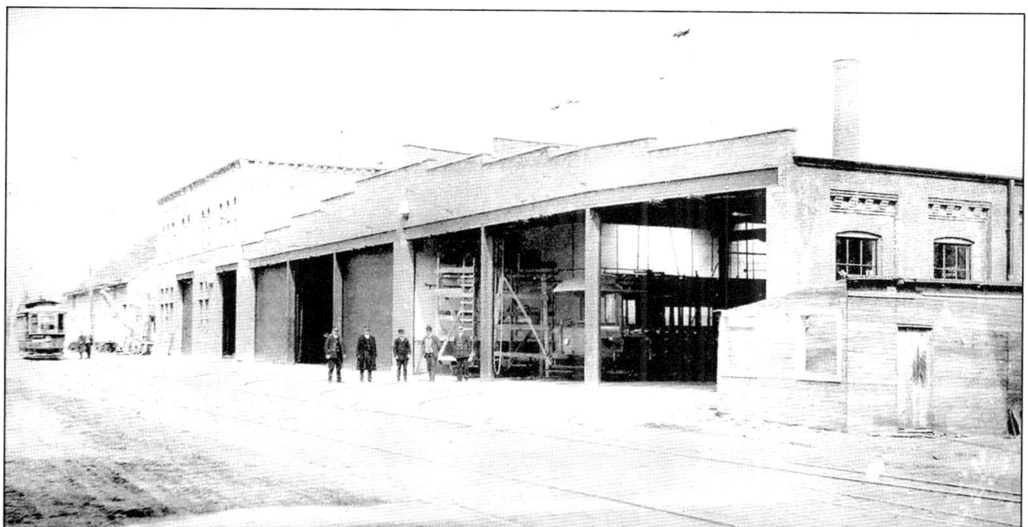

The Greenville barn in Norwich, shown here *c.* 1906, served as a bus garage from 1936 to 1968. After that, it was an antique shop operated by Alex Cohn of Norwich.

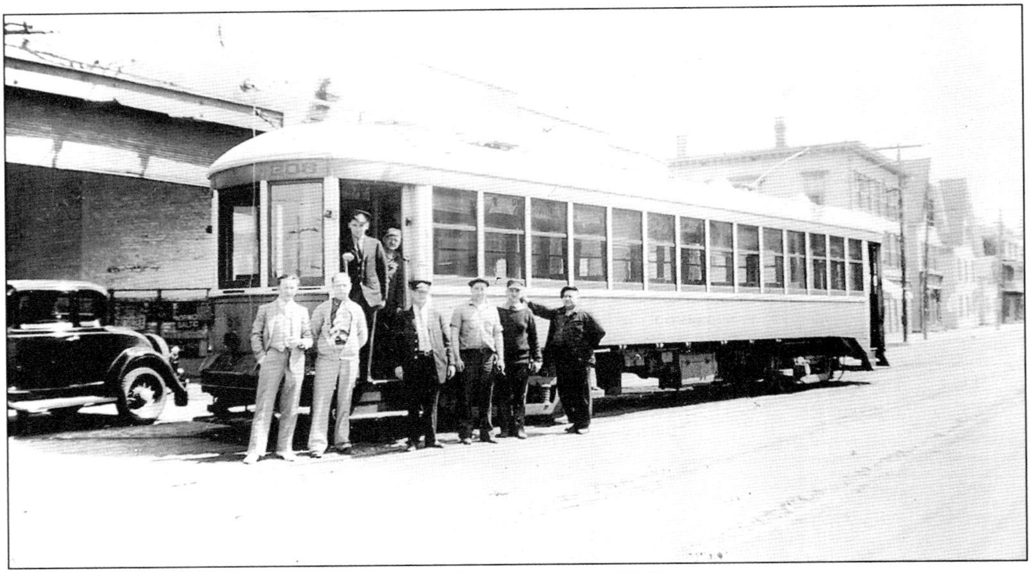

The Greenville barn shop crew poses for this picture in 1933.

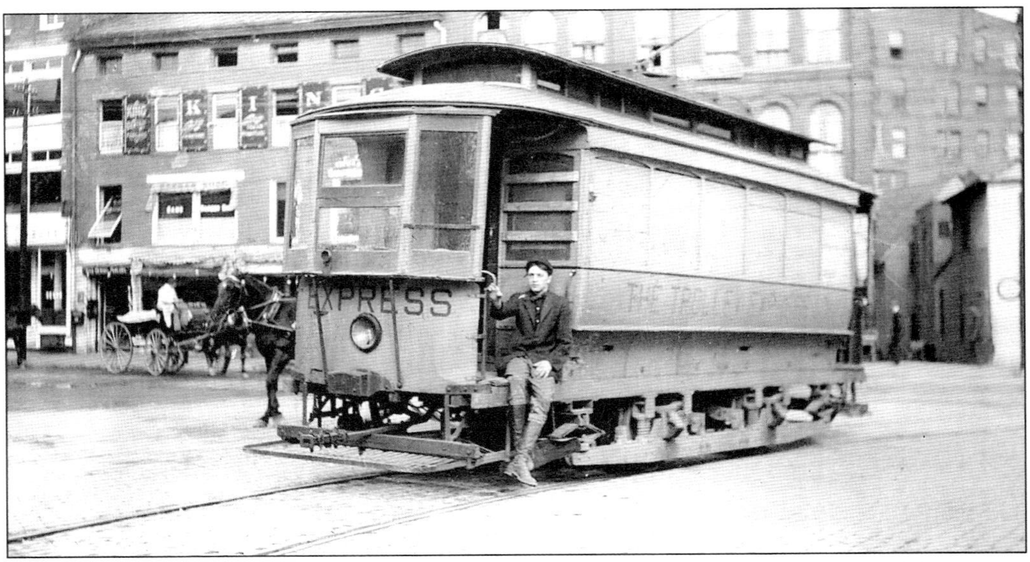

The Trolley Express provided door-to-door delivery service of packages to local businesses before UPS or FedEx. This car was formerly the New London Street Railway car No. 11, seen previously on page 12.

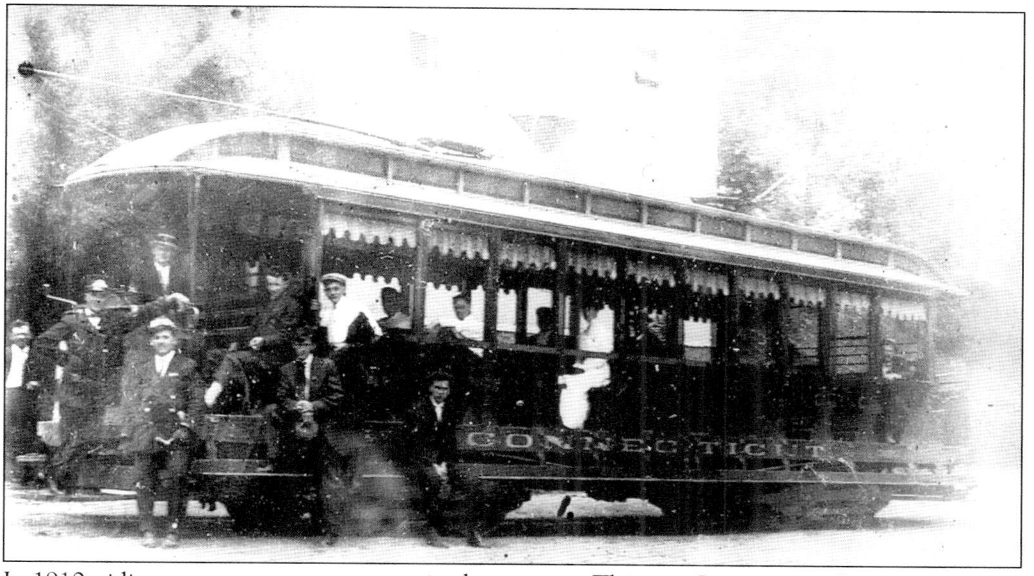

In 1910, riding on open cars was a treat in the summer. This car, Connecticut Company car No. 327, was built in 1903 by the Laconia Car Company. In 1916, it was rebuilt into a closed car.

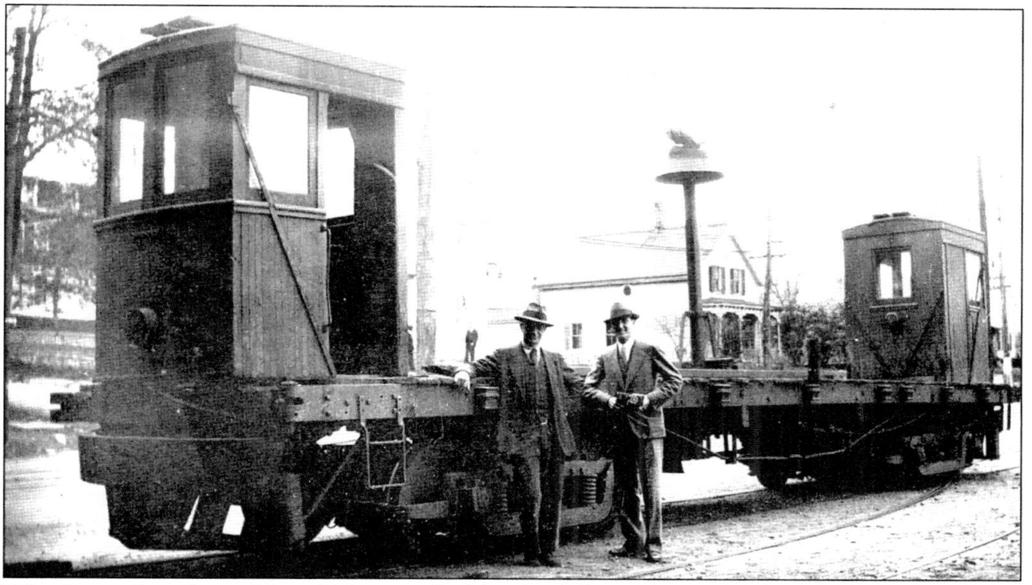

"The Barge," as flatcar No. 0335 was called by the folks in Norwich, serves as the background for a photograph of two company officials in 1935.

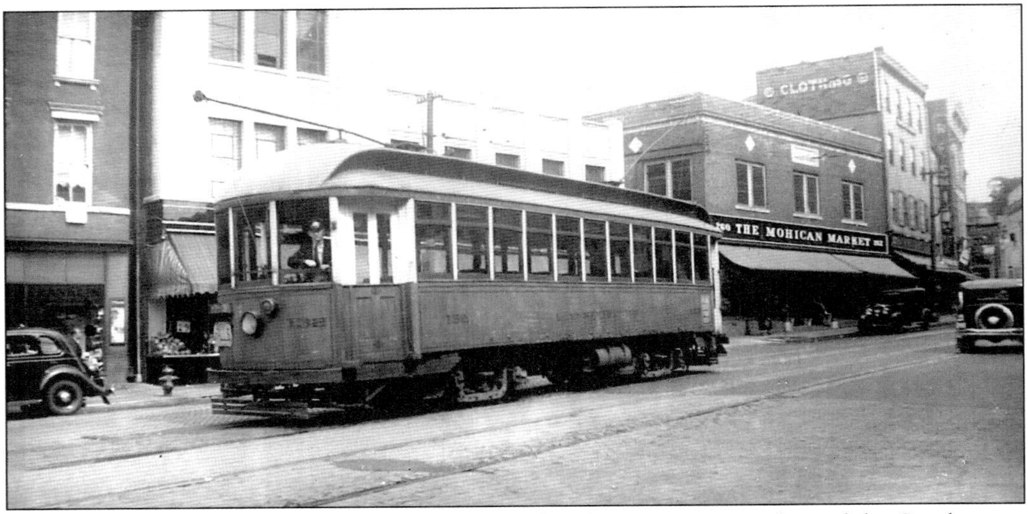

Car No. 132 is shown on Main Street in Norwich. This car was a product of the Stephenson Car Company and was built in 1903.

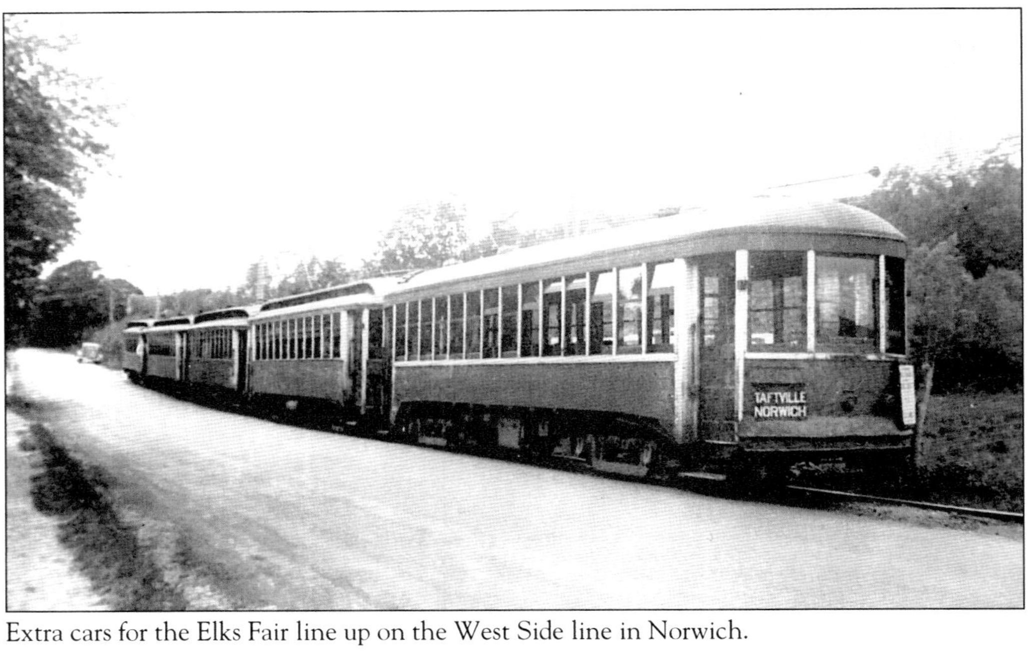

Extra cars for the Elks Fair line up on the West Side line in Norwich.

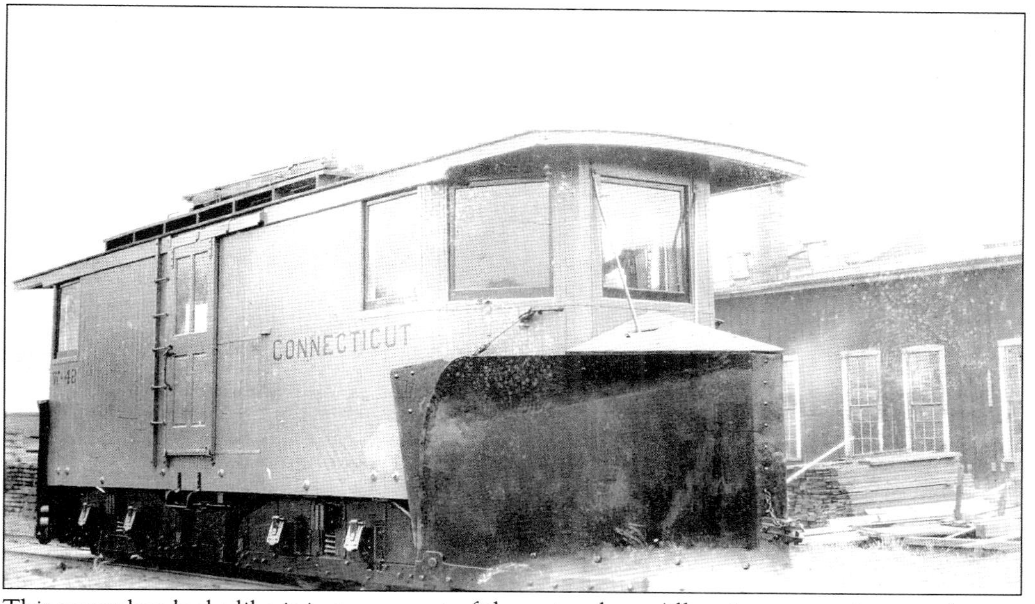

This snowplow looks like it just came out of the paint shop. All major car repairs were done at the Greenville barn in Norwich.

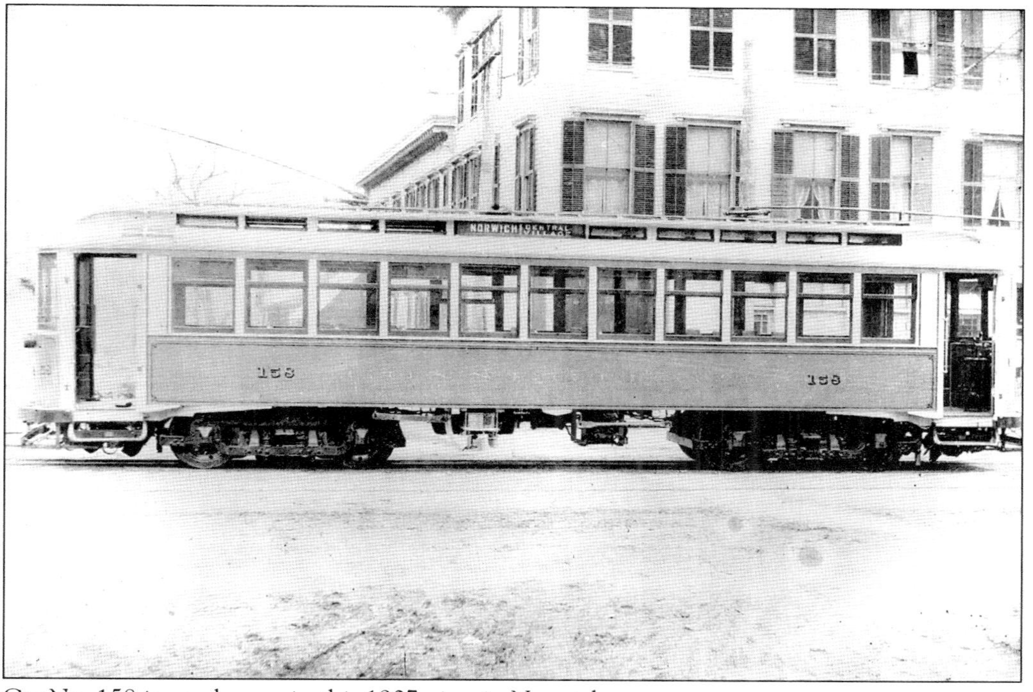

Car No. 158 is nearly new in this 1907 view in Norwich.

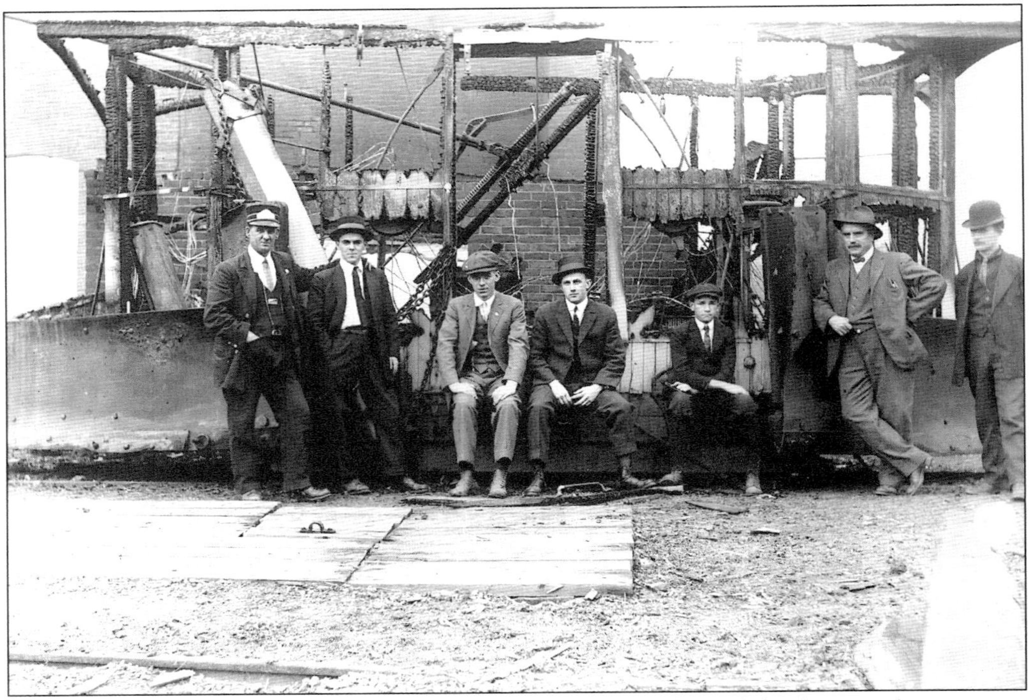

In 1916, the Thamesville carbarn burned. These men sit on what is left of a snowplow.

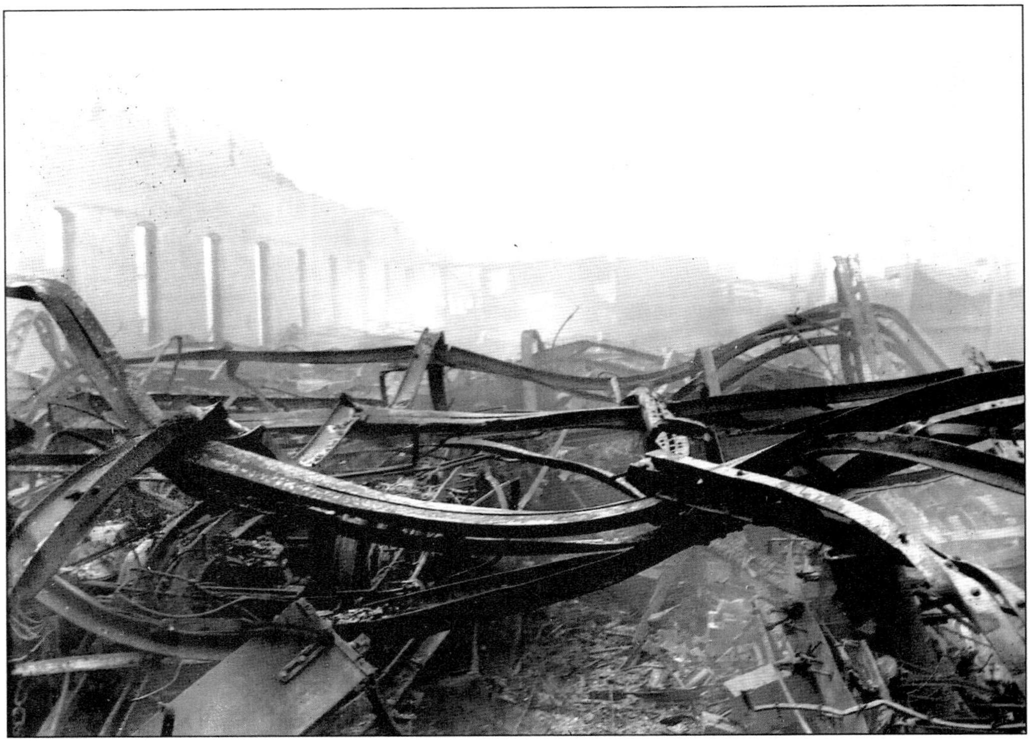

This shows the destruction inside the Thamesville barn following the fire of 1916.

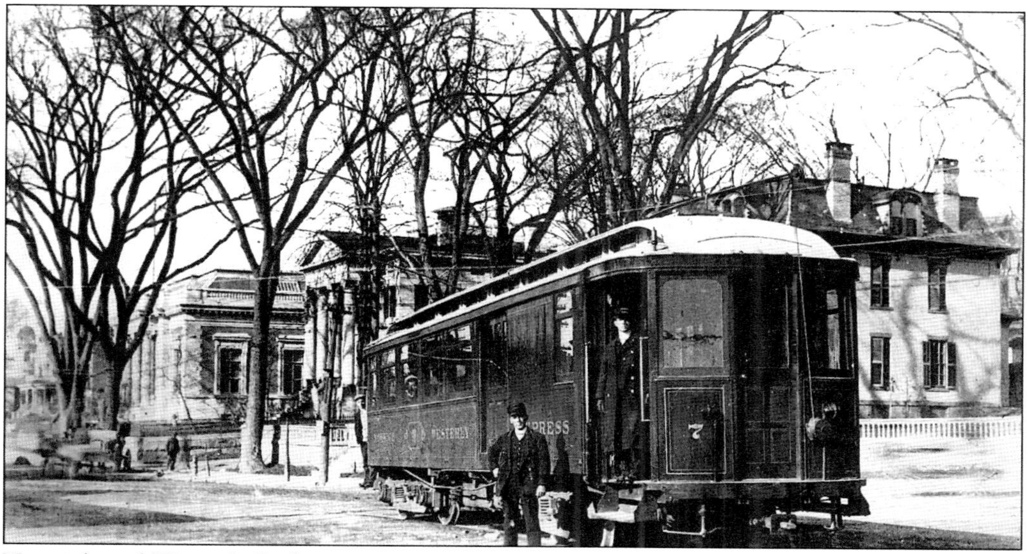

Norwich and Westerly Railway car No. 7 is pictured here with its crew in 1914. The cars were dark green with gold lettering.

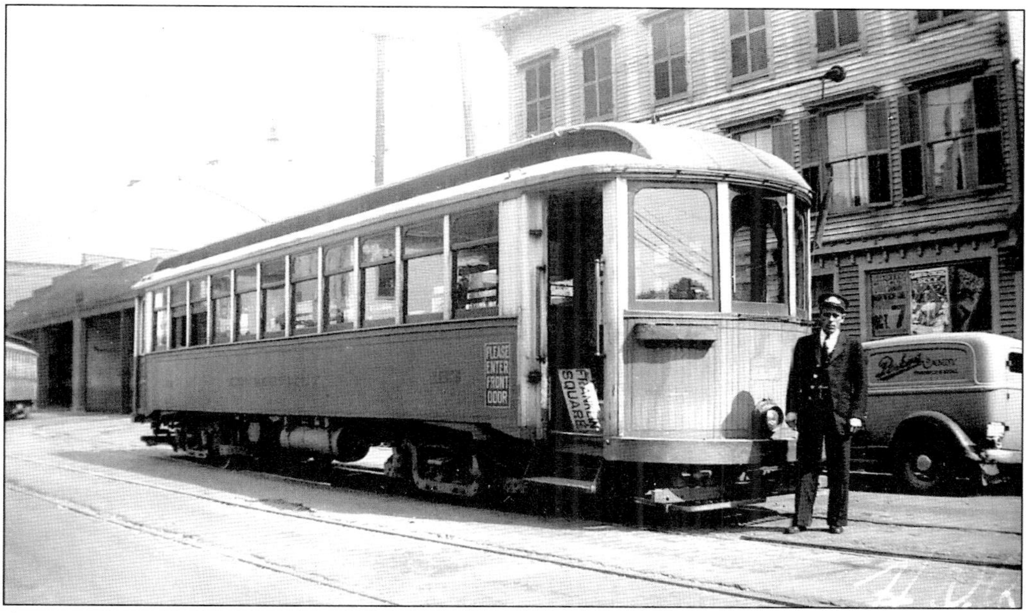

A two-man streetcar crew was initially the norm; however, by the 1930s, all of the Connecticut Company cars were operated by a one-man crew. Basically, there was no conductor, and the motorman ran the car and collected the fares. This unidentified operator is getting ready to start his run from the Greenville barn in Norwich c. 1934.

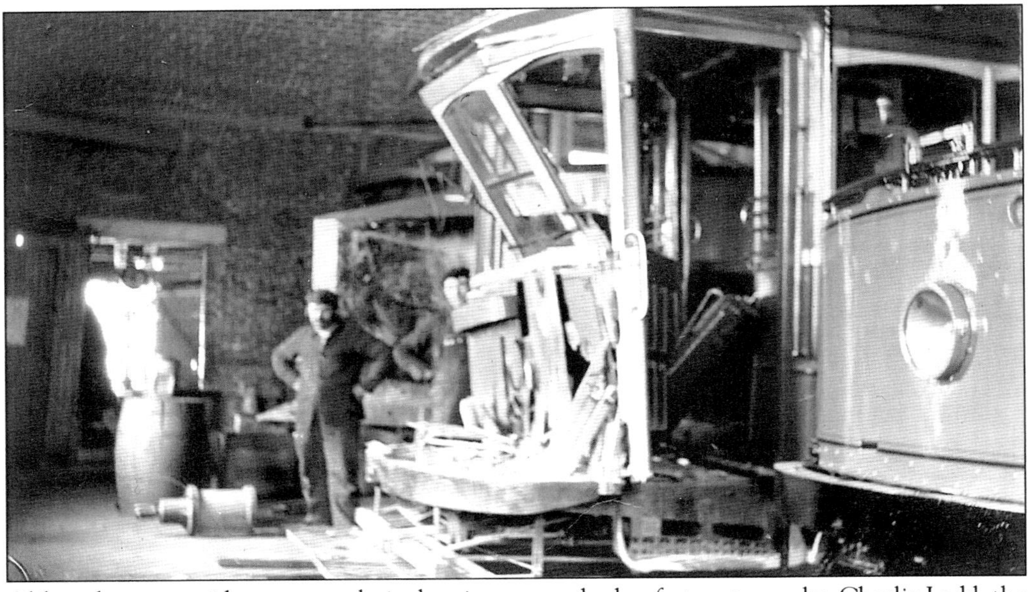

Although most accidents were relatively minor, some had unfortunate results. Charlie Ladd, the motorman of this car, was injured in 1918 when his car hit a wagon. Accidents with automobiles and trucks became more commonplace after the war, as the number of vehicles increased.

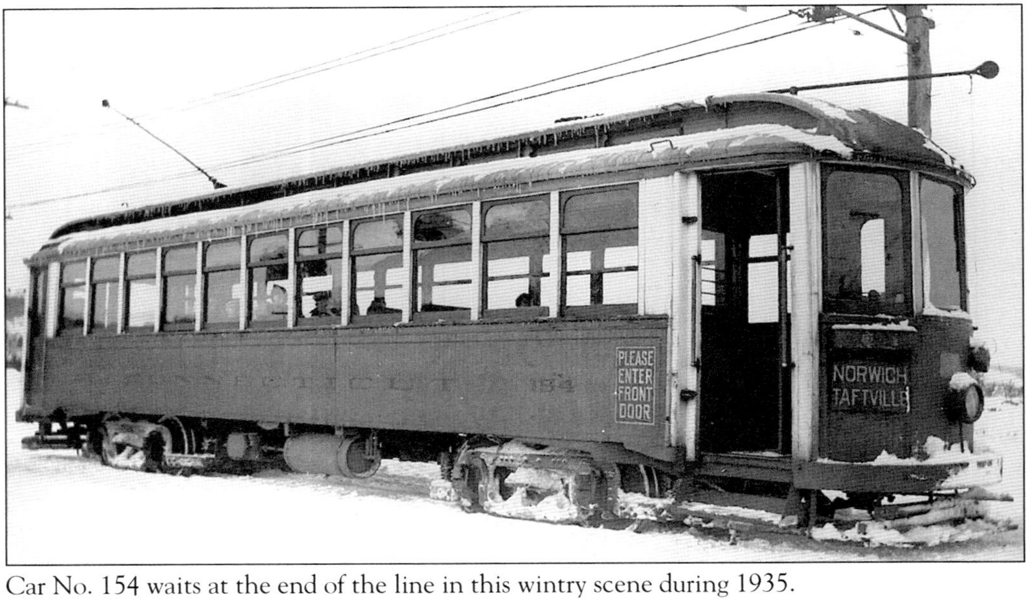

Car No. 154 waits at the end of the line in this wintry scene during 1935.

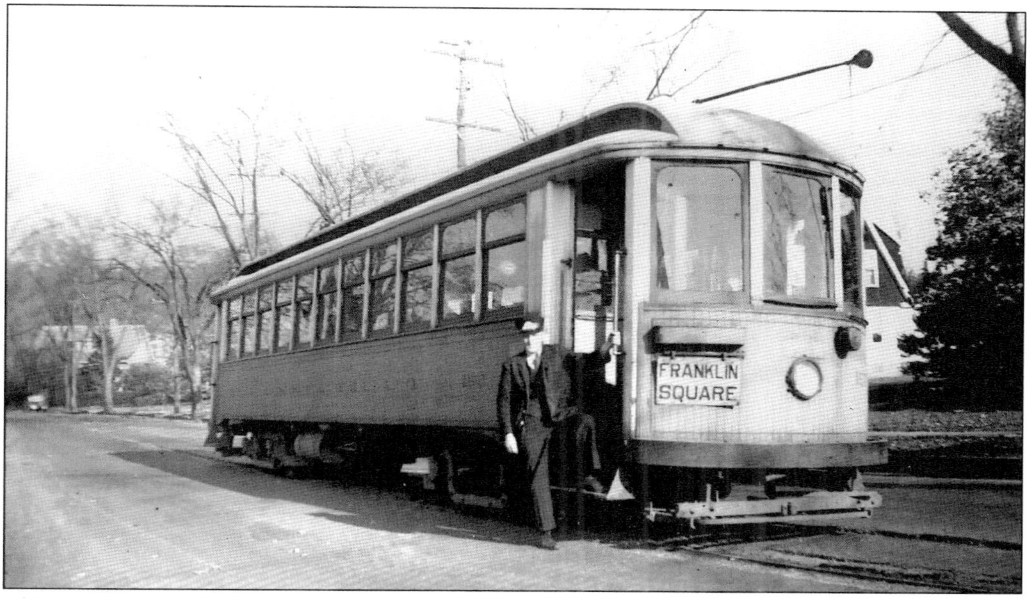

This operator was happy to stop and pose for this photograph in 1935.

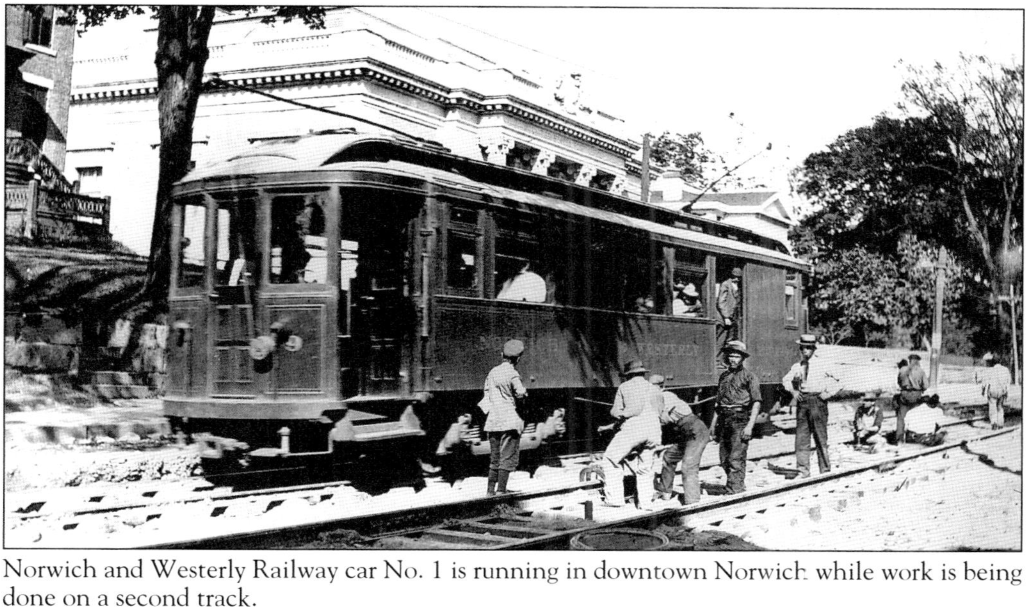
Norwich and Westerly Railway car No. 1 is running in downtown Norwich while work is being done on a second track.

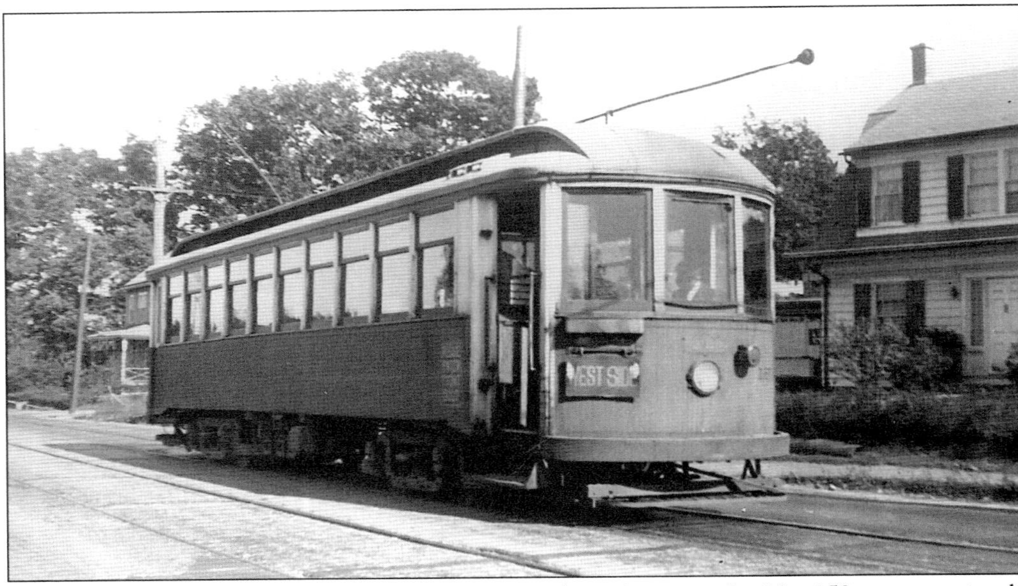

By 1936, the streetcars in Norwich were starting to show their age. Car No. 152, seen previously in 1915 and 1935, was built in 1905 and served in the fleet of the Connecticut Company for more than 30 years.

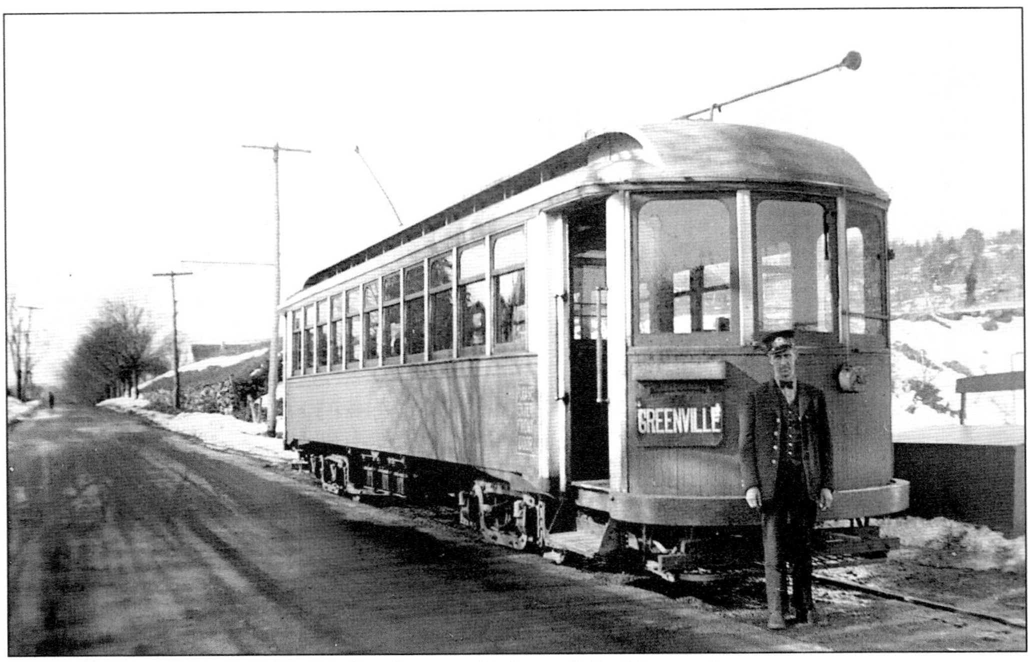

A proud motorman stands with his Greenville bound double-truck car.

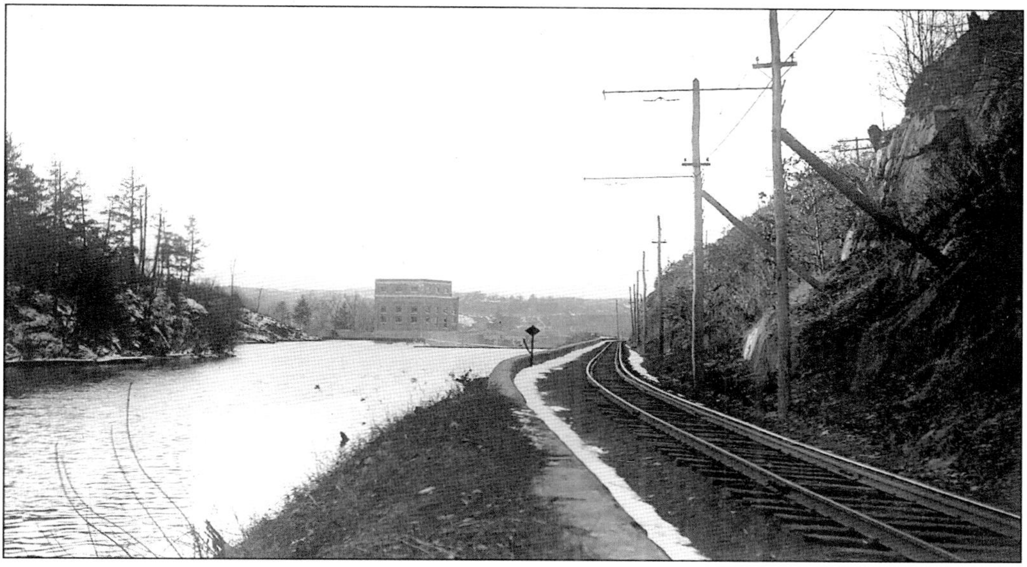

This portion of the New Haven Railroad main line, between Tafts Junction and Central Village, was used by both streetcars and railroad trains. The river on the left is the Shetucket River.

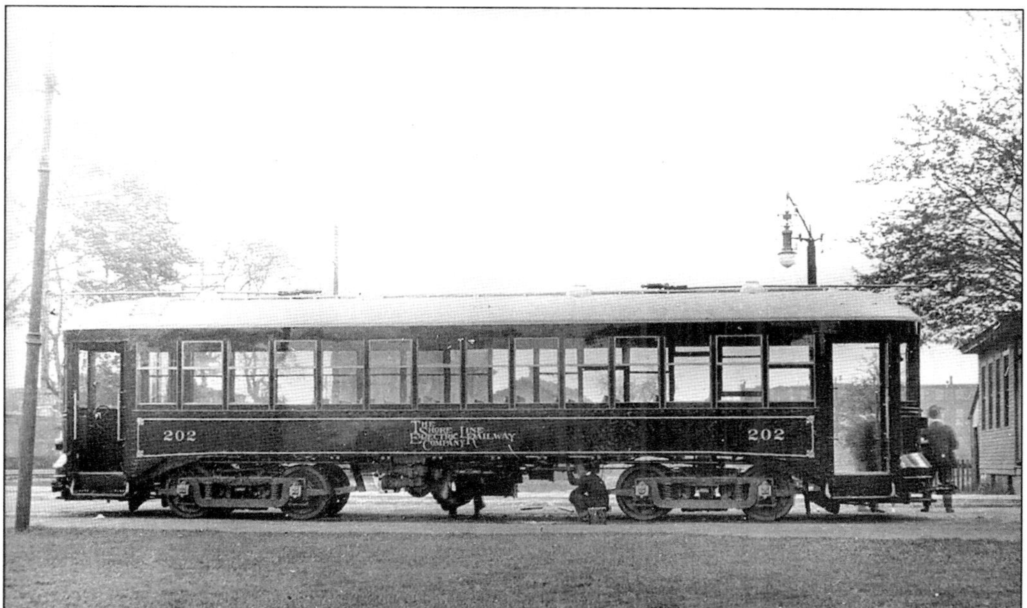

The Wason Manufacturing Company of Springfield, Massachusetts, built 10 passenger cars for the Shoreline Electric Railway in 1915. The Shoreline Electric Railway leased the line that they operated from the Connecticut Company. When the lease was cancelled in 1919, the lines were returned to the Connecticut Company along with the ownership of these cars.

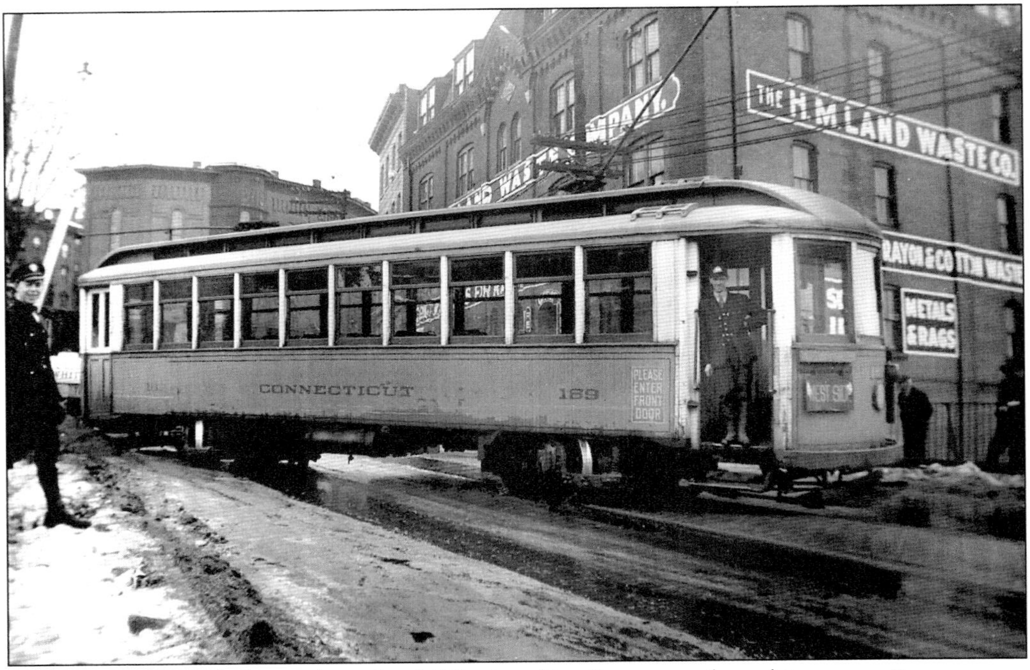

Car No. 159 has left the track in this 1935 view. Derailments such as this were quite common, especially where the track was in pavement. Typically, these derailments were not fatal, and the cars were usually back on the track in a short time, after being rerailed by an experienced shop crew, like the one in the Greenville barn.

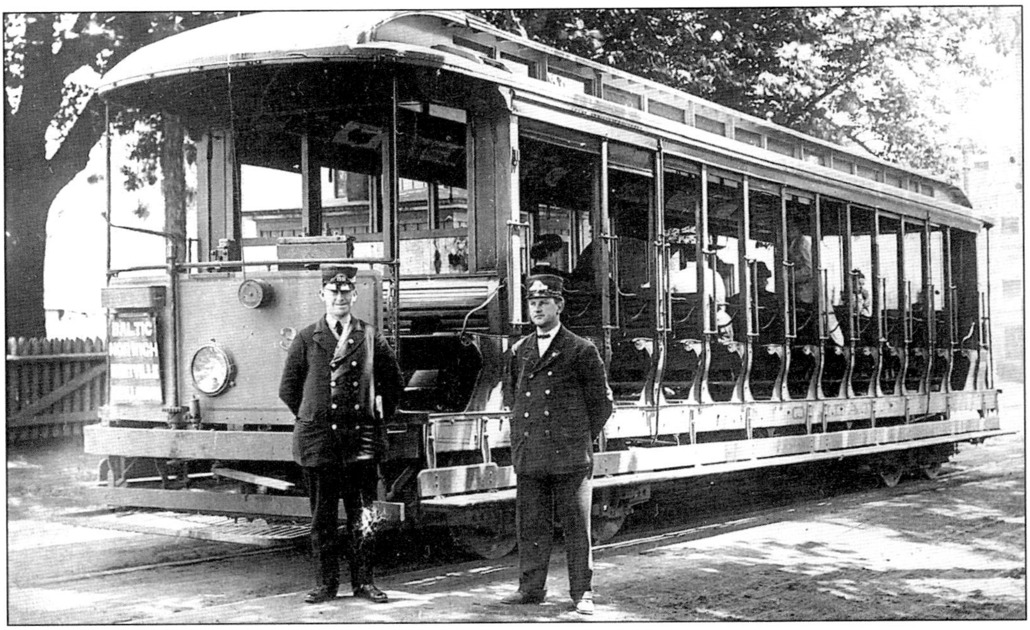

This distinguished crew poses for a picture in 1910.

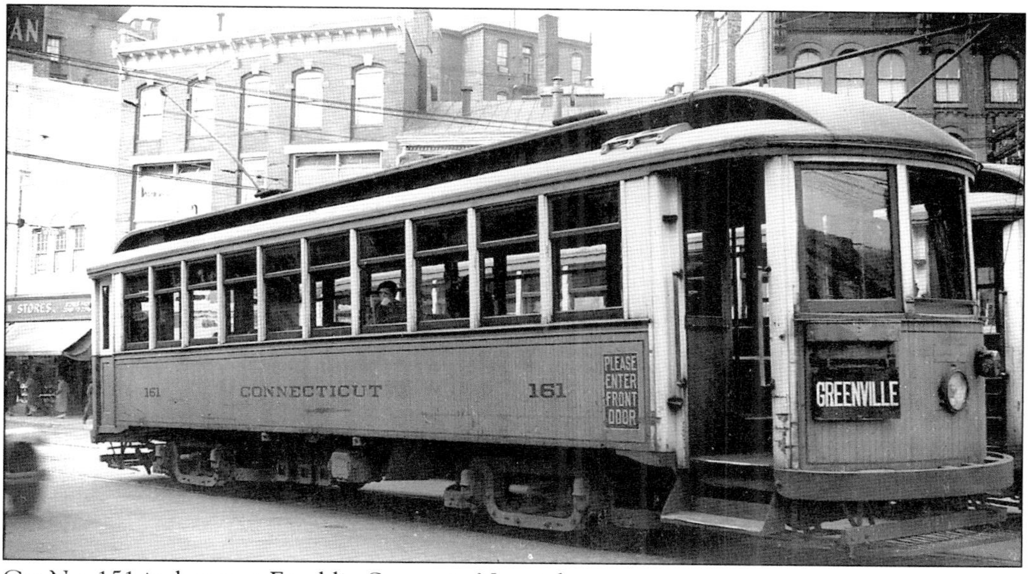

Car No. 151 is shown at Franklin Square in Norwich.

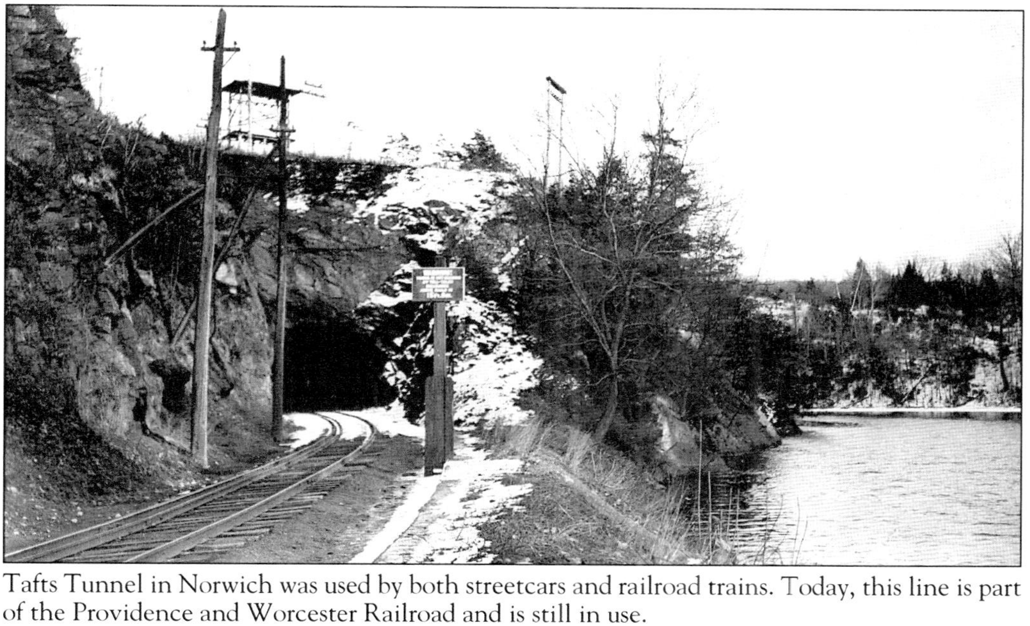

Tafts Tunnel in Norwich was used by both streetcars and railroad trains. Today, this line is part of the Providence and Worcester Railroad and is still in use.

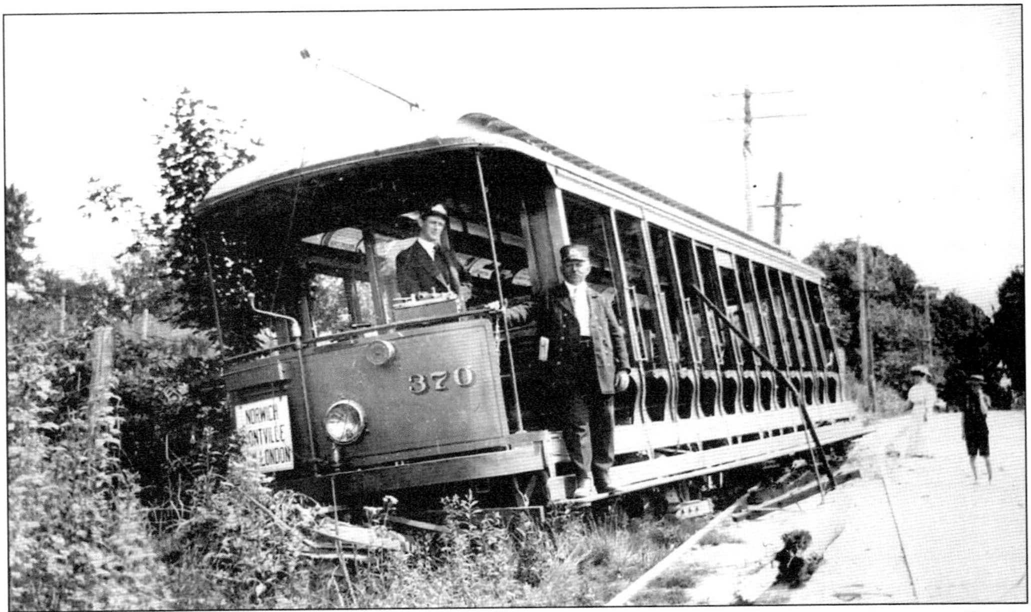

In this 1910 view, car No. 370 has had a problem staying on the track on its run between Baltic and New London.

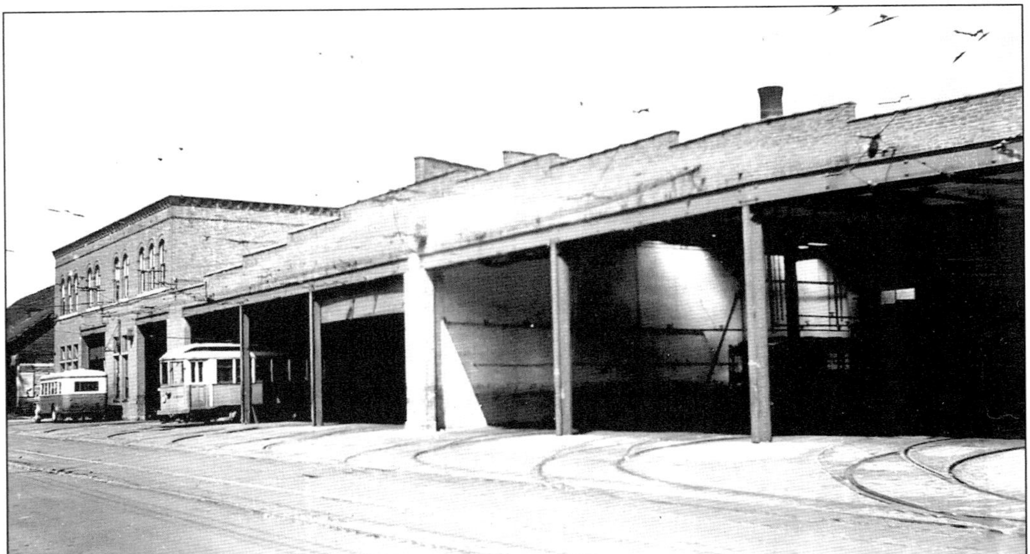

The Greenville barn in Norwich is shown in this 1930 photograph, which also shows an early bus. Buses would take the place of streetcars in Norwich in less than seven years.

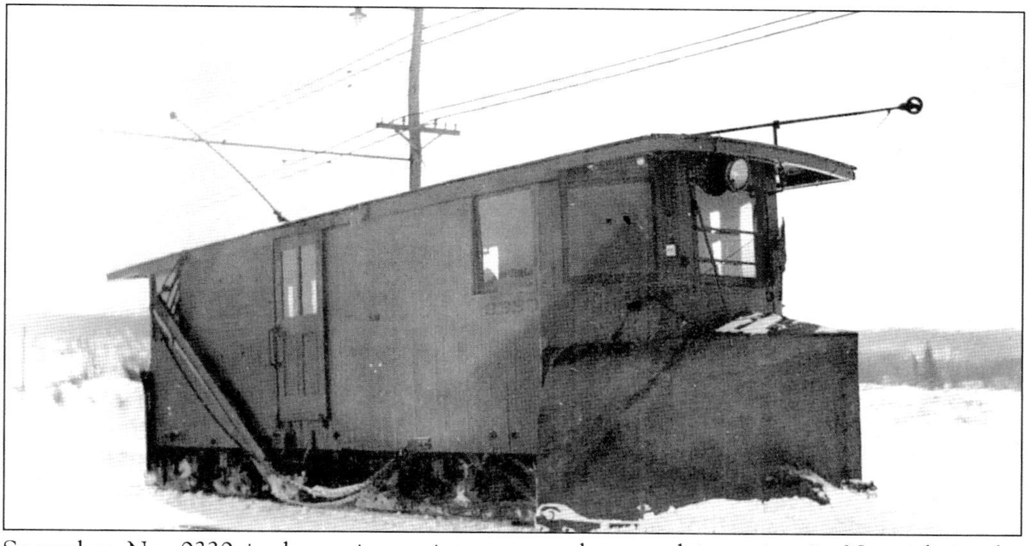

Snowplow No. 0330 is shown in a winter scene above and in action in Norwich in the 1930s below.

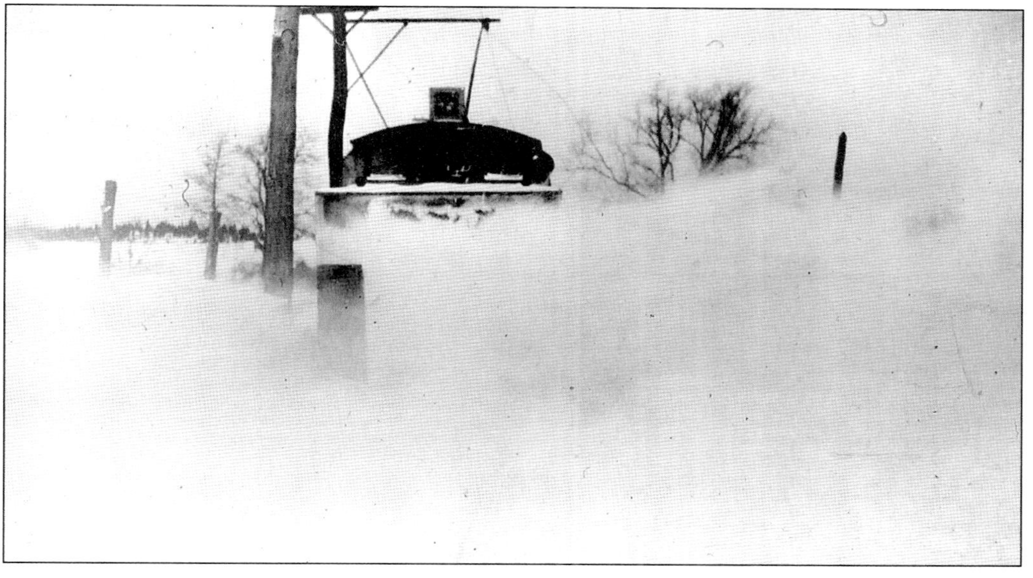

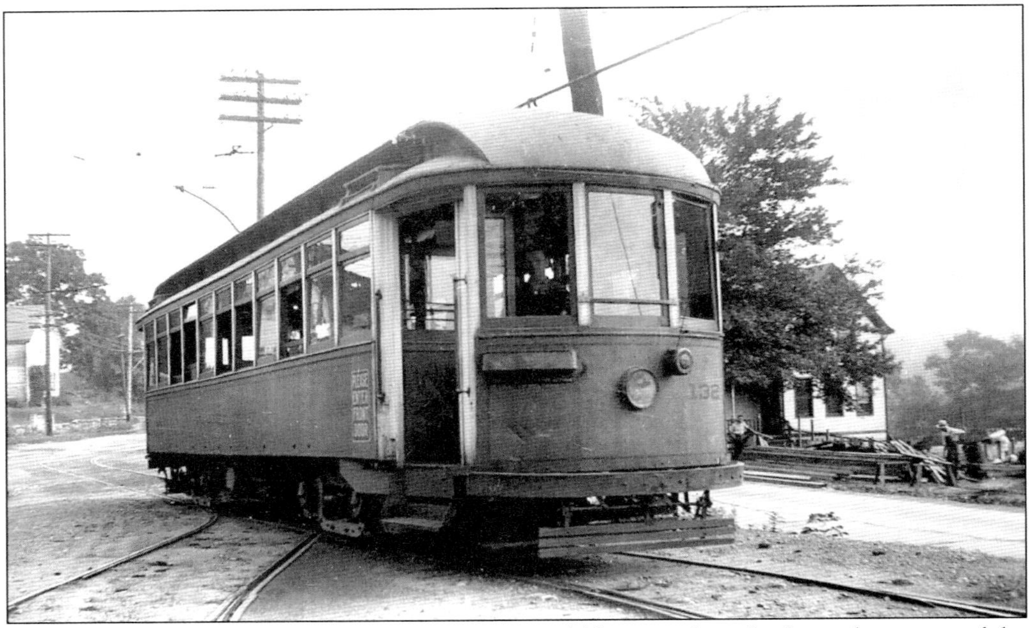

Cars in Norwich transported people from what would become the suburbs to the center of the city, usually to work or transact any business they needed to do.

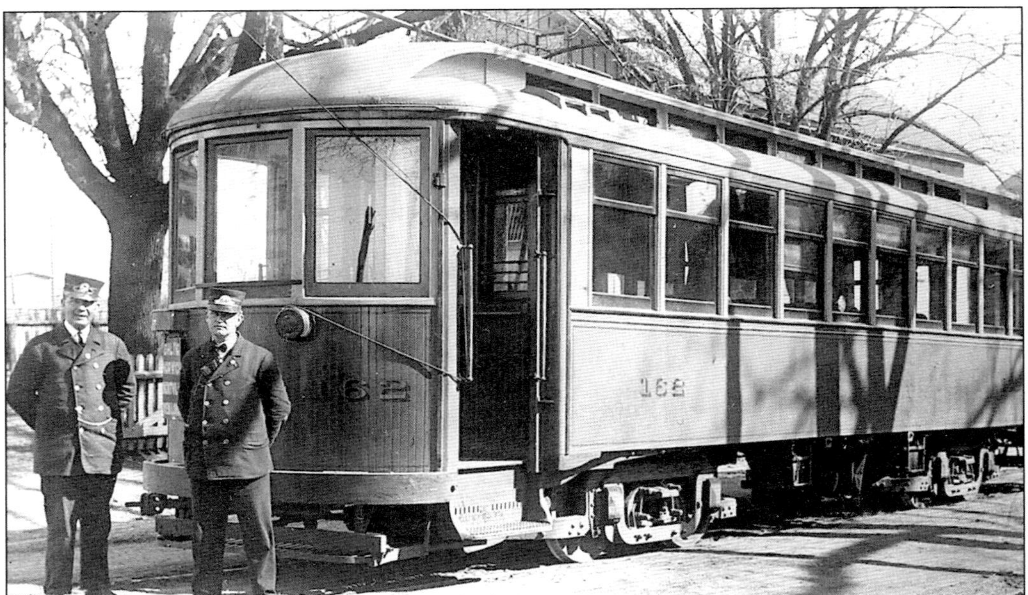

These well-groomed operators were proud to be photographed with their car in 1914.

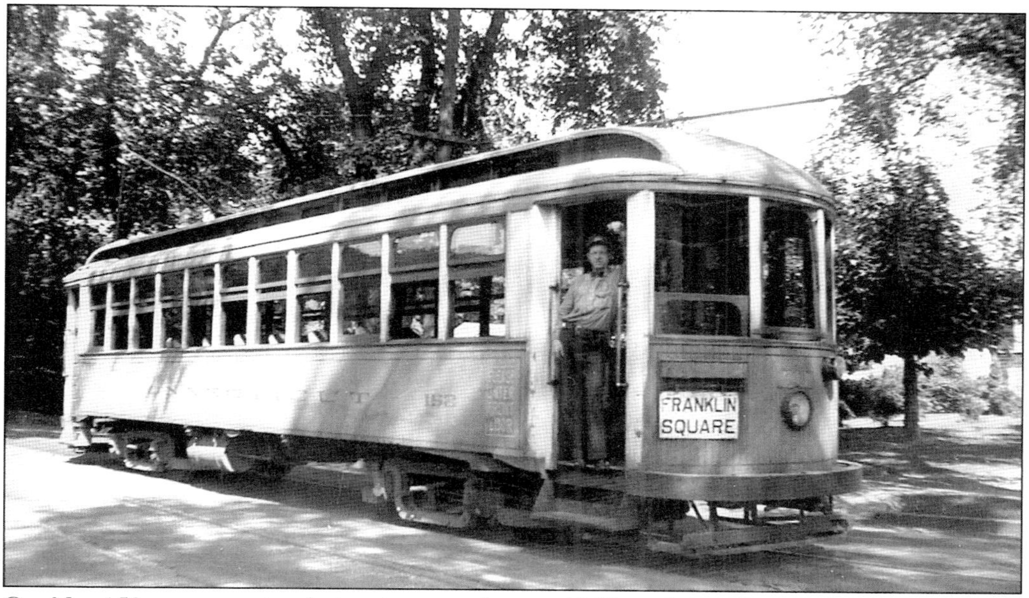

Car No. 152, seen previously in pictures taken in 1915, is shown here with an unidentified motorman in Norwich in 1935.

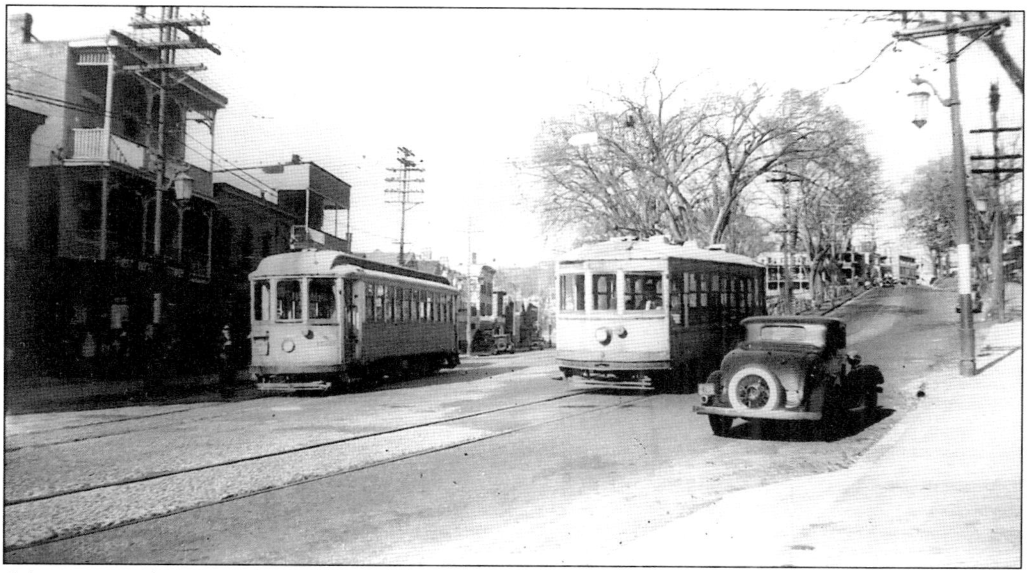

Often, more than one streetcar ran on the same line at the same time. This photograph of the junction of Boswell Avenue and Franklin Street in Norwich shows single-truck car No. 2304, which will follow car No. 152 to Franklin Square.

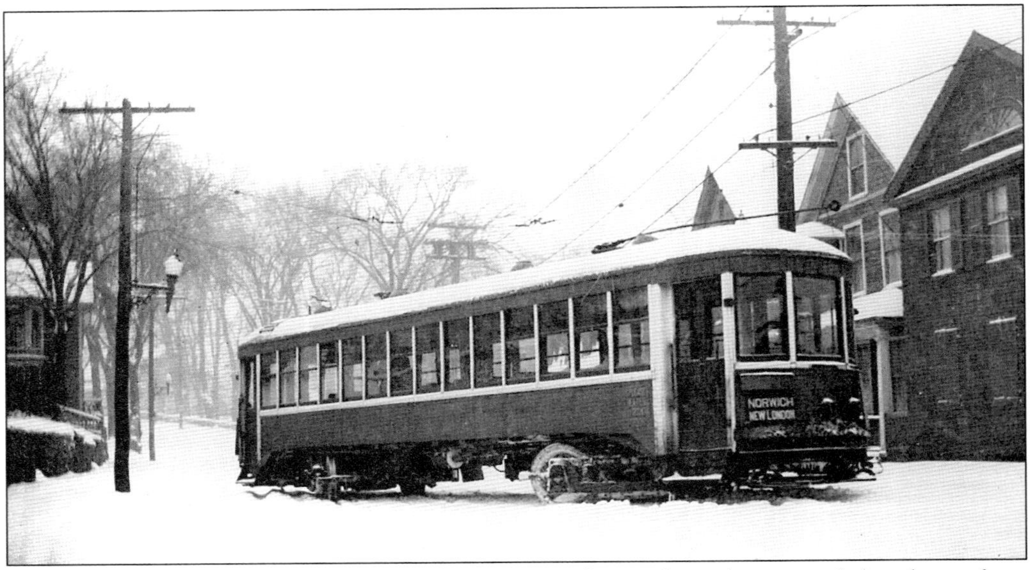

Streetcars ran throughout the year, and sometimes the road conditions prohibited cars from getting to their destination, as shown in this photograph of car No. 210 in Norwich during the winter of 1933. Ice and snow buildup on and around the rails caused this derailment.

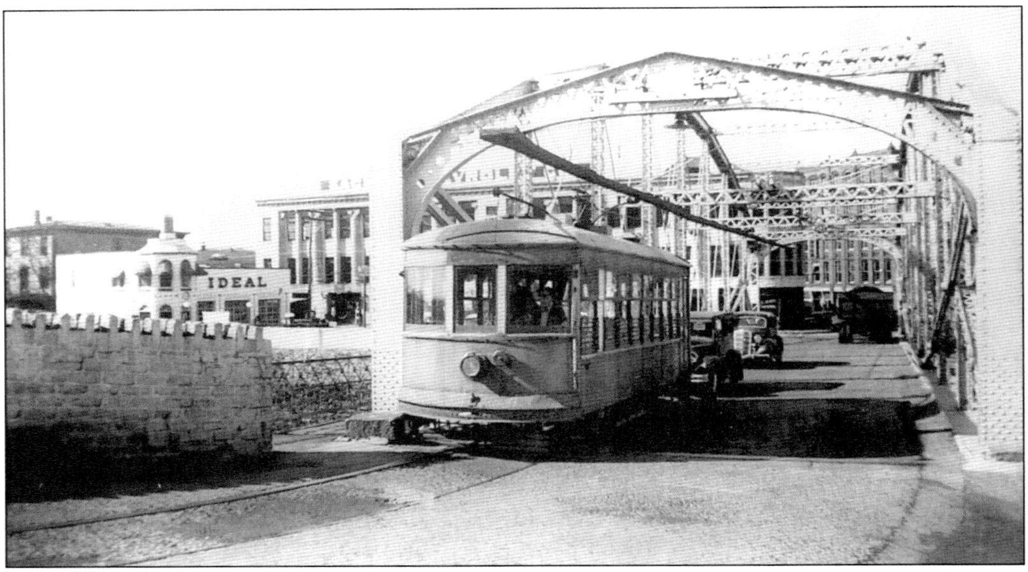

Often, streetcar lines shared the roadway with other forms of transportation, such as cars, as shown here with this single-truck passenger car on the Layren Bridge in Norwich in 1935.

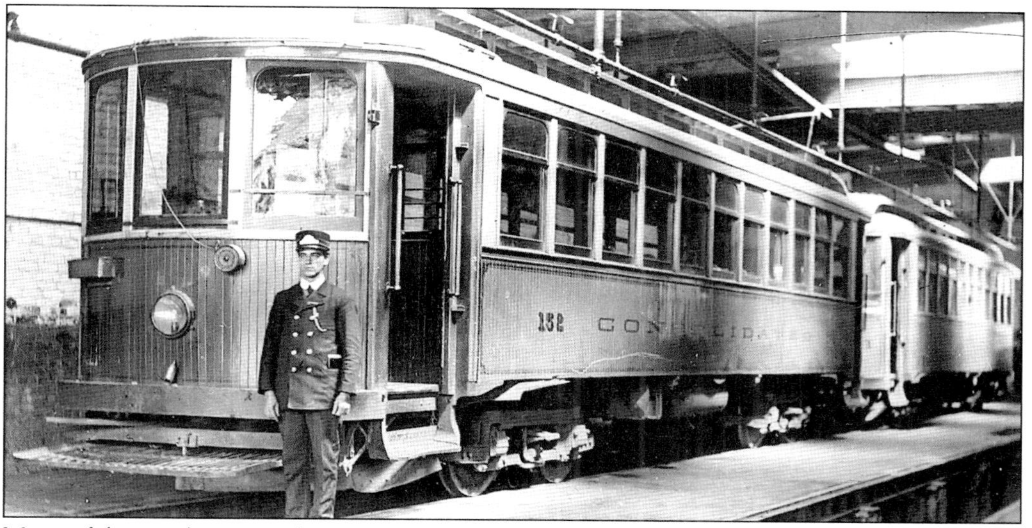

Many of the conductors and motormen paid professional photographers to take pictures of them in their uniforms next to their cars, as shown in these two photographs featuring car No. 152, inside of the Greenville carbarn in Norwich (above) and again on the line in 1915 (below).

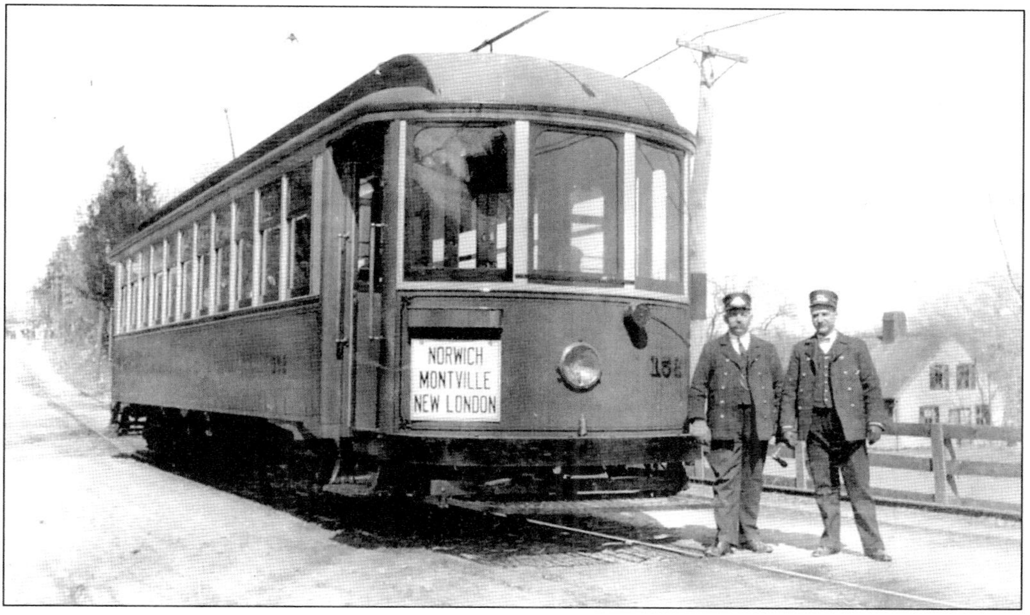

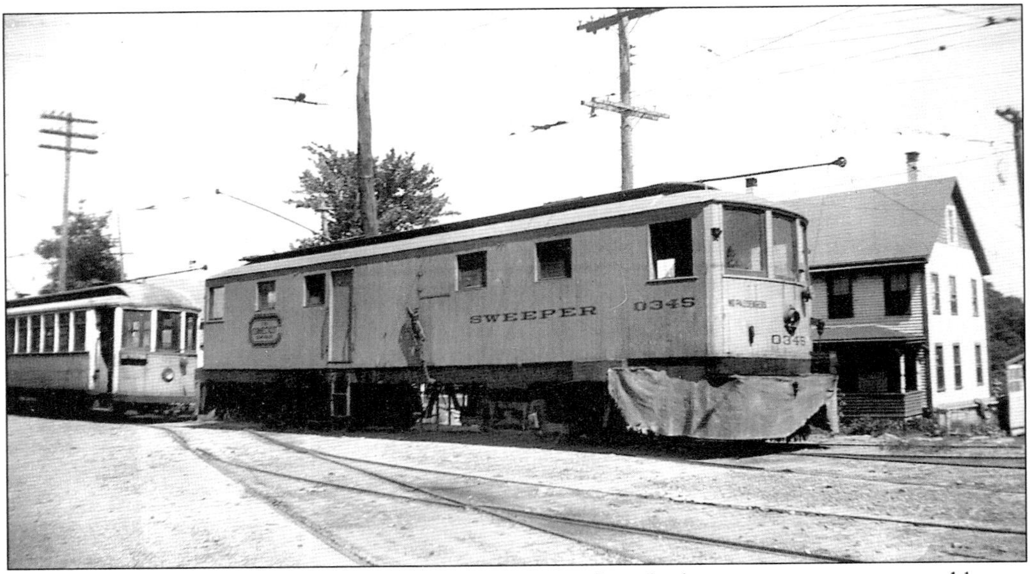

The Connecticut Company took obsolete open cars and made them into snow sweepers, like car No. 0345. They were outfitted with big rattan brooms that rotated, clearing the track of snow.

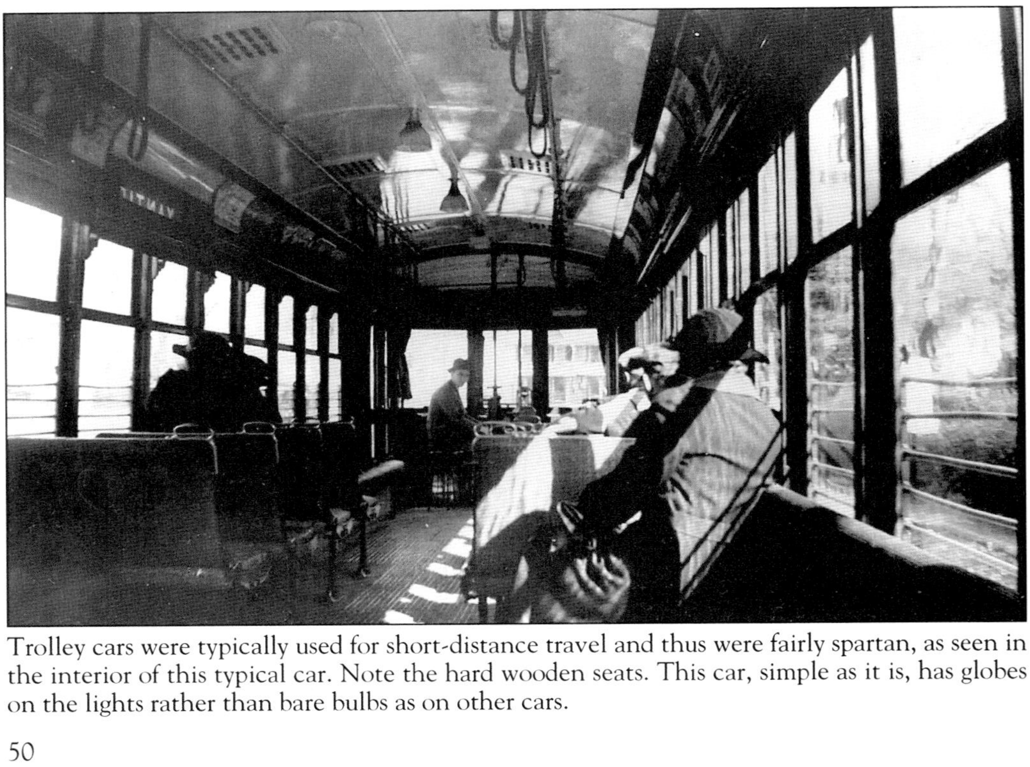

Trolley cars were typically used for short-distance travel and thus were fairly spartan, as seen in the interior of this typical car. Note the hard wooden seats. This car, simple as it is, has globes on the lights rather than bare bulbs as on other cars.

Operator Charlie Ladd stands in the door of car No. 205 in 1935.

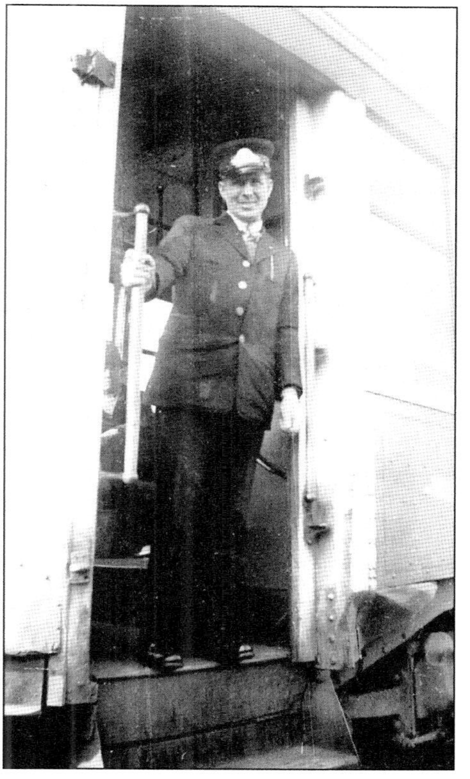

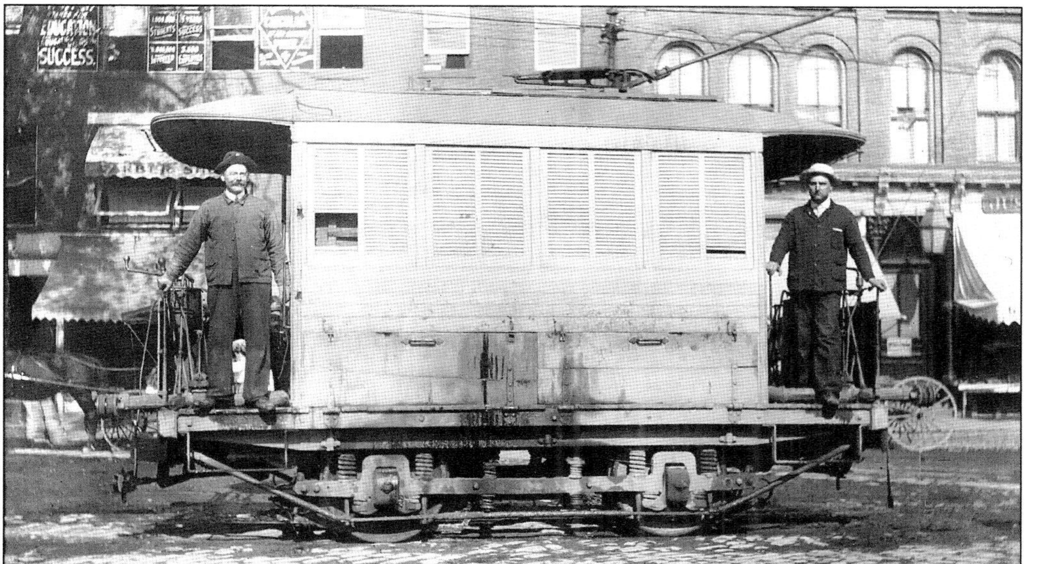

This Norwich Street Railway work car was most likely a converted horse car. Known for their thriftiness, many New England transportation companies converted older passenger cars they were no longer using into work cars that they could use in streetcar maintenance operations.

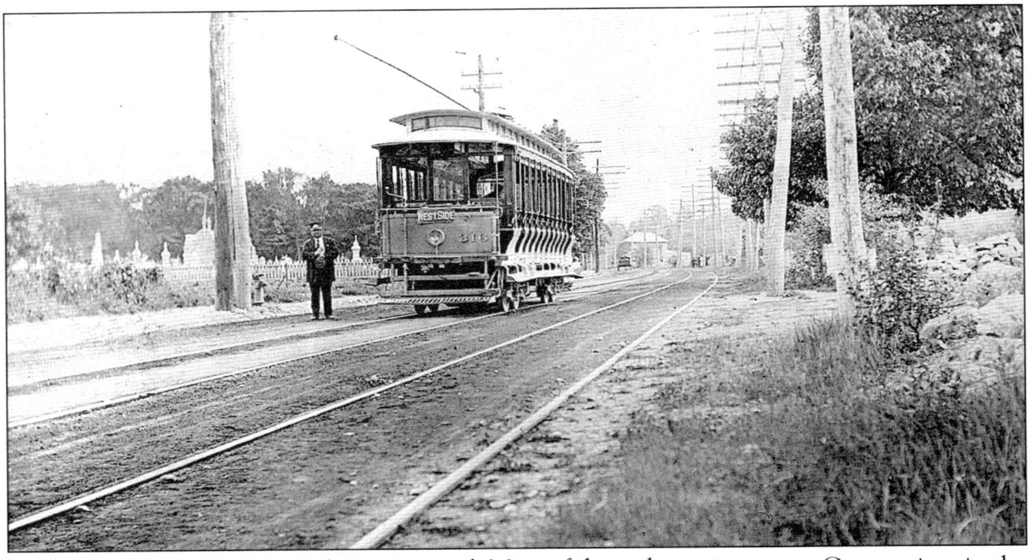

Note that this road in Norwich is not paved. Most of the industry in eastern Connecticut in the early 1900s was textile mills, and there were few cars that were affordable to the average mill worker. This made streetcars the natural choice for local travel.

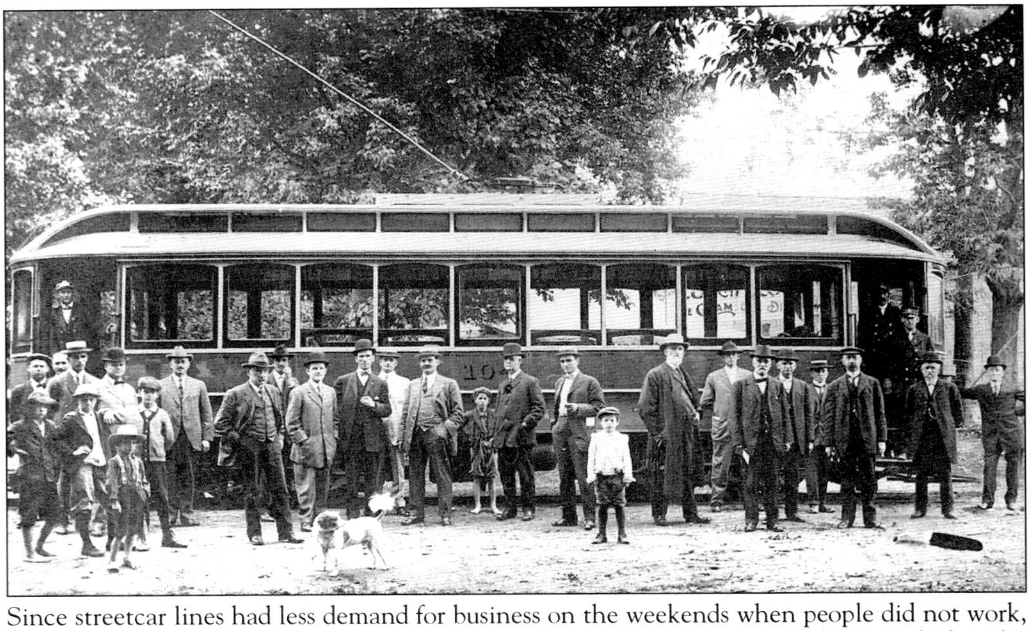

Since streetcar lines had less demand for business on the weekends when people did not work, many local groups were able to charter streetcars for picnics and other social outings before the availability of family cars or motor coaches.

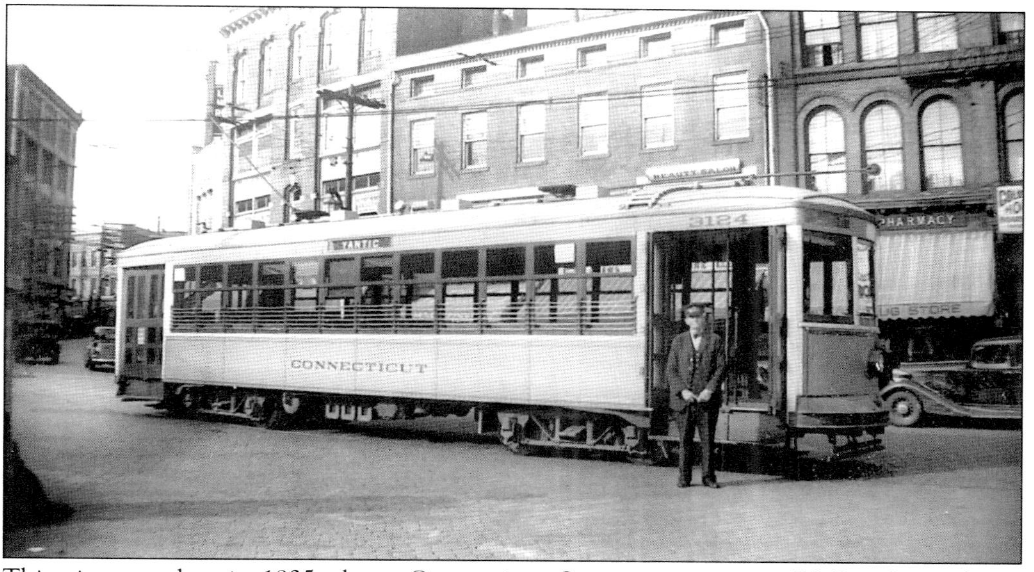

This picture, taken in 1935, shows Connecticut Company supervisor Ed Douglas with car No. 3124 in Franklin Square in Norwich.

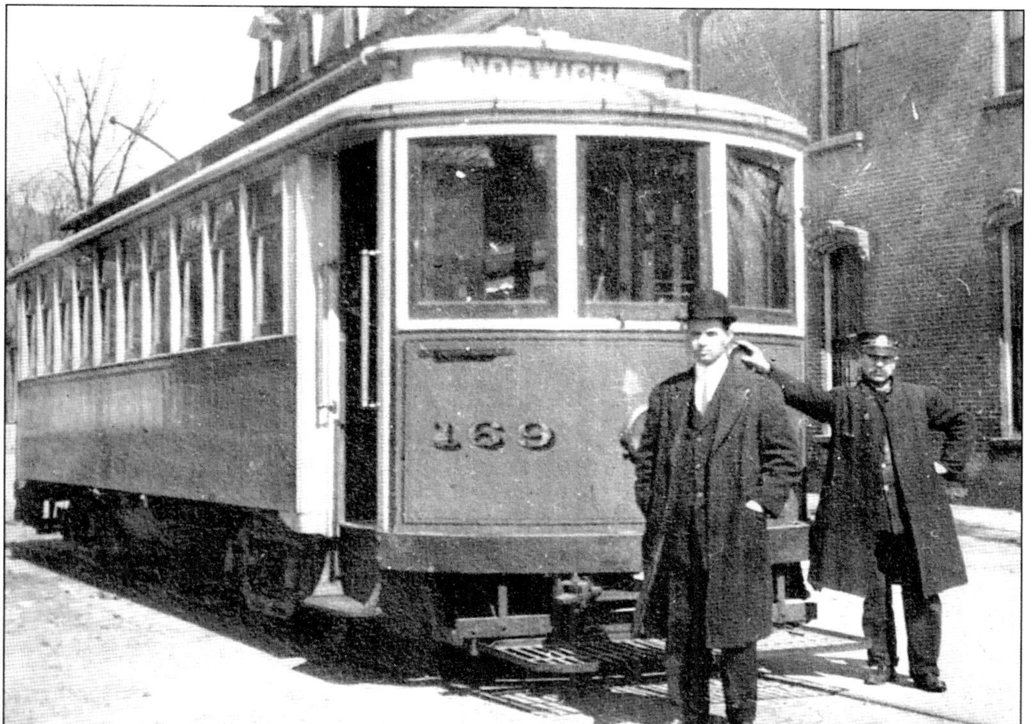

Two unknown Connecticut Company employees, most likely a manager and a motorman, pose with car No. 169 in 1911 in downtown Norwich.

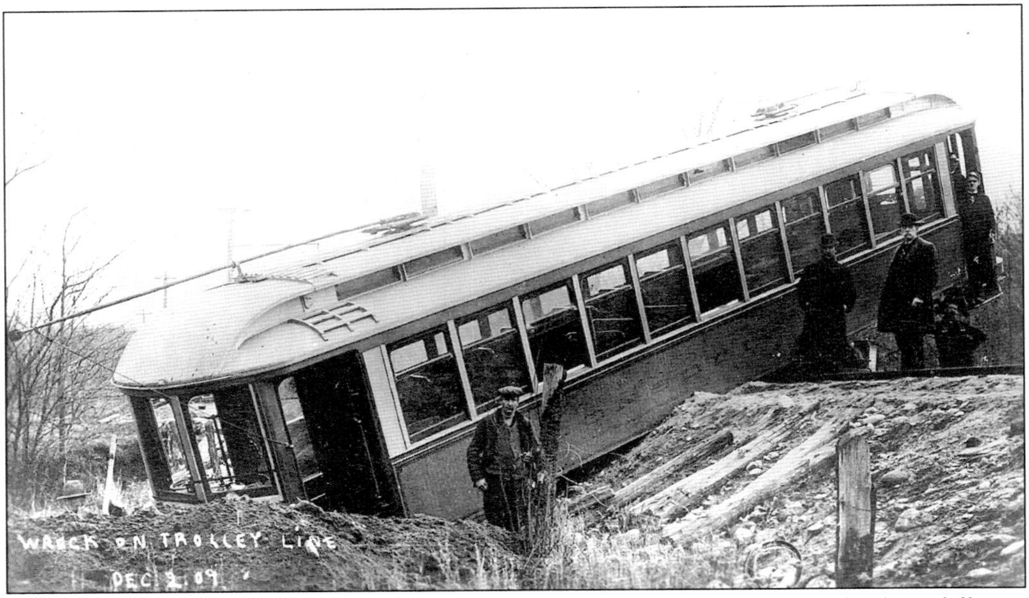

As with any form of transportation, accidents happened. These two photographs show different views of the derailment of Consolidated Railroad Company car No. 152 in December 1909. It is interesting to note that there were no injuries as a result of this accident.

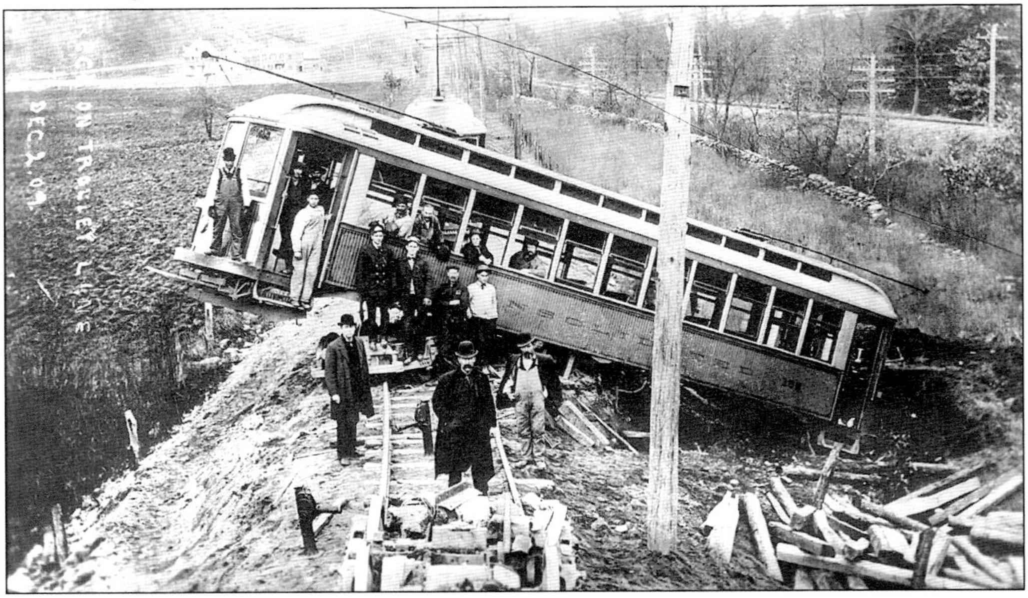

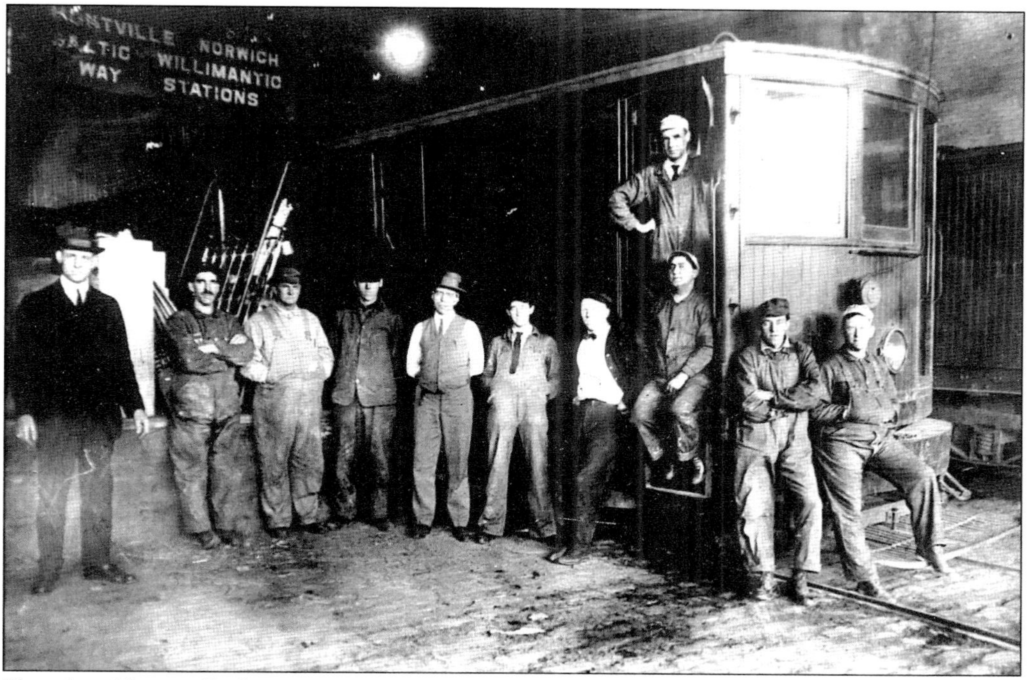

Shoreline Electric Railway car No. 01 is shown at the New London Freight House in 1915.

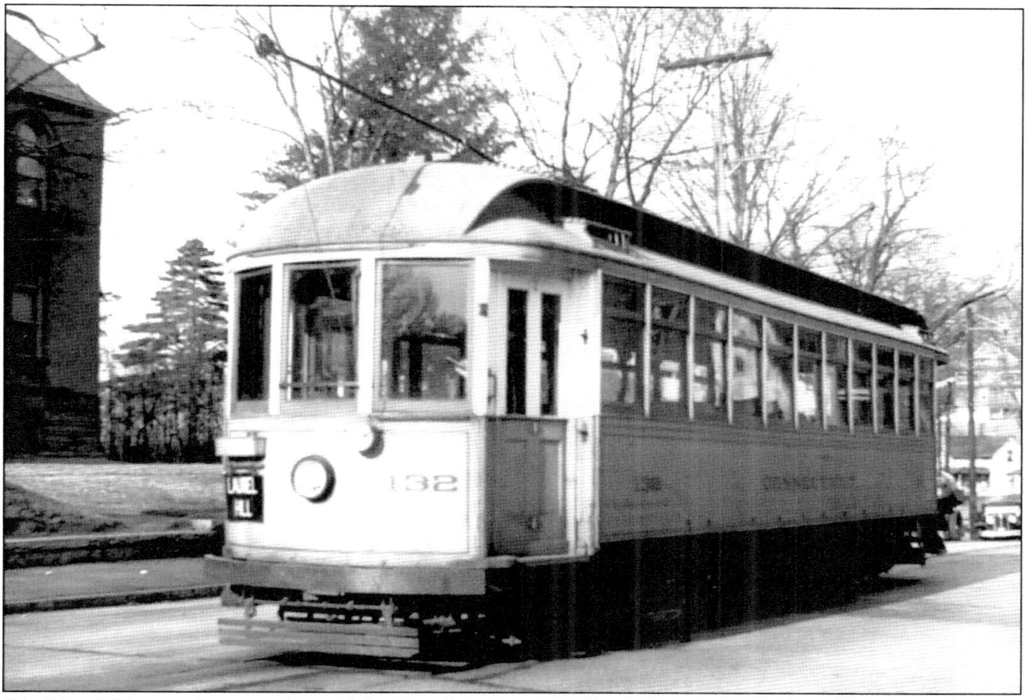

Car No. 132, another product of the Stephenson Car Company, was used in the Norwich area. This picture was taken on the Laurel Avenue line in 1934.

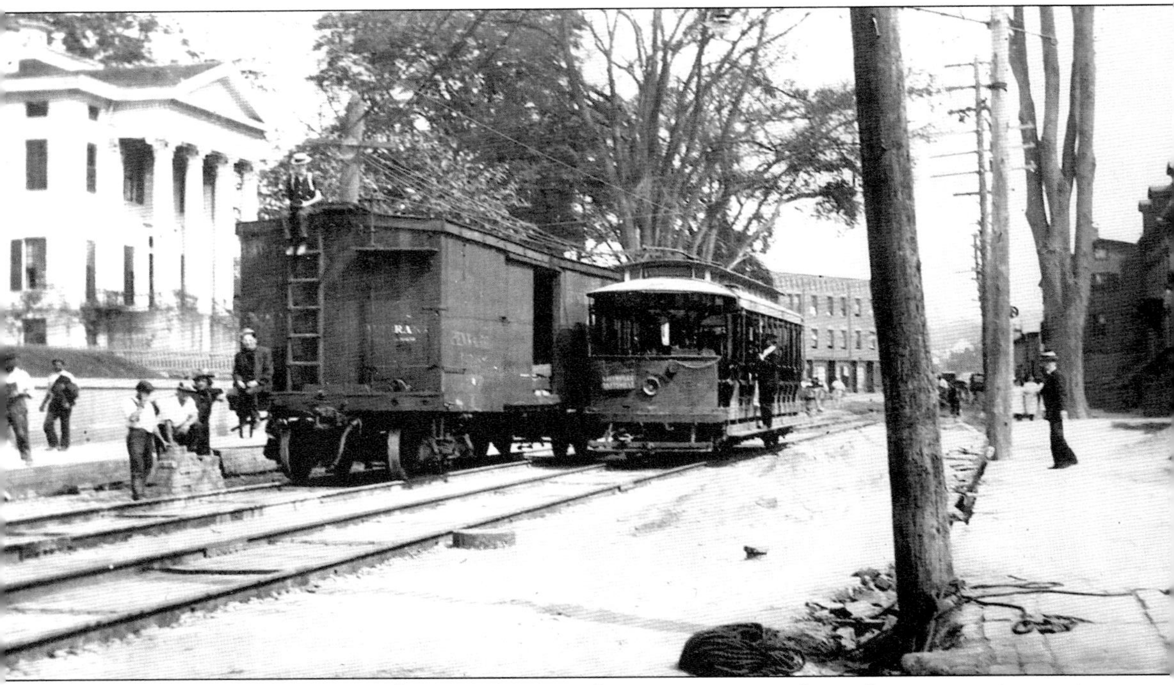

The ability to deliver supplies on-site, as in this picture, certainly made construction projects easier for streetcar companies. In this scene, a "steam road" boxcar, the term used for a boxcar from a steam railroad operation, delivers cobblestone directly to the work site, eliminating the need to move it again other than for its utilization on the line.

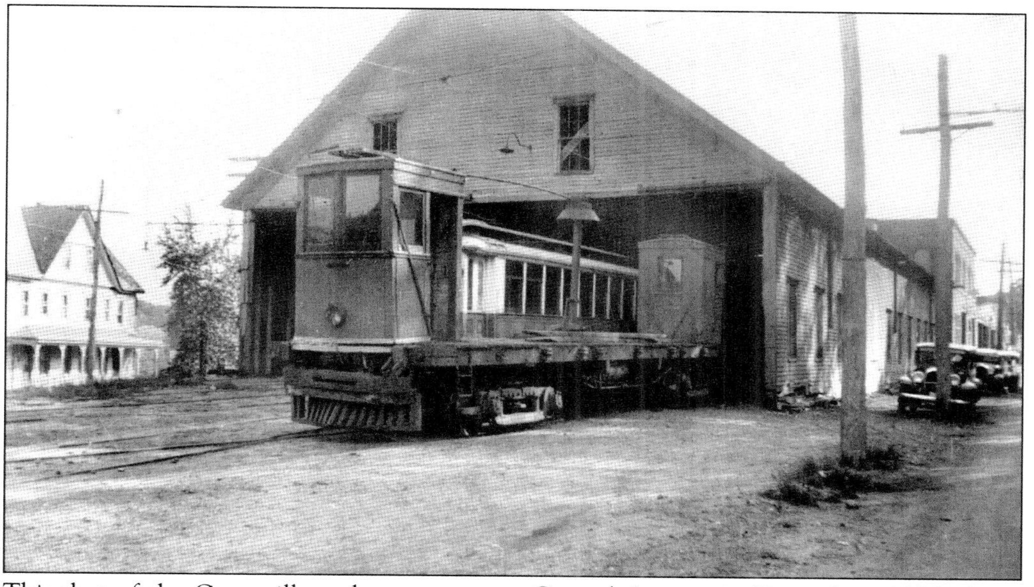

This shot of the Greenville carbarn annex, on Central Avenue in Norwich *c.* 1935, shows adequate room for the streetcar fleet. All equipment in Norwich was stored inside when not out on the line.

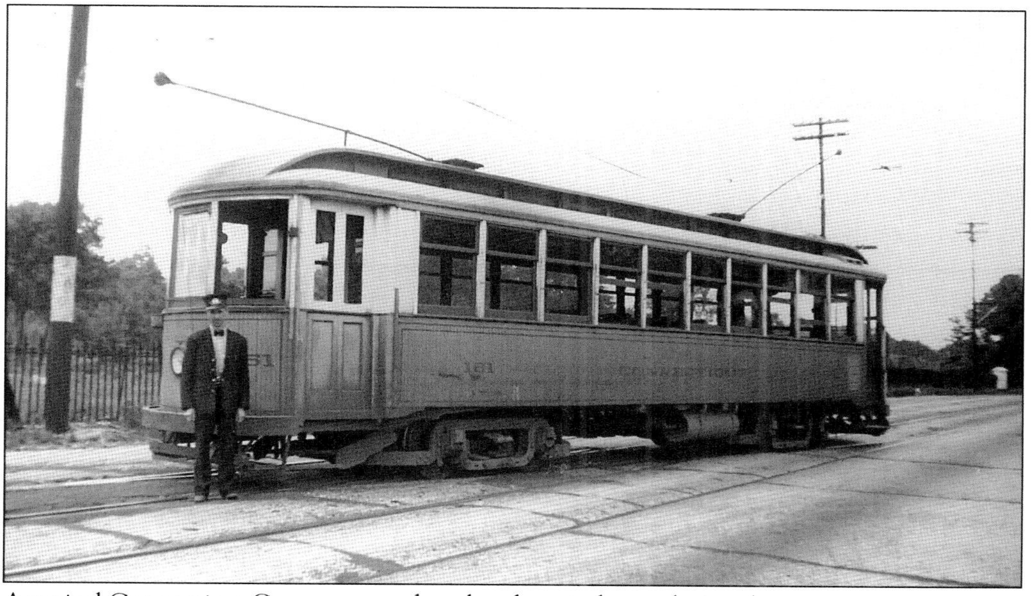

A typical Connecticut Company wooden closed car is shown during the one-man operator era.

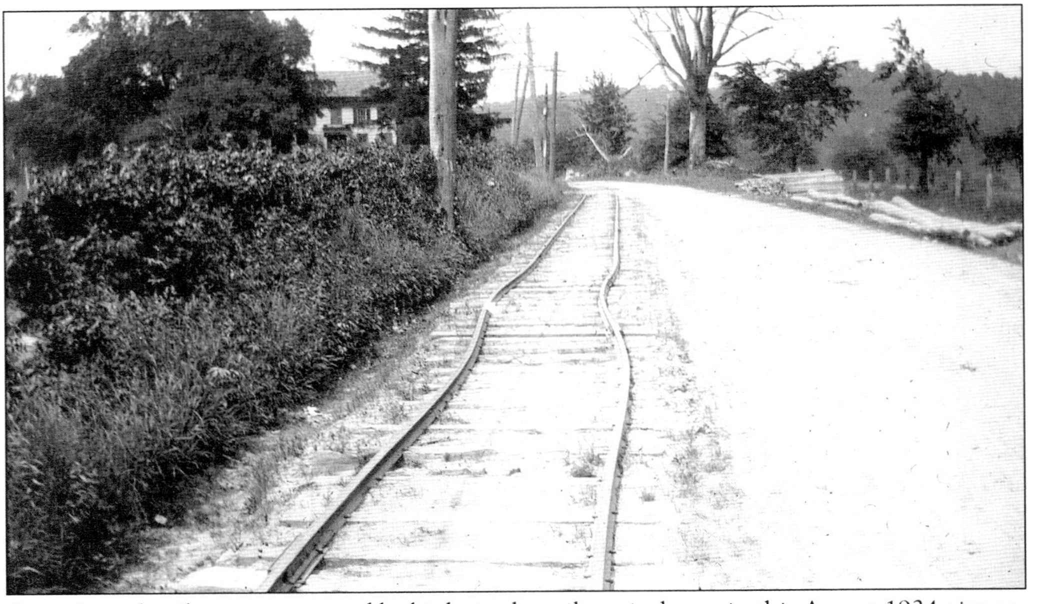

Sometimes derailments are caused by kinks in the rails, as is shown in this August 1934 picture. This particular kink was caused by the heat of the sun.

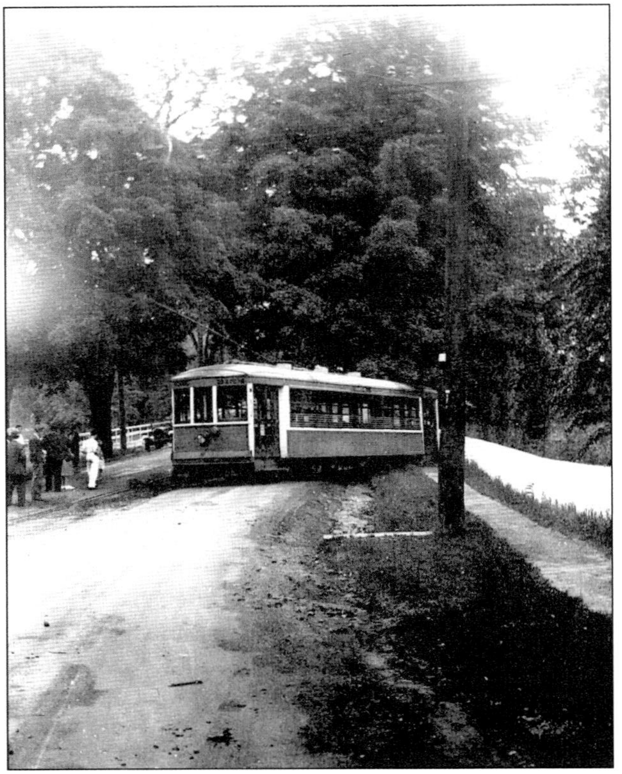

As is true with any rail operation, the trolley cars occasionally had problems with derailments, such as car No. 3124 shown in this picture. The car is a lightweight double-truck car, built in 1923 by the Osgood Bradley Car Company in Worcester, Massachusetts. This company was purchased by the Pullman Company in the 1930s.

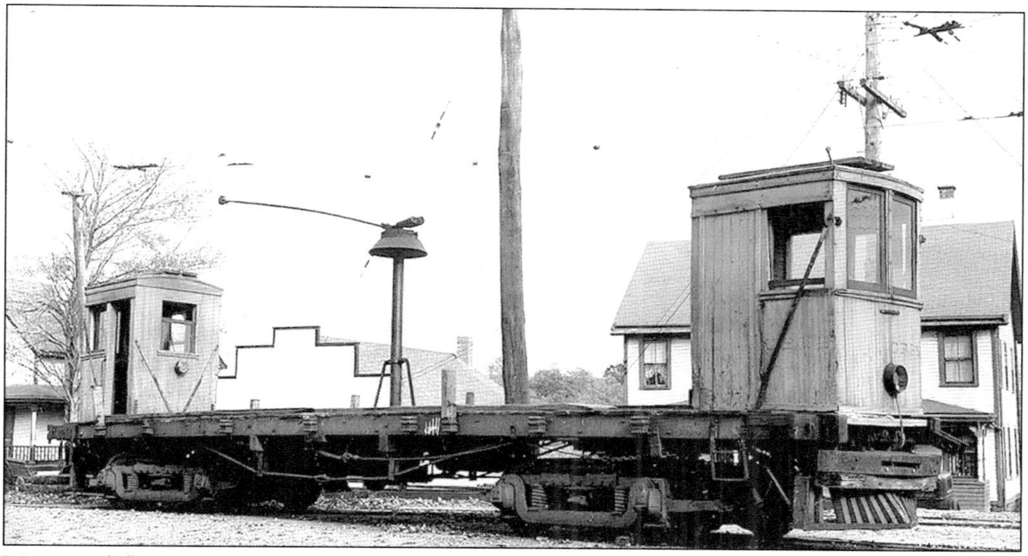

Motorized flatcar No. 0335 was used throughout the Norwich and New London lines. Work cars like this one were used to move track supplies to where they were needed. Since there is no roof to mount the trolley pole on, a shaft was installed in the middle of the car to provide the power it needed to run the motors.

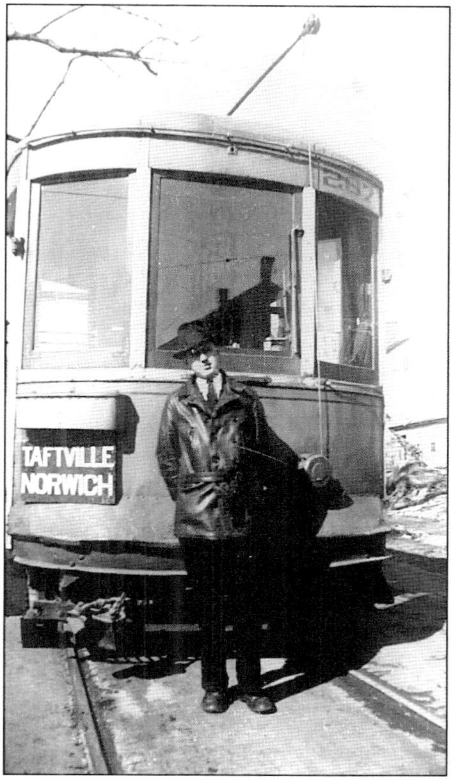

Horace Bromley is shown in this 1935 photograph with car No. 207.

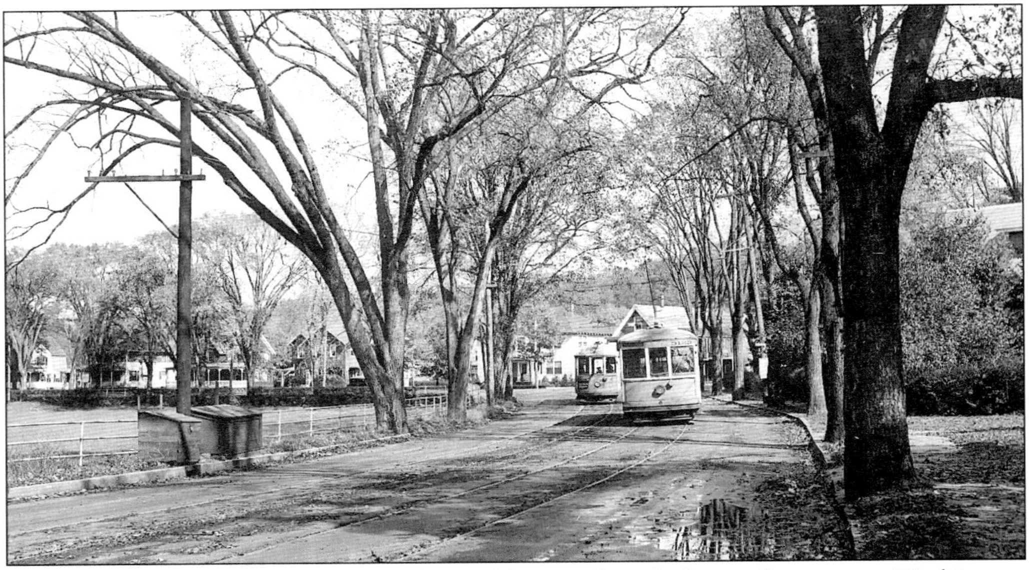

These two cars are shown meeting at the Buckley switch on Lafayette Street, near Washington Street in Norwich. These switches allowed cars going in opposite directions to pass each other. Meets were scheduled so that delays to passengers were minimal.

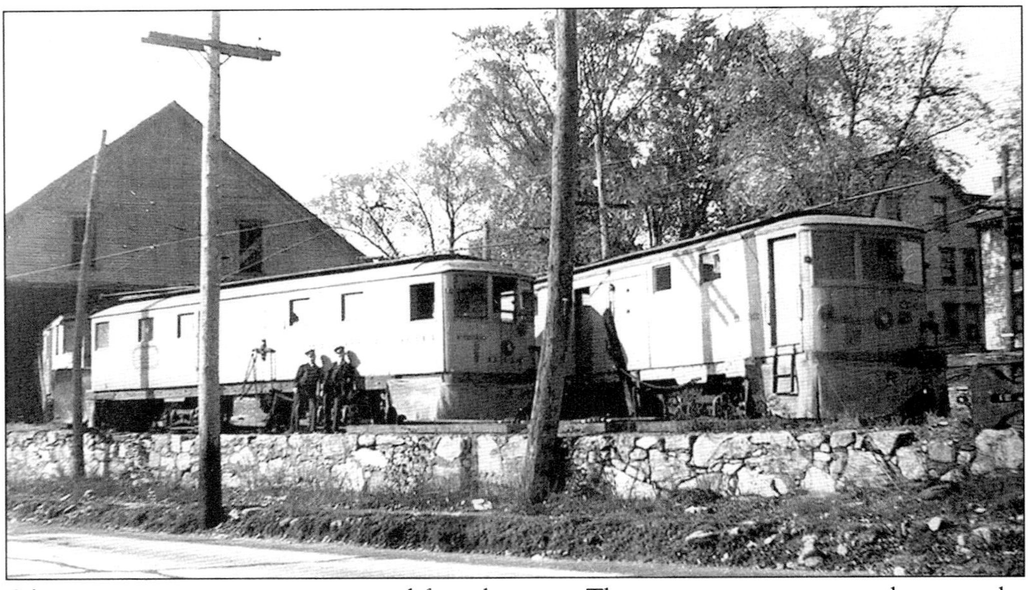

Often, passenger cars were converted for other uses. These two snow sweepers, shown at the Thamesville barn, were built as open cars by the Cincinnati Car Company in 1915. They were converted to snow sweepers by the Waterbury shops of the Connecticut Company in 1923. Car No. 0345 survived the closing of the Norwich lines in 1936 when it was sold to the Hoboken Shore Railroad in Hoboken, New Jersey. It was later scrapped in the 1950s.

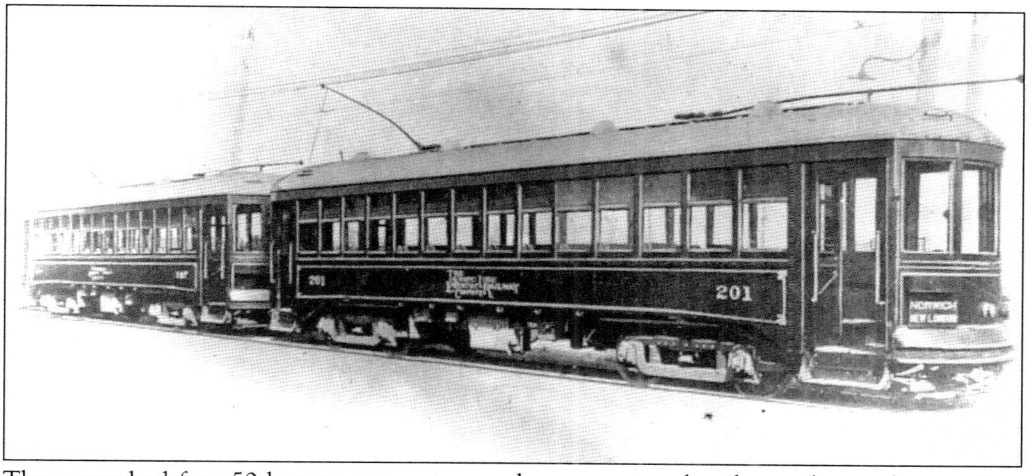

These cars had four 50-horsepower motors and were equipped with couplers and controllers for multiple unit operation so two or more cars could be run together in a train, as shown in this picture. Interestingly enough, this type of operation was never regularly used. The 200 series cars ran their entire life as single units between New London, Norwich, and Willimantic. However, in the 1920s, car No. 209 ran through to Webster, Massachusetts, on a public utilities commission inspection.

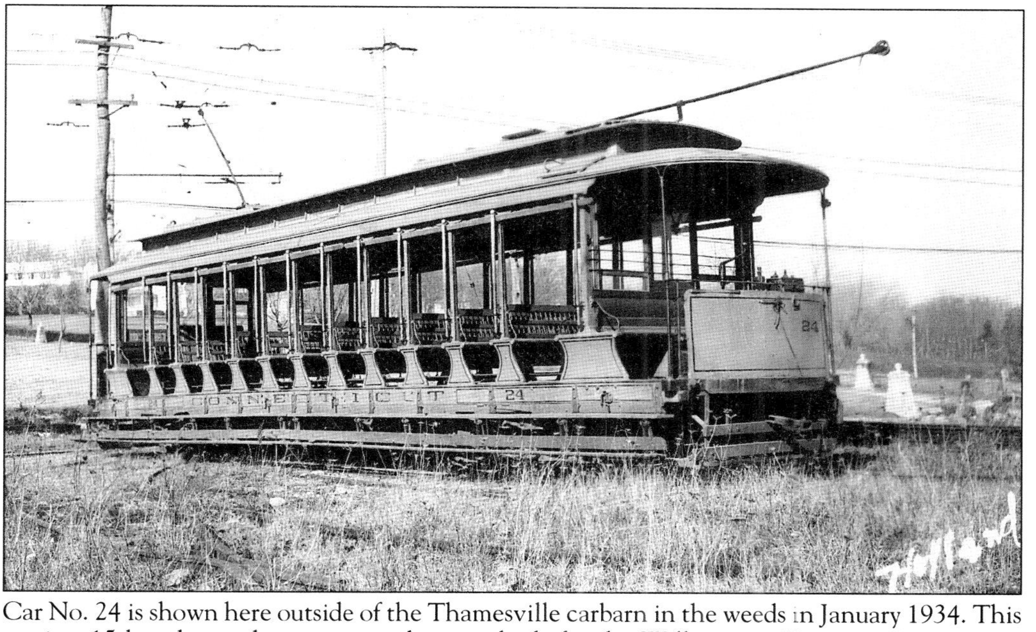

Car No. 24 is shown here outside of the Thamesville carbarn in the weeds in January 1934. This car is a 15-bench wooden open car that was built for the Willimantic Traction Company in 1900 by the Jones Car Company in Watervliet, New York.

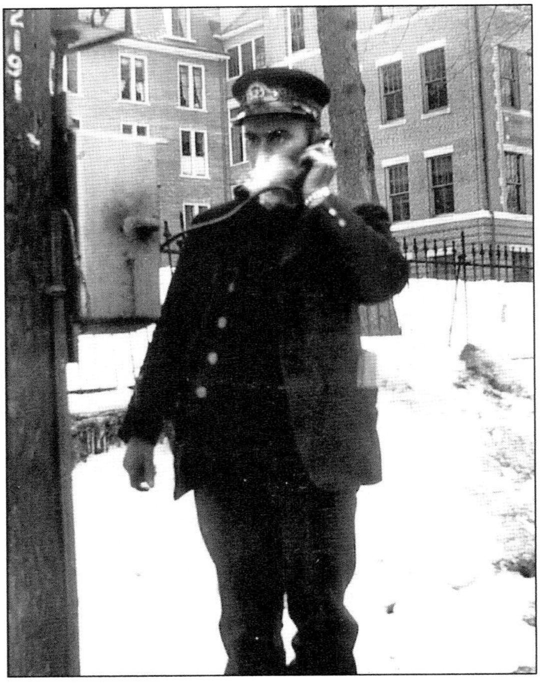

Communication between the operator and the dispatcher was paramount in keeping the trolley cars running safely and on time. The Connecticut Company maintained an extensive telephone system along its lines for just this purpose. This picture shows an operator using one of these phones in Norwich. The phones were housed in steel boxes that were usually located on power poles. They were placed at all car meeting points and important junctions.

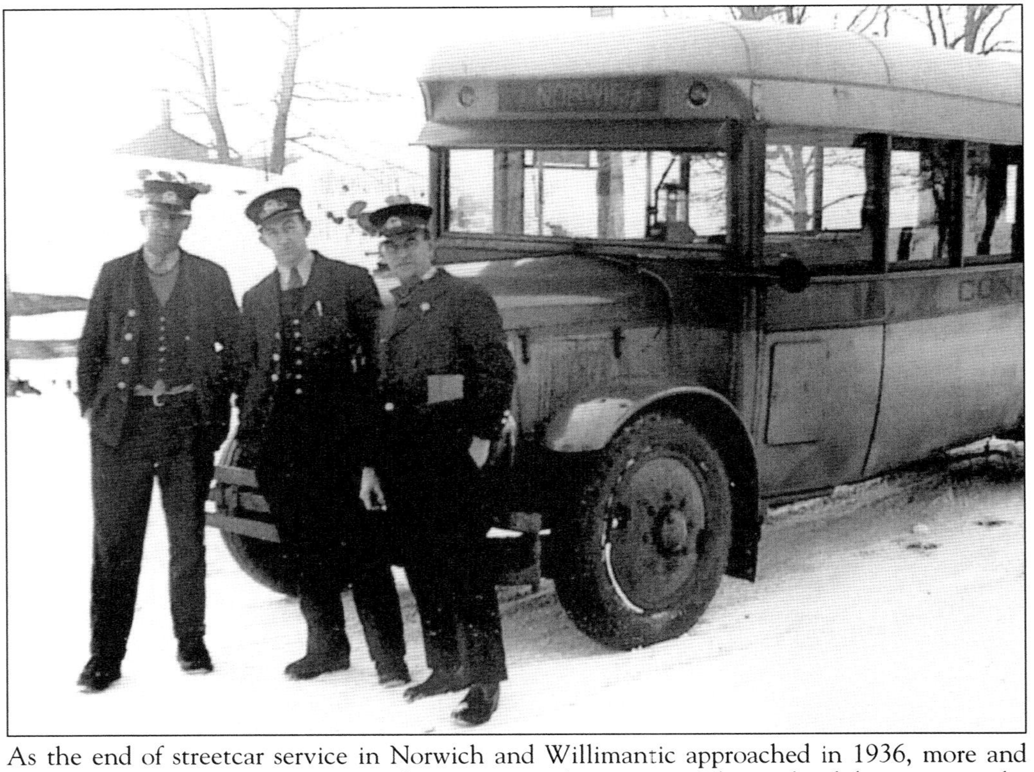

As the end of streetcar service in Norwich and Willimantic approached in 1936, more and more streetcar operators were trained as motor coach operators. Those who did not want to be trained to operate the buses did not have a job following the elimination of streetcar service.

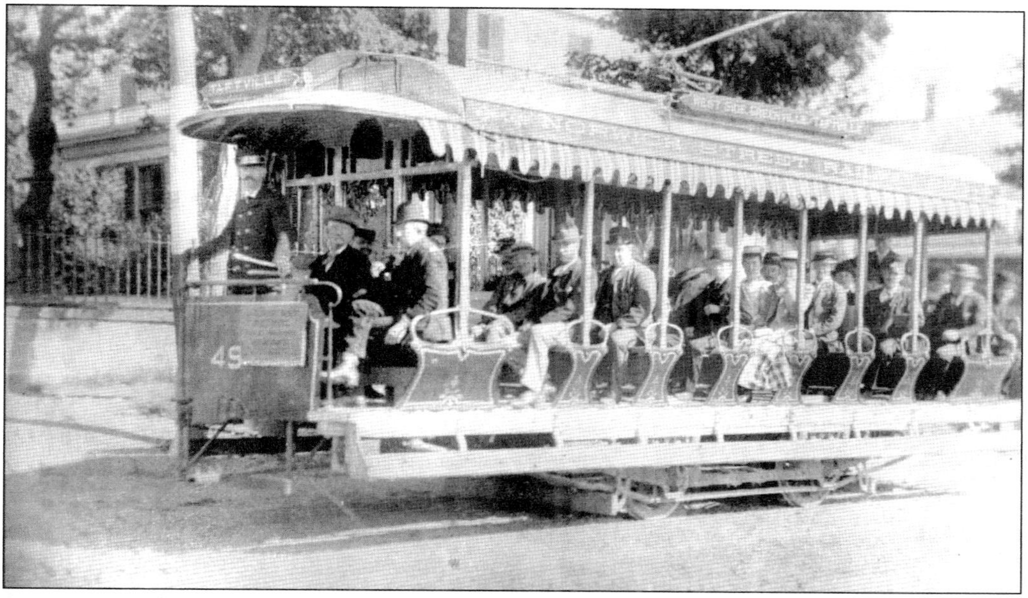

Seen is Norwich Street Railway open car No. 49, *c.* 1895, on Central Avenue en route to Taftville.

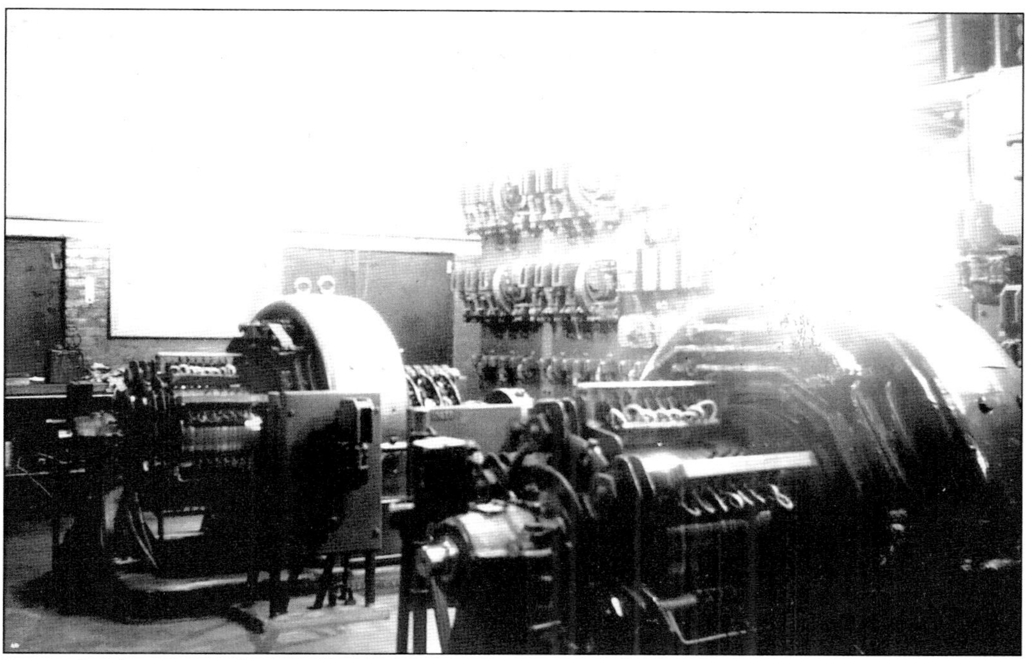

Power for the cars on the Connecticut Company lines was supplied by various power substations, like the power station shown here in Thamesville, which contained equipment that converted the power from 11,000 volts AC to 600 volts DC for the trolley cars to run on.

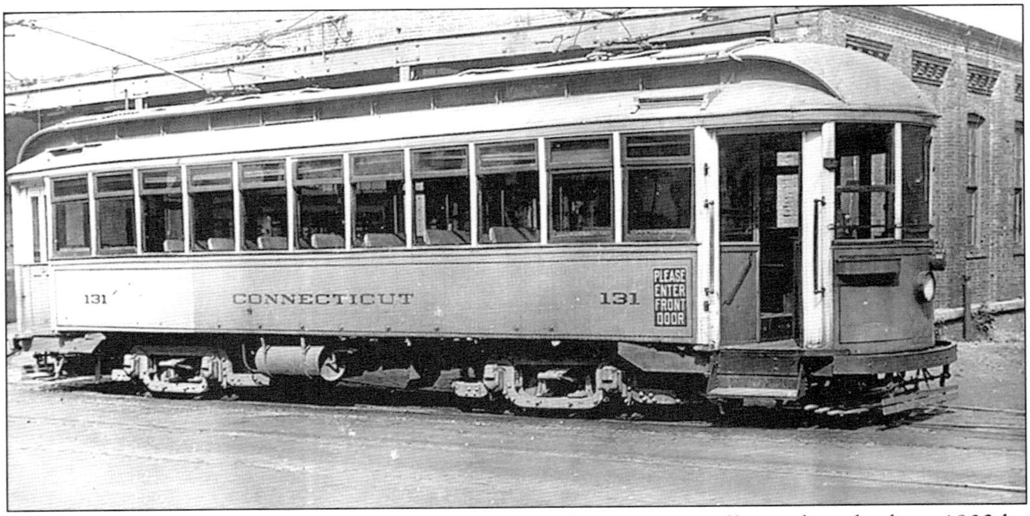

Car No. 131, shown here in front of the Greenville barn, was an all-wood car built in 1903 by the Stephenson Car Company in New York.

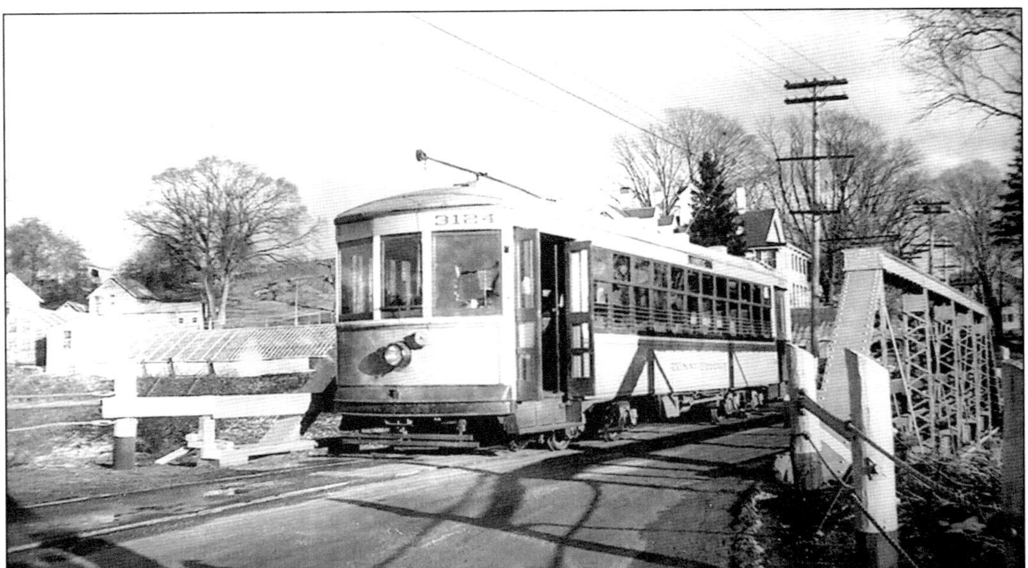
This double-truck car is shown in service on the Norwich to Yantic line crossing the bridge just south of Yantic.

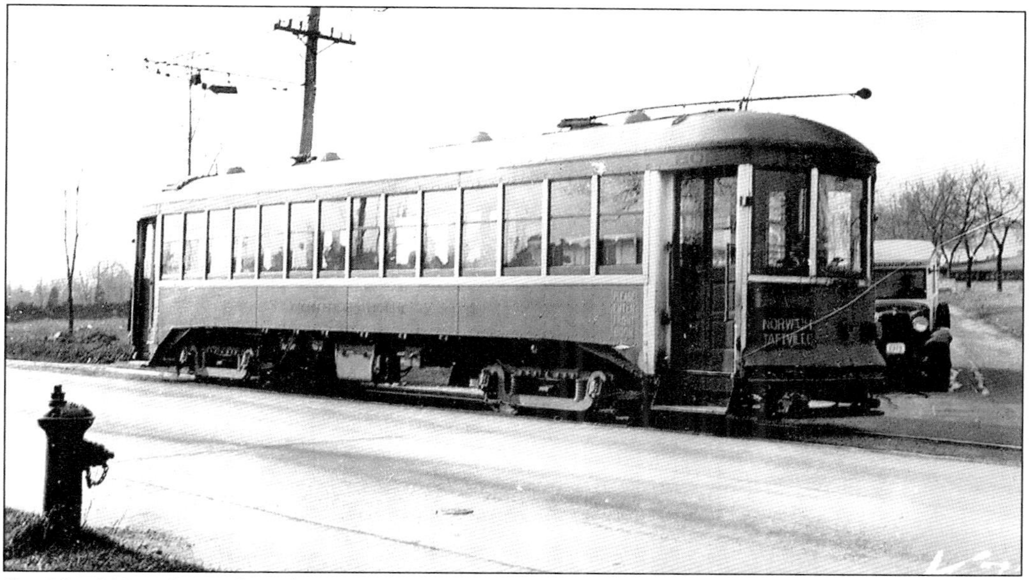

Car No. 209 is shown here laying over at Uncas-on-Thames Hospital on the New London line.

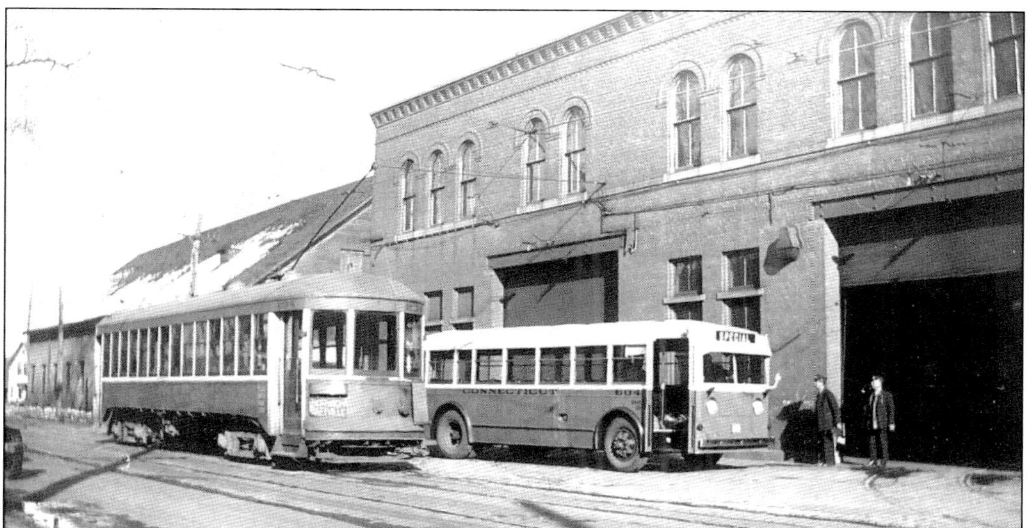

The future is apparent in this picture. Motor buses took over lines from the faithful trolley cars. The Greenville barn was even converted to a bus garage, and it served that purpose until the 1960s.

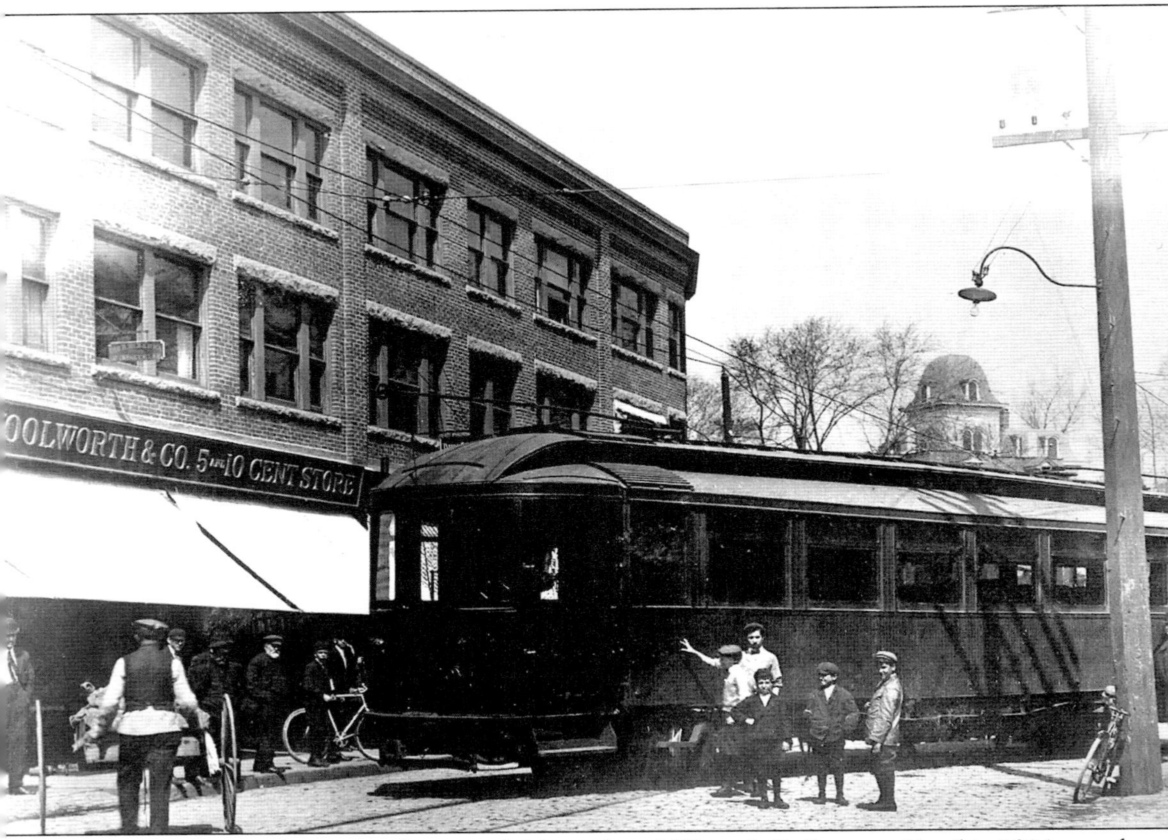

Derailments in the city, as shown with Norwich and Westerly Railway car No. 5 in 1914, posed difficult problems for traffic flow.

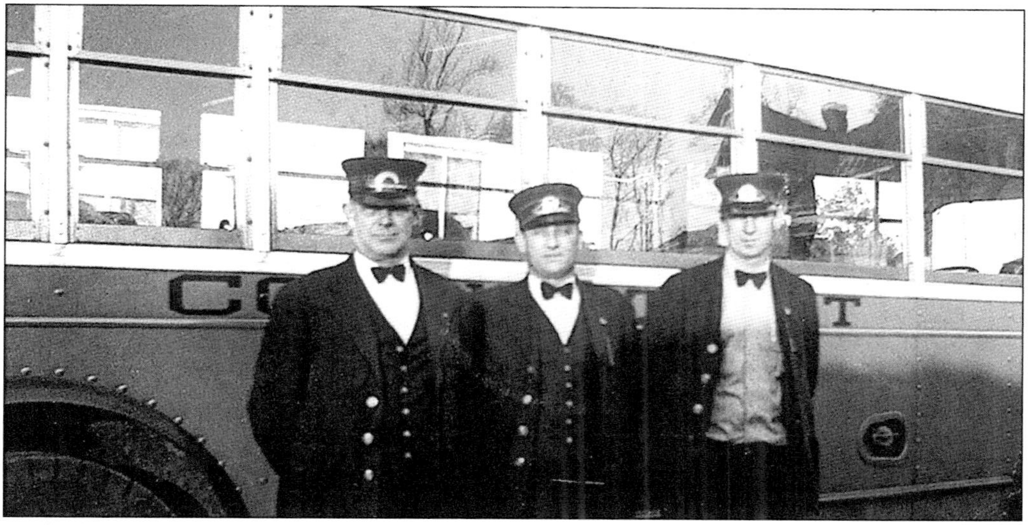

With the decline of the trolley systems, many former motormen became bus drivers. These students are still wearing their motorman's uniforms, complete with vests and bow ties. The bus they are learning on is a 1934 Yellow Coach.

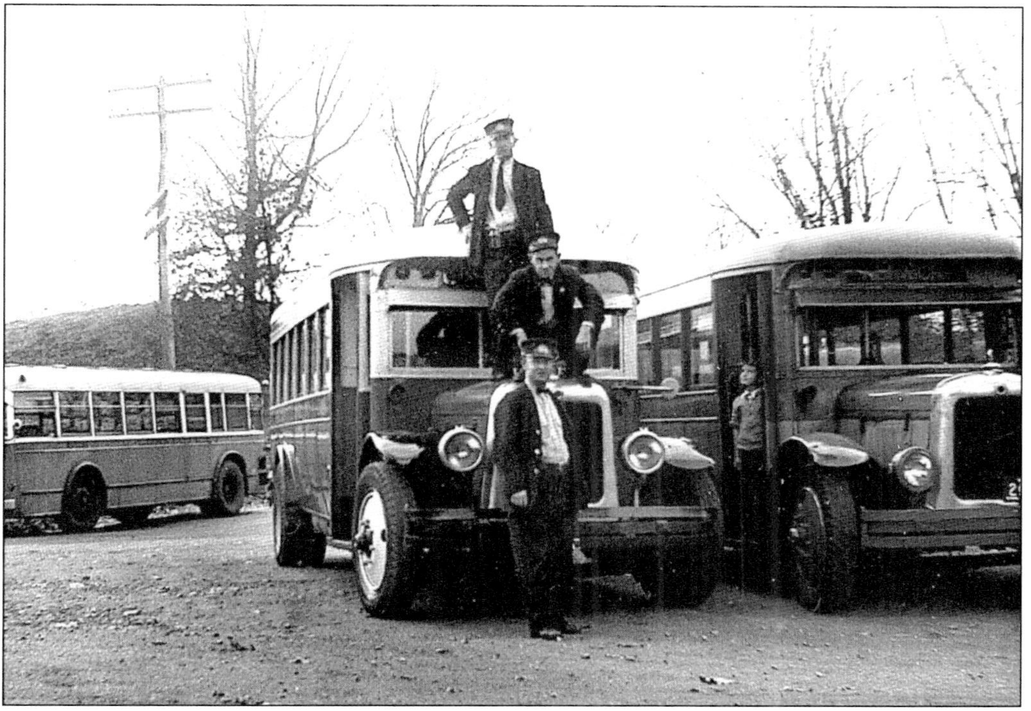

New routes and new drivers did not always mean new equipment. The two buses in this picture are Yellow Coaches from the 1920s.

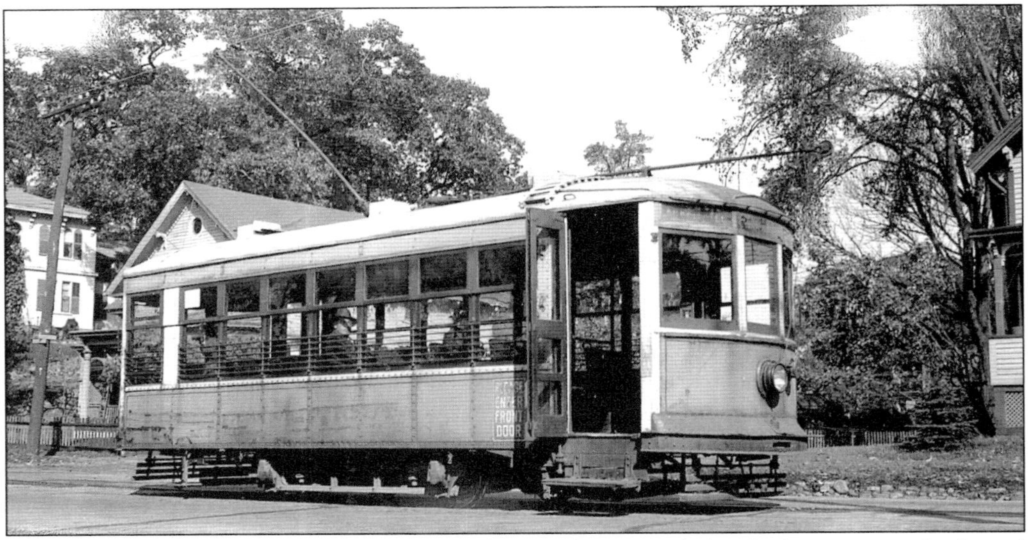

Car No. 2304 only held 20 passengers, but that was big enough for the business on the Laurel Hill line in Norwich. Single-truck cars were never popular with the riding public due to the poor ride they gave.

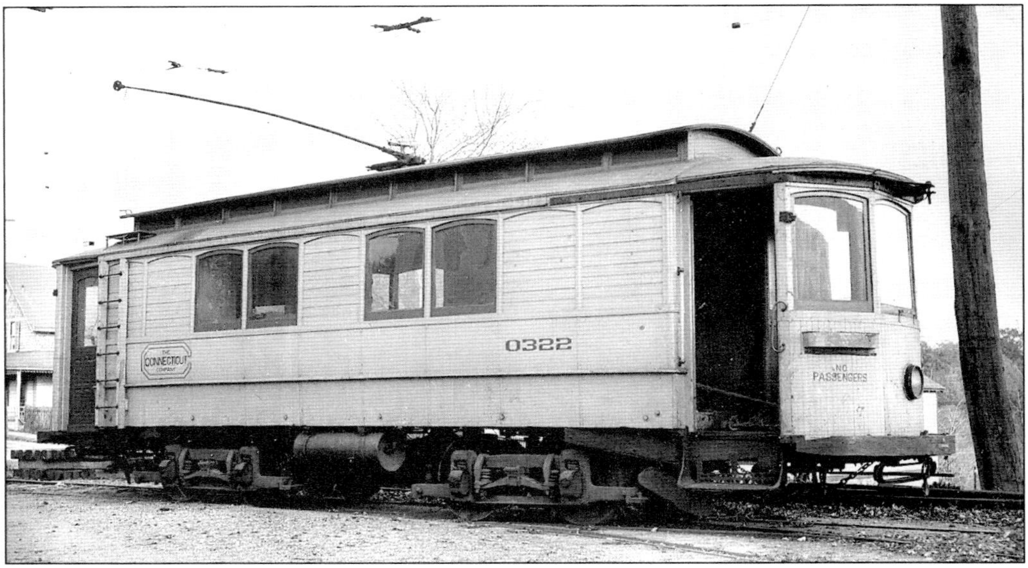

Many obsolete passenger cars were converted into work cars, like car No. 0322. This car was used in Norwich for line maintenance during the summer months and as a sand car in the winter months.

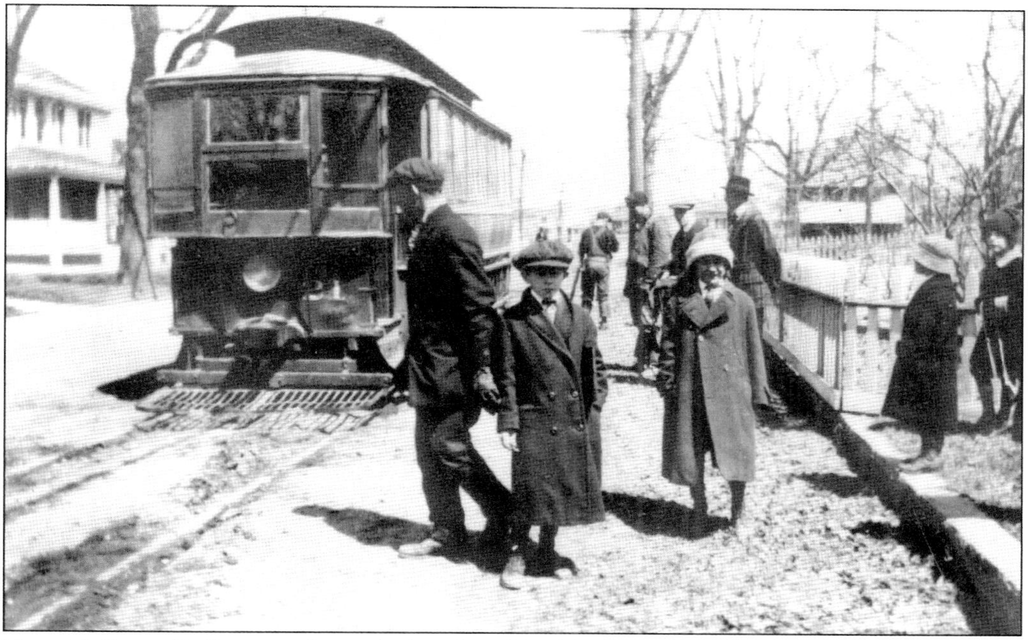

Norwich Street Railway single-truck closed-car No. 21 is getting ready to pick up schoolchildren in this 1894 scene. Note the homemade windshield added to the car, an afterthought to shelter the motorman from the wind and rain.

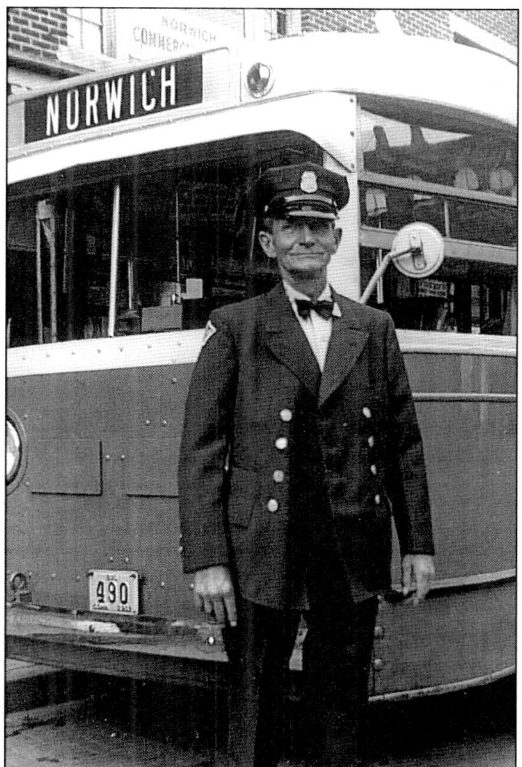

This employee's hat badge indicates that he is a supervisor. The supervisors rode with the operators to check their time schedule and operating skills and also made sure they treated the riding public with respect.

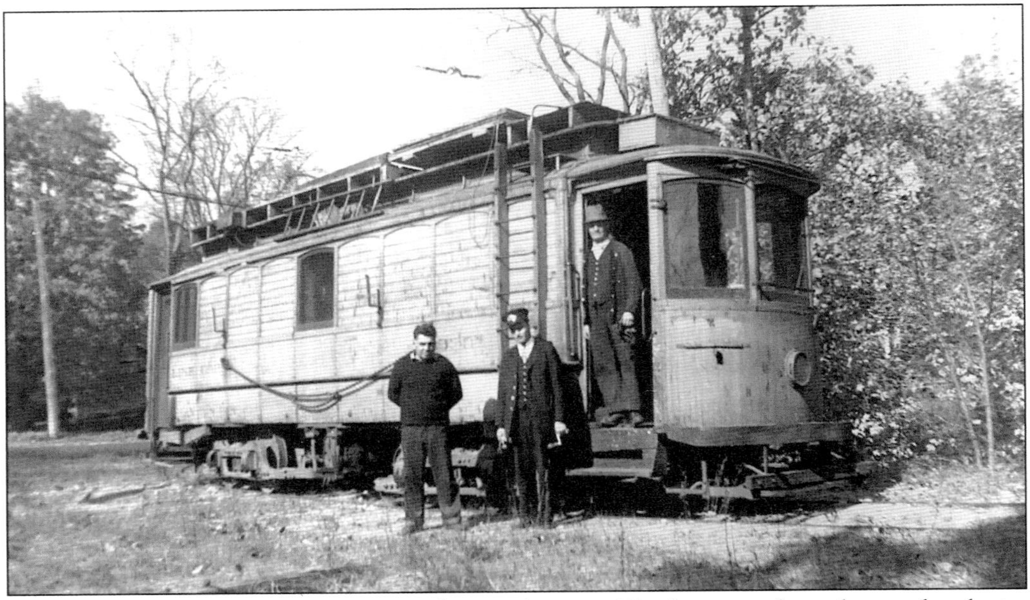

This former passenger car was converted into a line car. The line crew kept the overhead wire in good repair, which assured continued service.

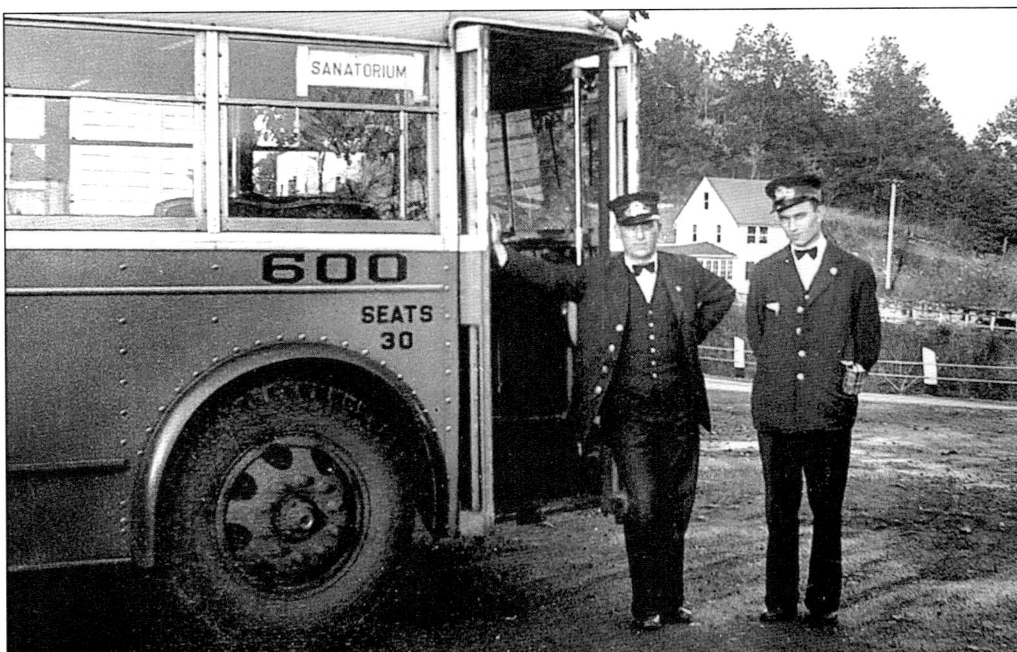

Streetcar operators train to be motor coach operators.

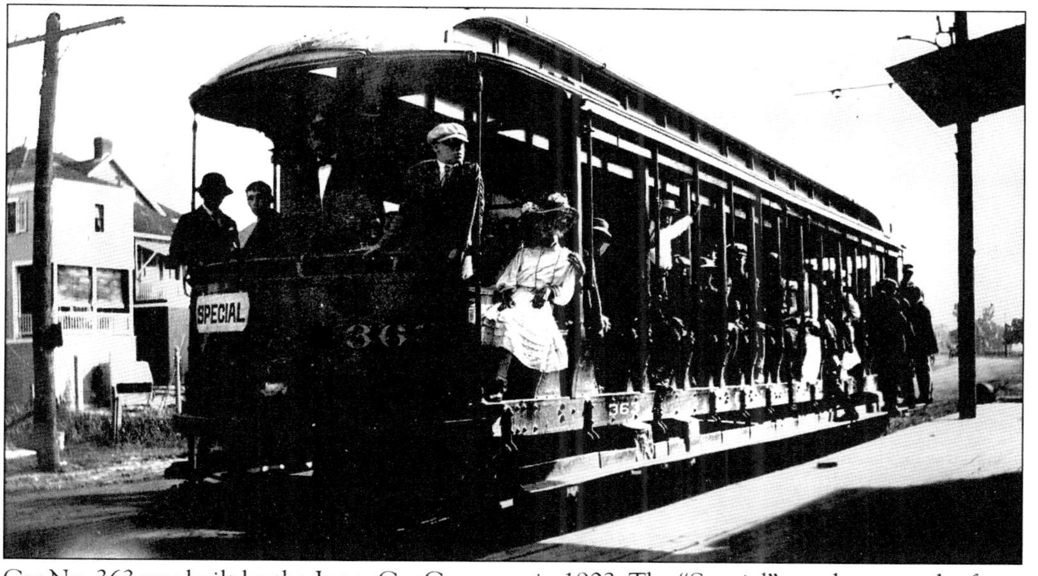

Car No. 363 was built by the Jones Car Company in 1902. The "Special" sign hung on the front of the car usually denoted a nonscheduled trip, possibly a picnic or other special outing.

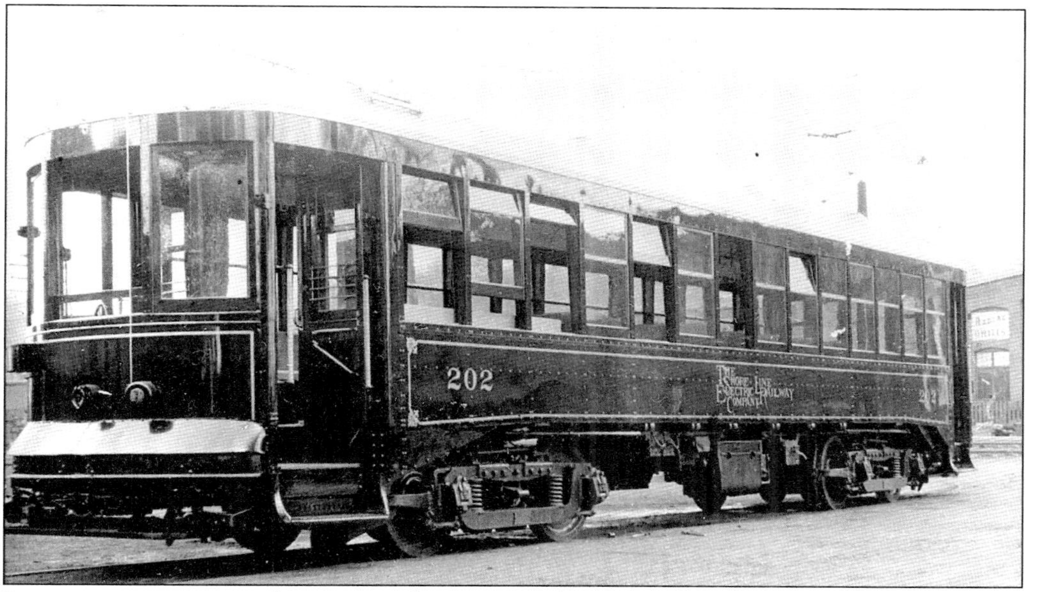

It was common practice for car manufacturers to take photographs of cars before they released them to the purchaser. This is a picture of Shoreline Electric Railway car No. 202 at the Wason Manufacturing Company plant in Springfield, Massachusetts, in 1915.

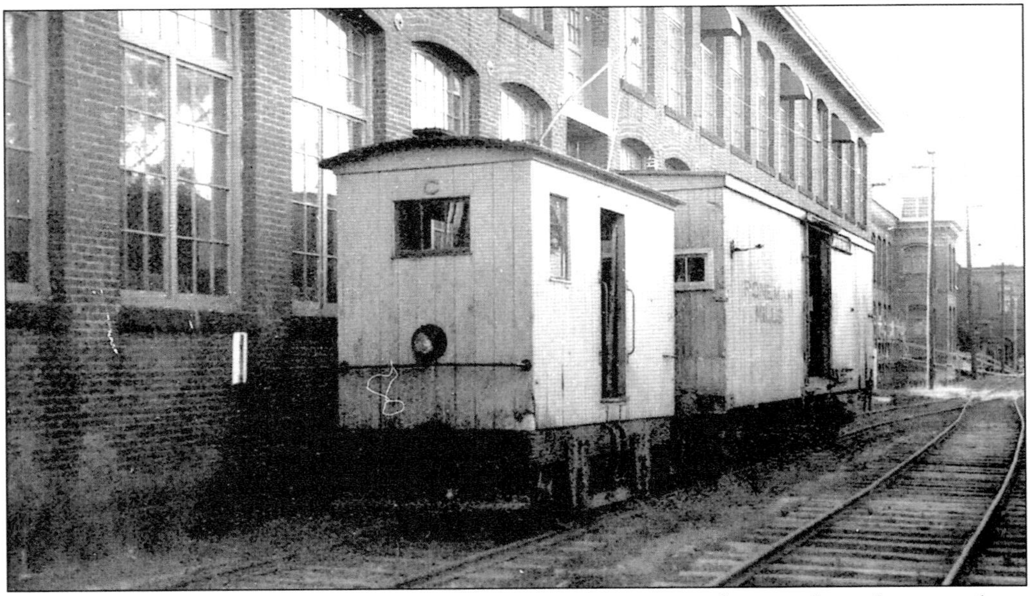

The Ponemah Mills, in the Taftville section of Norwich, operated an in-plant electric railway to move their products to the New Haven Railroad. Here, locomotive "C" moves a company boxcar in the yard. This car, line-repair car No. S193, can be seen in operation today at the Connecticut Trolley Museum in East Windsor.

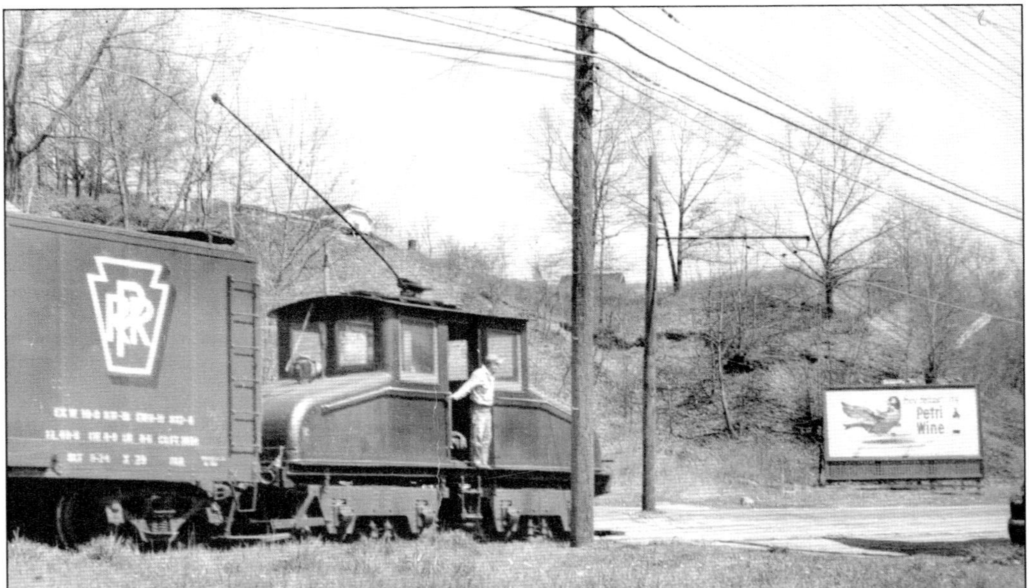

The Ponemah Mills electric railway moved freight cars, as shown in this 1950s-era picture, to the New Haven Railroad interchange. This engine was built in 1894 and ran in Norwich until the mill closed in 1965. When "Black Maria," as the engine was called by the locals, needed servicing, it was run over the streetcar tracks to the Greenville barn, where the Connecticut Company would do the necessary repair work. This locomotive has been preserved and can be seen at the Connecticut Trolley Museum in East Windsor.

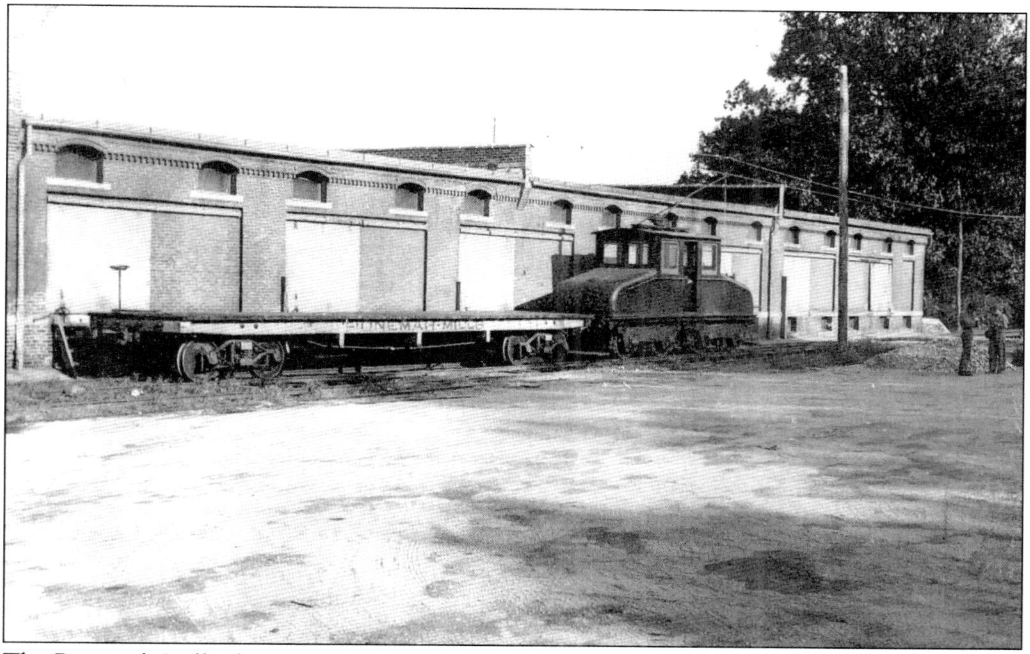

The Ponemah Mills electric locomotive sits in the mill yard in Taftville in 1934.

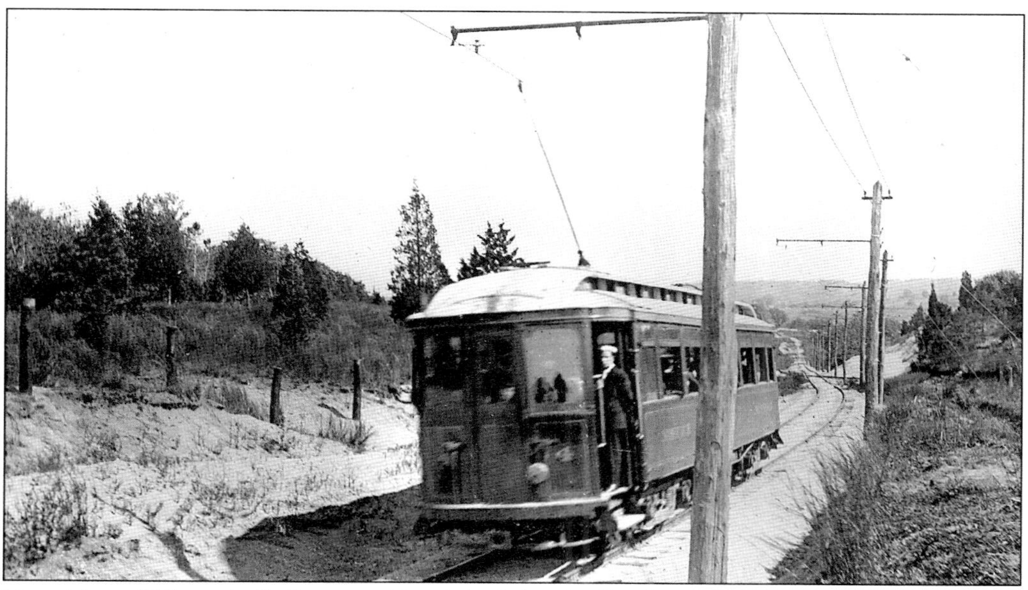

Norwich and Westerly Railway car No. 4, built by the Southern Car Company, is shown near the Norwich State Hospital in Preston in 1906.

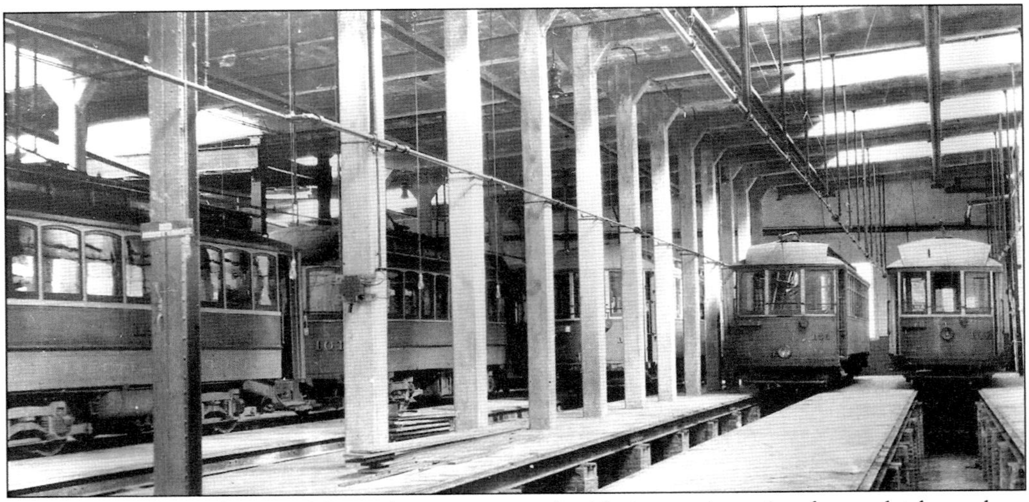

The Greenville carbarn in Norwich was equipped with inspection pits, from which workers could inspect the mechanical workings of the car and do repairs as necessary. This barn was also equipped with skylights, which afforded better lighting conditions for the workers while at the same time saving money for the company. A point of note is that this barn was also equipped with a fire sprinkler system, a luxury that many companies could not afford for their carbarns.

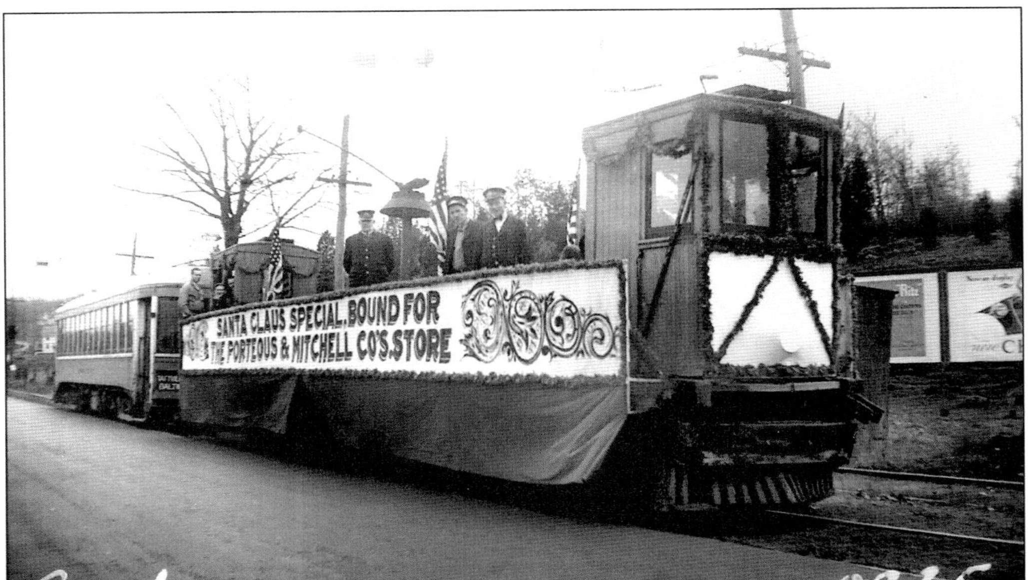

Work car No. 0335 is decorated for the annual Christmas parade sponsored by the Porteous and Mitchell department store in downtown Norwich.

During Period Daylight Saving Time is in effect read as Daylight Saving Time

THE CONNECTICUT COMPANY

Time given indicates when cars may be expected to arrive and depart. Subject to change without notice

Time: 12 01 midnight to 12 00 noon is indicated by light figures.
12 01 noon to 12 00 midnight is indicated by heavy figures.

April 30, 1933

NEW LONDON TO NORWICH AND WILLIMANTIC

EASTERN STANDARD TIME

	A.M.	A.M.	A.M.	A.M.	A.M.	A.M.	A.M.	A.M.	A.M.	A.M.	A.M.	A.M.	A.M.	A.M.	A.M.	A.M.	A.M.	P.M.	P.M.	P.M.
Parade, New London......Lv.	.....	.....	.....	.....	*5 45	*6 15	6 45	*7 15	7 45	*8 15	8 45	9 15	9 45	10 15	10 45	11 15	11 45	12 15	12 45	1 15
Conn. College, New London...	.....	.....	.....	.....	*6 00	*6 30	7 00	*7 30	8 00	*8 30	9 00	9 30	10 00	10 30	11 00	11 30	12 00	12 30	1 00	1 30
Quaker Hill, Waterford.......	.....	.....	.....	.....	*6 07	*6 37	7 07	*7 37	8 07	*8 37	9 07	9 37	10 07	10 37	11 07	11 37	12 07	12 37	1 07	1 37
Post Office, Montville.......	.....	.....	.....	.....	*6 16	*6 46	7 16	*7 46	8 16	*8 46	9 16	9 46	10 16	10 46	11 16	11 46	12 16	12 46	1 16	1 46
State Sanitarium, Norwich....	.....	.....	.....	.....	*6 33	*7 03	7 33	*8 03	8 33	*9 03	9 33	10 03	10 33	11 03	11 33	12 03	12 33	1 03	1 33	2 03
Franklin Square, Norwich.....	*4 30	*5 15	5 45	*6 15	6 45	7 15	7 45	8 15	8 45	9 15	9 45	10 15	10 45	11 15	11 45	12 15	12 45	1 15	1 45	2 15
Post Office, Taftville..........	*4 54	*5 37	6 07	*6 37	7 05	7 37	8 07	8 37	9 07	9 37	10 07	10 37	11 07	11 37	12 07	12 37	1 07	1 37	2 07	2 37
Baltic Center................	*5 13	*5 57	6 25	.....	W7 25	7 57	8 25	.....	.....	9 57	10 25	.....	.....	11 57	12 25	.....	.....	1 57	2 25	.....
Post Office, So. Windham......	*5 35	.....	6 45	.....	W7 45	.....	8 45	.....	.....	.....	10 45	.....	.....	.....	12 45	.....	.....	.....	2 45	.....
R. R. Crossing, Willimantic. Ar.	*5 50	.....	6 55	.....	W7 57	.....	8 57	.....	.....	.....	10 57	.....	.....	.....	12 57	.....	.....	.....	2 57	.....
	A.M.	A.M.	A.M.	A.M.	A.M.	A.M.	A.M.	A.M.	A.M.	A.M.	A.M.	A.M.	A.M.	N'N	P.M.	P.M.	P.M.	P.M.	P.M.	P.M.

	P.M.	P.M.	P.M.	P.M.	P.M.	P.M.	P.M.	P.M.	P.M.	P.M.	P.M.	P.M.	P.M.	P.M.	P.M.	P.M.	P.M.	P.M.	N'HT	
Parade, New London......Lv.	1 45	2 15	2 45	3 15	3 45	4 15	4 45	5 15	5 45	6 15	6 45	7 15	7 45	8 15	8 45	S 9 15	9 45	10 45	12 00	.....
Conn. College, New London...	2 00	2 30	3 00	3 30	4 00	4 30	5 00	5 30	6 00	6 30	7 00	7 30	8 00	8 30	9 00	S 9 30	10 00	11 00	12 10	.....
Quaker Hill, Waterford.......	2 07	2 37	3 07	3 37	4 07	4 37	5 07	5 37	6 07	6 37	7 07	7 37	8 07	8 37	9 07	S 9 37	10 07	11 07	12 18	.....
Post Office, Montville.......	2 16	2 46	3 16	3 46	4 16	4 46	5 16	5 46	6 16	6 46	7 16	7 46	8 16	8 46	9 16	S 9 46	10 16	11 16	12 23	.....
State Sanitarium, Norwich....	2 33	3 03	3 33	4 03	4 33	5 03	5 33	6 03	6 33	7 03	7 33	8 03	8 33	9 03	9 33	S10 03	10 33	11 33	12 37	.....
Franklin Square, Norwich.....	2 45	3 15	3 45	4 15	4 45	5 15	5 45	6 15	6 45	7 15	7 45	8 15	8 45	9 15	9 45	10 15	10 45	11 45	12 45	.....
Post Office, Taftville..........	3 07	3 37	4 07	4 37	5 07	5 37	6 07	6 37	7 07	7 37	8 07	8 37	9 07	9 37	10 07	10 33	11 07	.....	.....	.....
Baltic Center................	W3 25	3 57	4 25	.....	.....	5 57	6 25	.....	.....	7 57	8 25	.....	9 25	.....	10 25	.....	11 25	.....	.....	.....
Post Office, So. Windham......	W3 45	.....	4 45	.....	.....	.....	6 45	.....	.....	.....	8 45	.....	S9 45	.....	.....	.....	.....	.....	.....	.....
R. R. Crossing, Willimantic Ar.	W3 57	.....	4 57	.....	.....	.....	6 57	.....	.....	.....	8 57	.....	S9 57	.....	.....	.....	.....	.....	.....	.....
	P.M.	P.M.	P.M.	P.M.	P.M.	P.M.	P.M.	P.M.	P.M.	P.M.	P.M.	P.M.	P.M.	P.M.	P.M.	P.M.	P.M.	P.M.	A.M.	

WILLIMANTIC AND NORWICH TO NEW LONDON

	A.M.	A.M.	A.M.	A.M.	A.M.	A.M.	A.M.	A.M.	A.M.	A.M.	A.M.	A.M.	A.M.	A.M.	A.M.	A.M.	P.M.	P.M.	P.M.	P.M.
R. R. Crossing, Willimantic.Lv.	.....	.....	.....	.....	.....	*5 55	.....	7 00	.....	W8 00	.....	9 00	.....	.....	.....	11 00	.....	.....	.....	1 00
Post Office, So. Windham.....	.....	.....	.....	.....	.....	*6 10	.....	7 12	.....	W8 12	.....	9 12	.....	.....	.....	11 12	.....	.....	.....	1 12
Baltic Center................	.....	.....	.....	.....	*6 00	*6 25	.....	7 32	8 02	W8 32	.....	9 32	10 02	.....	.....	11 32	12 02	.....	.....	1 32
Post Office, Taftville..........	.....	.....	.....	.....	*6 20	*6 45	*7 20	7 50	8 20	8 50	9 20	9 50	10 20	10 50	11 20	11 50	12 20	12 50	1 20	1 50
Franklin Square, Norwich.....	*4 45	*5 15	5 45	*6 15	6 45	*7 15	7 45	8 15	8 45	9 15	9 45	10 15	10 45	11 15	11 45	12 15	12 45	1 15	1 45	2 15
State Sanitarium, Norwich....	*4 57	*5 27	5 57	*6 27	6 57	*7 27	7 57	8 27	8 57	9 27	9 57	10 27	10 57	11 27	11 57	12 27	12 57	1 27	1 57	2 27
Post Office, Montville.........	*5 14	*5 44	6 14	*6 44	7 14	*7 44	8 14	8 44	9 14	9 44	10 14	10 44	11 14	11 44	12 14	12 44	1 14	1 44	2 14	2 44
Quaker Hill, Waterford.......	*5 23	*5 53	6 23	*6 53	7 23	*7 53	8 23	8 53	9 23	9 53	10 23	10 53	11 23	11 53	12 23	12 53	1 23	1 53	2 23	2 53
Conn. College, New London...	*5 30	*6 00	6 30	*7 00	7 30	*8 00	8 30	9 00	9 30	10 00	10 30	11 00	11 30	12 00	12 30	1 00	1 30	2 00	2 30	3 00
Parade, New London......Ar.	*5 40	*6 10	6 40	*7 10	7 40	*8 10	8 40	9 10	9 40	10 10	10 40	11 10	11 40	12 10	12 40	1 10	1 40	2 10	2 40	3 10
	A.M.	A.M.	A.M.	A.M.	A.M.	A.M.	A.M.	A.M.	A.M.	A.M.	A.M.	A.M.	A.M.	P.M.	P.M.	P.M.	P.M.	P.M.	P.M.	P.M.

	P.M.	P.M.	P.M.	P.M.	P.M.	P.M.	P.M.	P.M.	P.M.	P.M.	P.M.	P.M.	P.M.	P.M.	P.M.	P.M.	P.M.	P.M.	P.M.	
R. R. Crossing, Willimantic Lv.	.....	.....	.....	3 00	.....	W4 00	.....	5 00	.....	.....	.....	7 00	.....	.....	.....	9 00	.....	S10 00	.....	.....
Post Office, So. Windham.....	.....	.....	.....	3 12	.....	W4 12	.....	5 12	.....	.....	.....	7 12	.....	.....	.....	9 12	.....	S10 12	.....	.....
Baltic Center...............	2 02	.....	.....	3 32	4 02	W4 32	.....	5 32	6 02	.....	.....	7 32	8 02	.....	.....	9 32	.....	10 32	11 30	.....
Post Office, Taftville..........	2 20	2 50	3 20	3 50	4 20	4 50	5 20	5 50	6 20	6 50	7 20	7 50	8 20	8 50	9 20	9 50	10 34	10 50	11 50	.....
Franklin Square, Norwich.....	2 45	3 15	3 45	4 15	4 45	5 15	5 45	6 15	6 45	7 15	7 45	S8 15	8 45	9 15	9 45	10 15	10 50	11 15	12 15	.....
State Sanitarium, Norwich.....	2 57	3 27	3 57	4 27	4 57	5 27	5 57	6 27	6 57	7 27	7 57	S8 27	8 57	9 27	9 57	.....	10 58	.....	.....	.....
Post Office, Montville.........	3 14	3 44	4 14	4 44	5 14	5 44	6 14	6 44	7 14	7 44	8 14	S8 44	9 14	.....	10 14	.....	11 14	.....	.....	.....
Quaker Hill, Waterford.......	3 23	3 53	4 23	4 53	5 23	5 53	6 23	6 53	7 23	7 53	8 23	S8 53	9 23	.....	10 23	.....	11 23	.....	.....	.....
Conn. College, New London...	3 30	4 00	4 30	5 00	5 30	6 00	6 30	7 00	7 30	8 00	8 30	S9 00	9 30	.....	10 30	.....	11 30	.....	.....	.....
Parade, New London......Ar.	3 40	4 10	4 40	5 10	5 40	6 10	6 40	7 10	7 40	8 10	8 40	S9 10	9 40	.....	10 40	.....	11 40	.....	.....	.....
	P.M.	P.M.	P.M.	P.M.	P.M.	P.M.	P.M.	P.M.	P.M.	P.M.	P.M.	P.M.	P.M.	P.M.	P.M.	P.M.	P.M.	P.M.	A.M.	

S Saturdays and Sundays only.

* Does not run on Sundays or Holidays.

W Runs on weekdays only.

A 1933 New London and Norwich to Willimantic schedule is shown here.

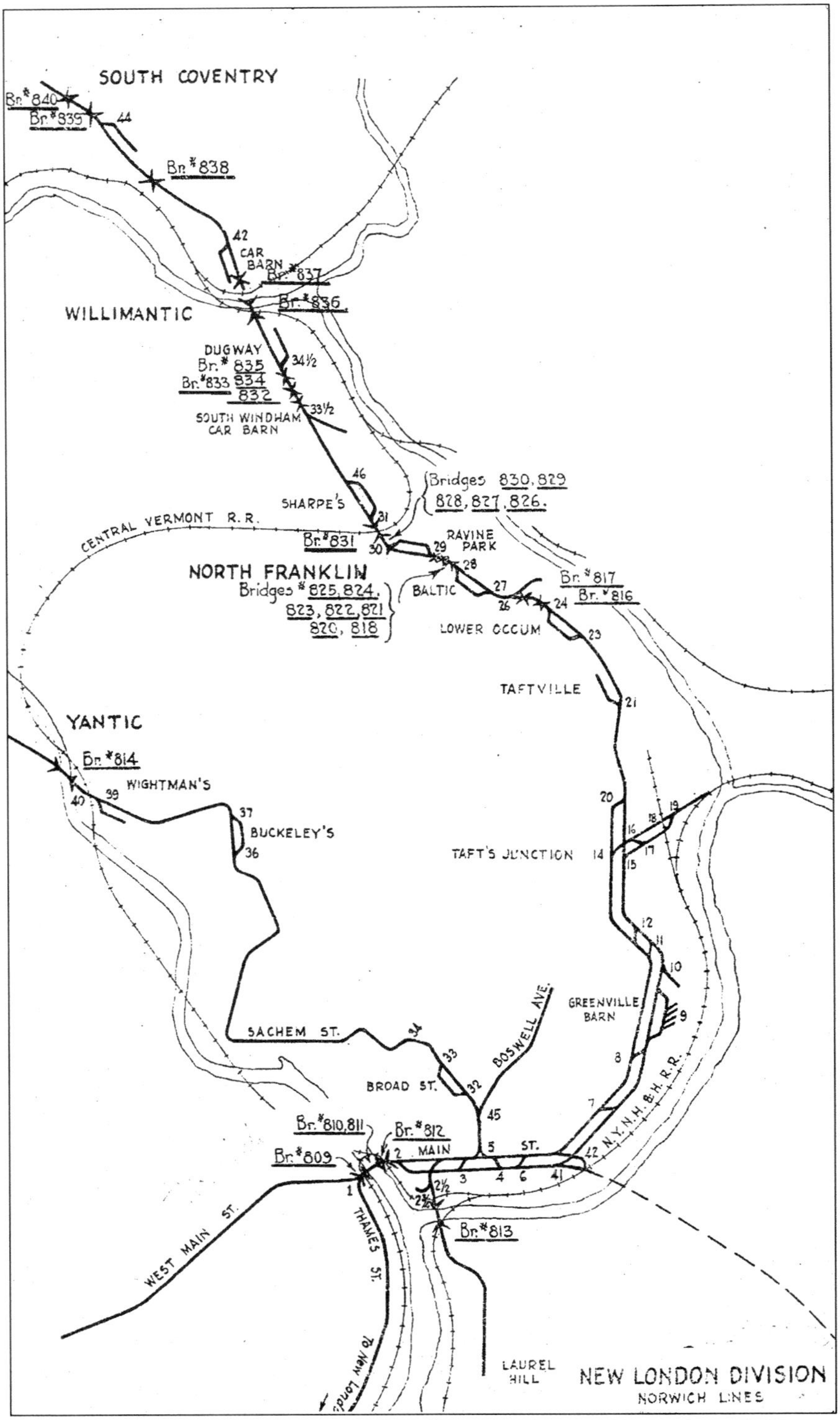

A map is shown of the Norwich and Willimantic lines in December 1919.

Three

Putnam Lines

The longest route on the Norwich lines was up to Putnam and beyond to Worcester, Massachusetts. Construction first started in Putnam in 1899 when the Peoples Tramway began running between the railroad station in Putnam and Alexander Lake. In 1902, another small line north of Putnam, the Thompson Tramway, was merged with the Peoples Tramway to form the Worcester and Connecticut Eastern Railway (W&CE), a subsidiary of the New York, New Haven & Hartford Railroad (NYNH&H). Later, in 1902, the W&CE purchased the Danielson & Norwich Street Railway. This created a system that was 39 miles long, running from the Massachusetts border to Central Village. Trackage rights on the Worcester Consolidated allowed W&CE cars to operate directly into downtown Worcester. Other short branch lines included the short line that ran between Central Village and Moosup (approximately two miles) and another line that ran between Danielson and East Killingly (approximately six miles).

The Worcester and Connecticut Eastern Railway was purchased by the New Haven Railroad and renamed the Consolidated Railway Company in May 1904. By the end of 1904, the New London and Norwich local lines, the Willimantic line, and the Putnam lines were all under single ownership.

At the same time, the Consolidated Railway entered into an agreement with the NYNH&H to electrify a section of the old Norwich & Worcester Railroad between Tafts Station and Central Village, a distance of 16 miles. This connected the Norwich lines with the lines through Putnam and Danielson. A connection was made at Tafts Station between the former Norwich Street Railway and the Norwich & Worcester Railroad. This now allowed cars from Franklin Square in Norwich to operate all the way to Central Village. Streetcars never ran all the way from either New London or Norwich to Putnam. A cross platform change continued to be made in Central Village to either a Putnam or a Moosup car. The track arrangement in Central Village was never designed for one car to be operated all the way through to Worcester without involving a complicated reverse move in Central Village. Cars did not travel to Worcester except during the 1920s, as part of an inspection of all the street railway lines in eastern Connecticut for the Connecticut Public Utilities Commission.

The Connecticut Company eventually acquired land for a right of way on which to build its own line from Occum through the town of Lisbon, but the track was never built.

At the beginning of the 1920s, operating expenses increased, and the cost of operating the lightly patronized lines north of Norwich caused the management to look closely at cost-cutting measures. The first line to have service discontinued was the Moosup line from Central Village. This line had one car that met all the cars from Norwich and Putnam. The line was abandoned in November 1925. The next service to be discontinued was the entire Putnam division from Norwich to Putnam in December of the same year. Motor coaches were substituted and ran along the same route that the streetcar took, mostly along Route 12. All motor coach operations north of Norwich were discontinued in 1960 due to a lack of riders.

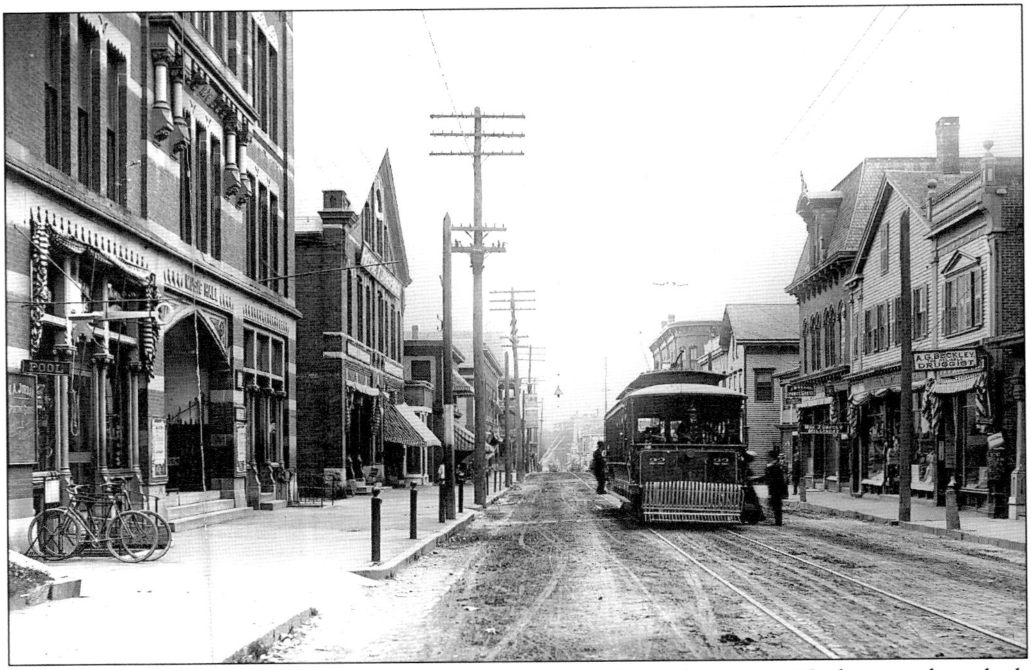

While there are bicycles in this scene of Main Street in Danielson in 1905, there is also a lack of automobiles, indicating the usefulness of the trolley system for this area.

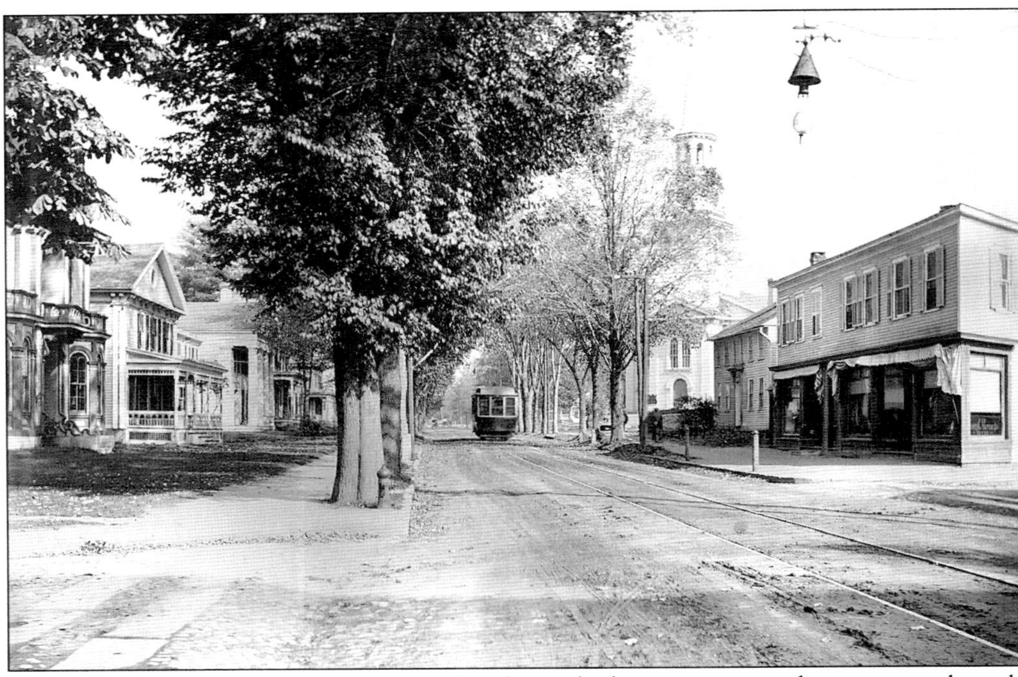

The trolley lines enabled the people who lived outside the city to get to the city in a relatively quick and economical fashion, as shown in this photograph of a Worcester and Connecticut Eastern Railway streetcar on Main Street in Danielson in 1905.

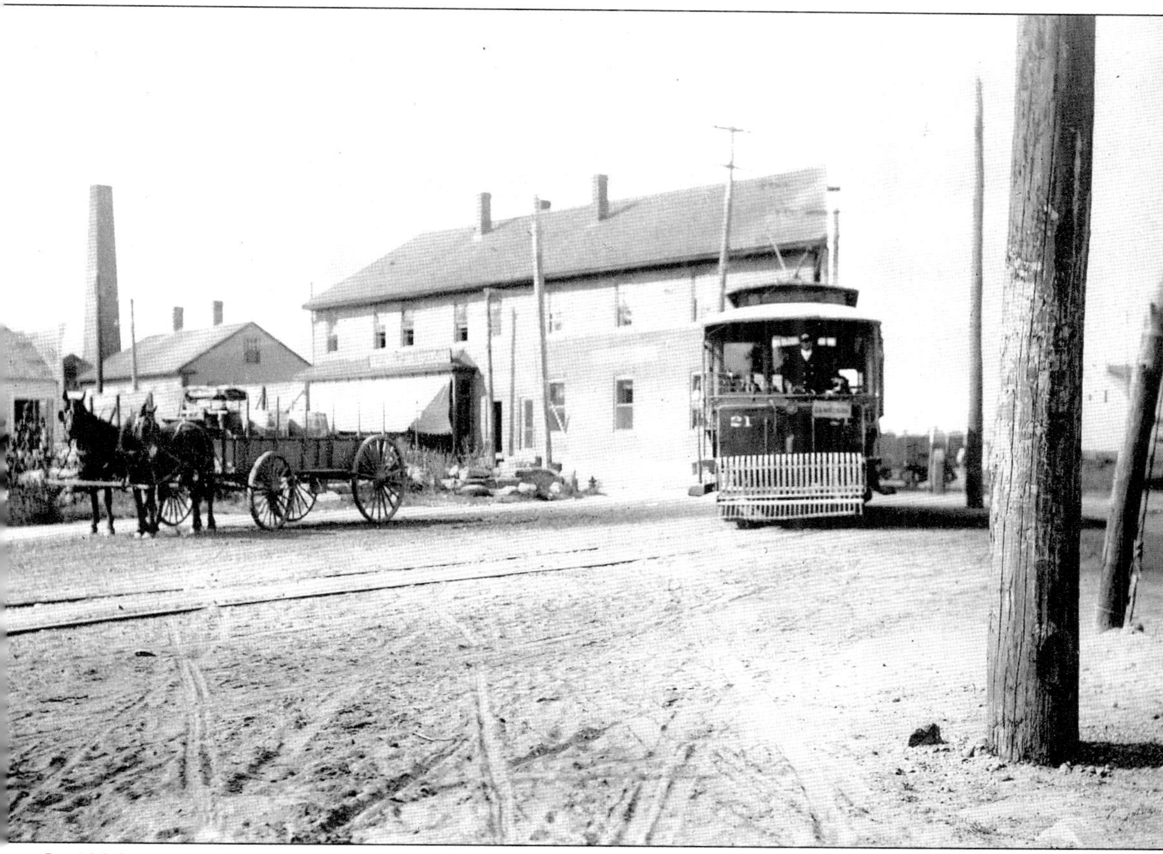

In 1906, it was not unusual to see trolley cars and carriages with horses on the same roads, as shown in this photograph taken in North Grosvernorsdale. Car No. 21 is a 15-bench open car that was built in 1900 by the Jones Car Company for the Worcester and Connecticut Eastern Railway.

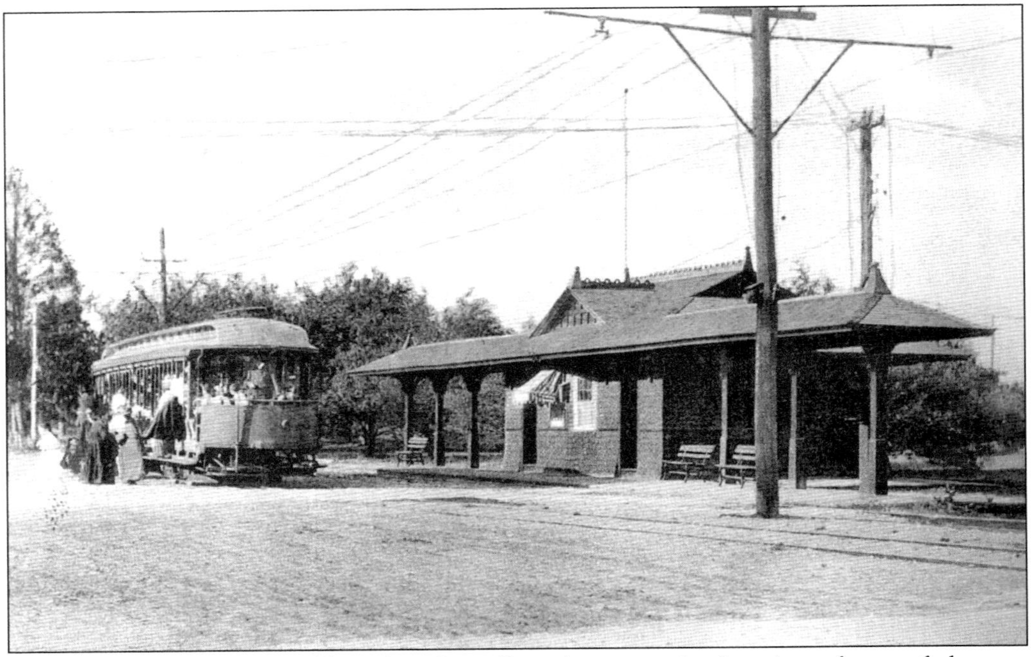

The waiting station at Wildwood Park in Danielson was the location of one of the two amusement parks in eastern Connecticut built by the streetcar company to encourage riding on evenings and weekends.

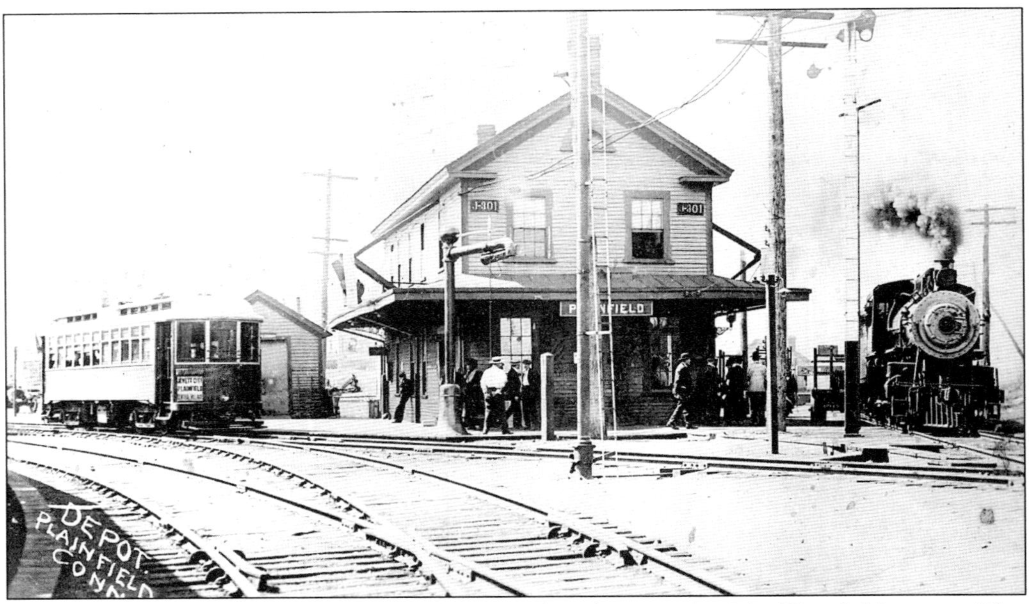

Sharing tracks is not a new practice, as shown in this photograph of the Plainfield station. This view shows a Connecticut Company Norwich to Central Village trolley car, along with a New Haven Railroad Hartford to Providence passenger train.

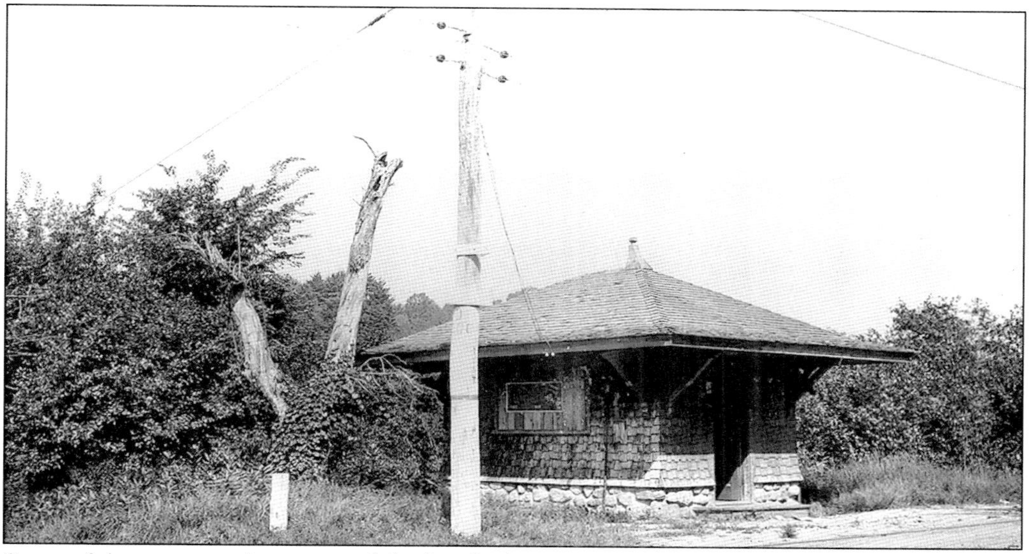

Some of the more rural portions of the line had waiting stations where riders could wait during more inclement weather. This picture is taken in West Thompson on August 24, 1921.

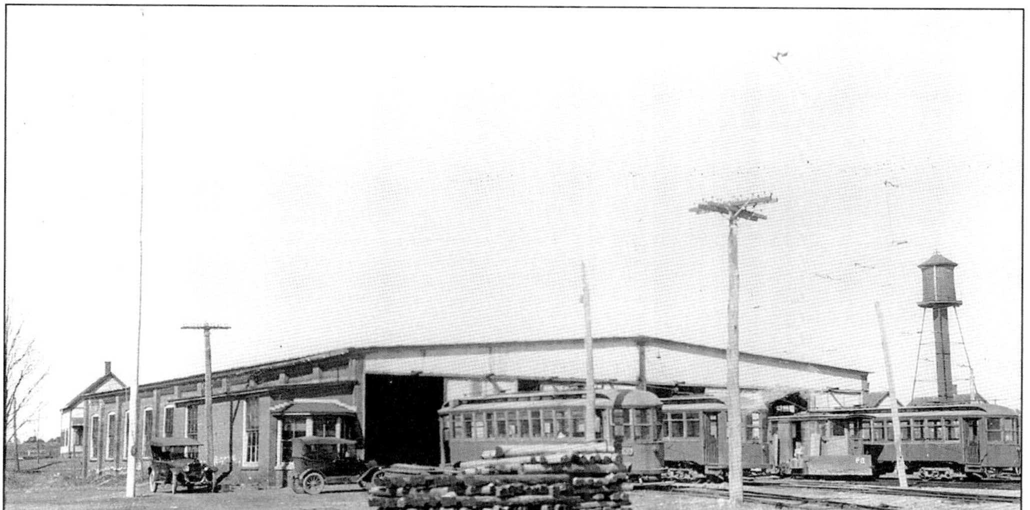

The Dayville carbarn in this 1923 picture closed in 1925, when trolley service from Tafts Junction to the Massachusetts state line was discontinued.

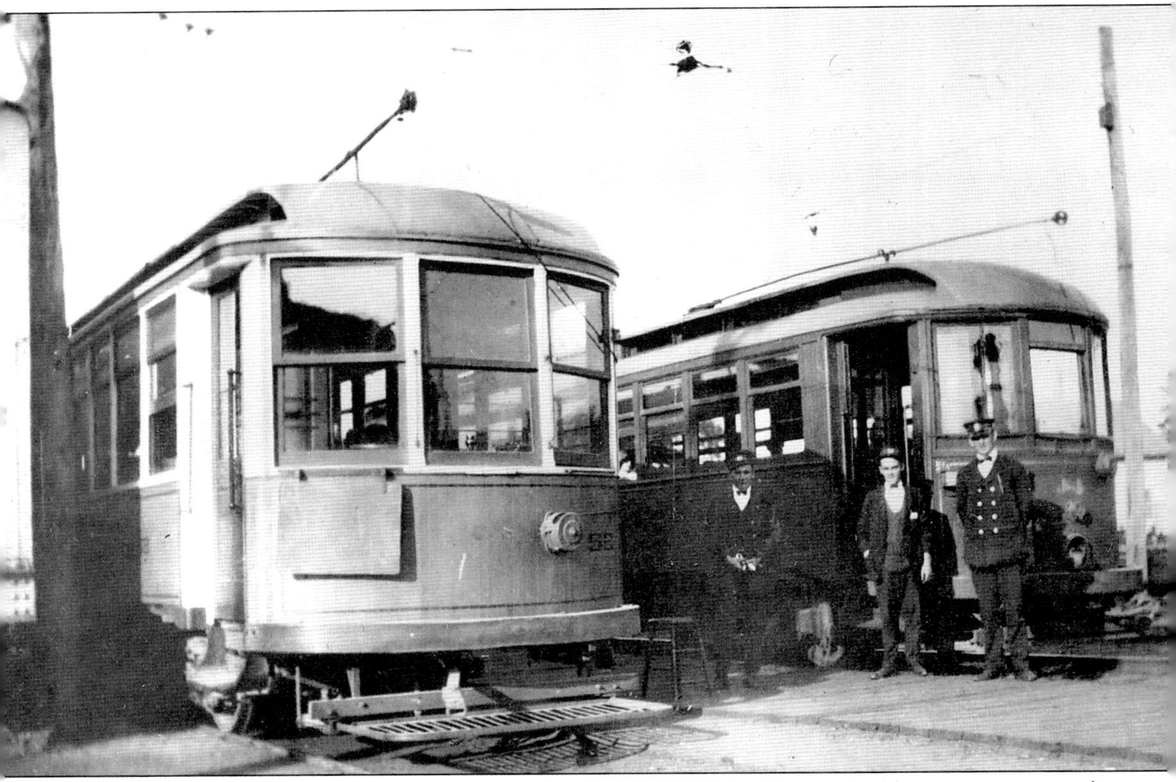

Connecticut Company cars that operated over the New Haven Railroad lines were required to have a railroad employee with the crew. A three-man crew is shown in this 1911 picture taken in Central Village.

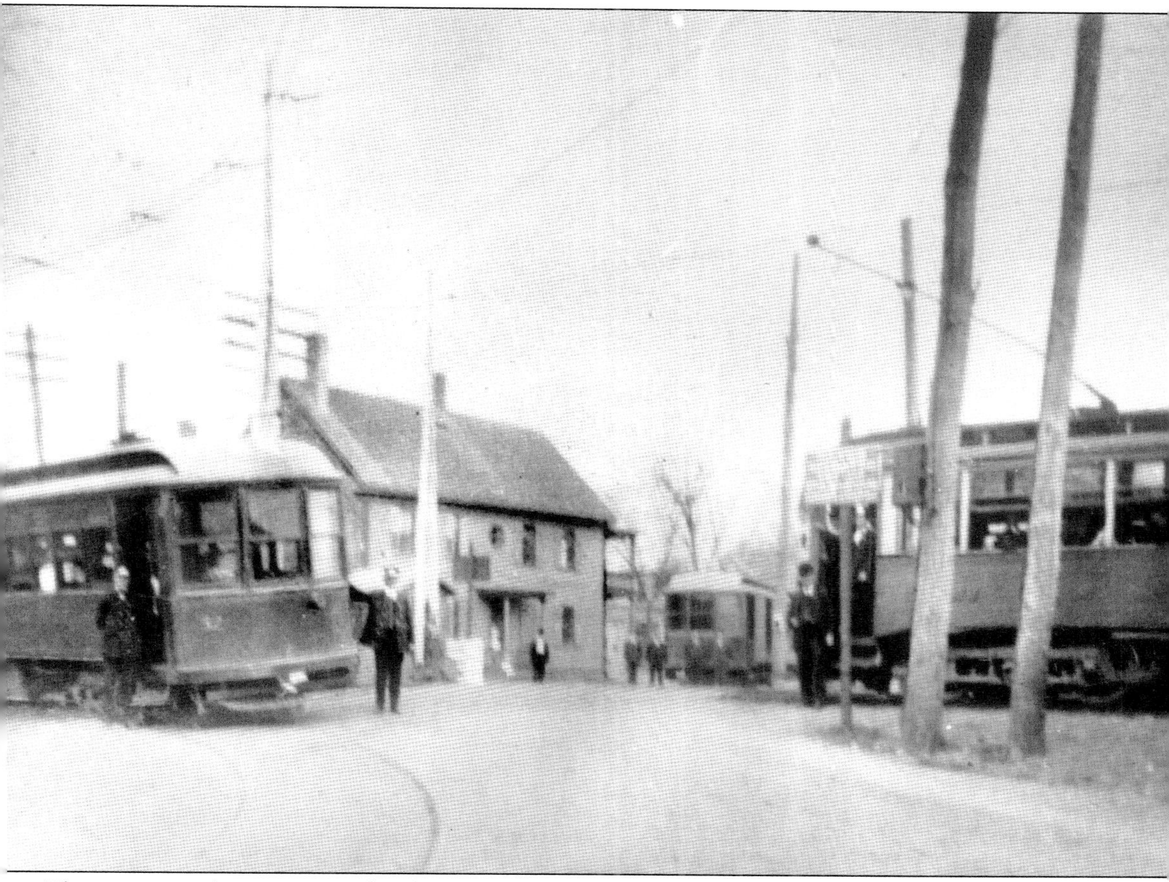

This picture, taken in Central Village c. 1920, shows a car heading south to Norwich on the right, a car bound for Putnam on the left, and a car bound for Moosup across the New Haven Railroad line. The Moosup line was never directly connected to either the New Haven Railroad or the Connecticut Company trackage. There was one car that provided service on that section. When that car needed to be worked on, a temporary, or shoe-fly, track was built, the car was transferred to the New Haven Railroad track, and the temporary track was removed.

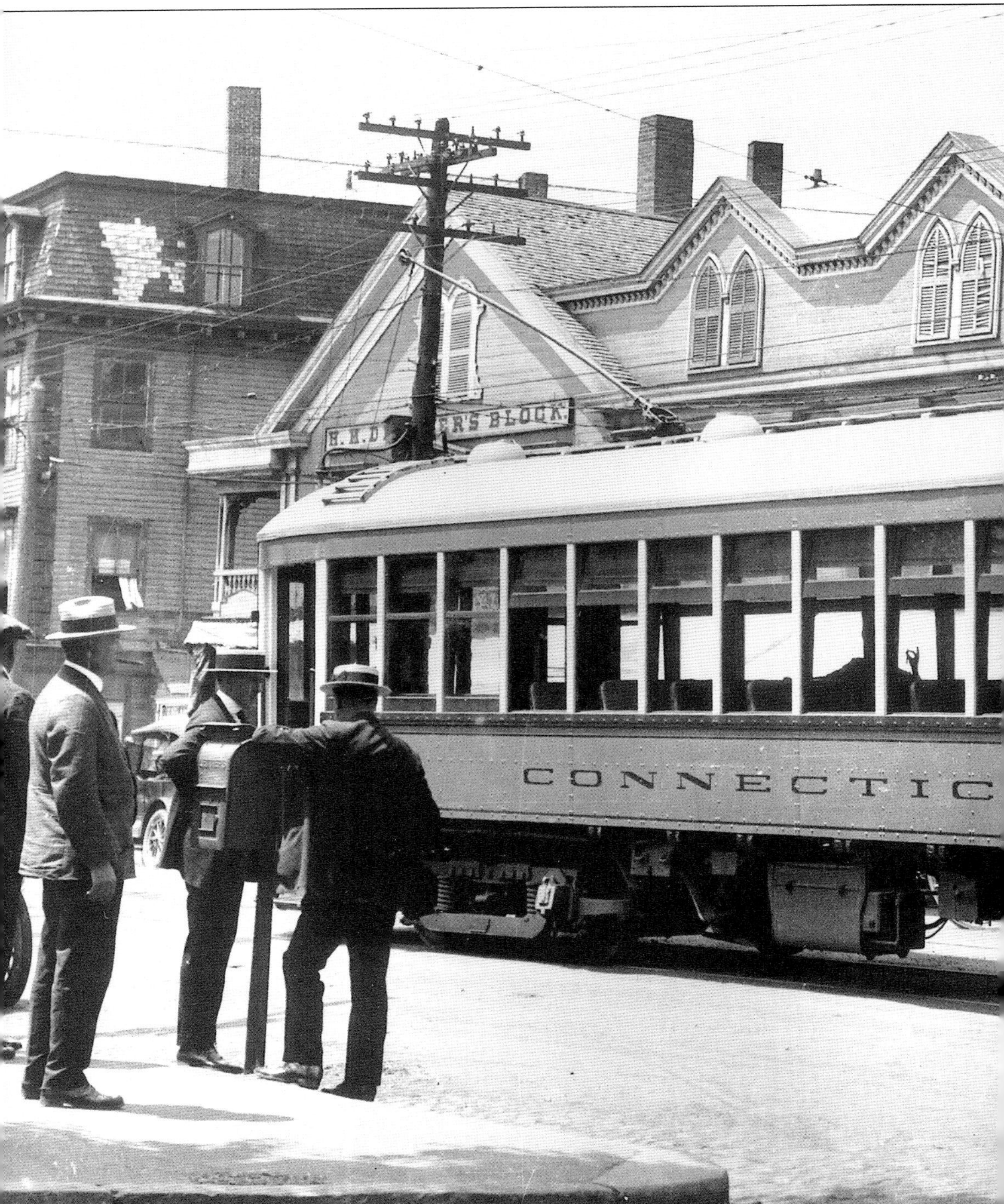

This heavyweight Connecticut Company car No. 209 is in Webster, Massachusetts, *c.* 1920. While the tracks connected New London, Connecticut, and Worcester, Massachusetts, one streetcar never ran the full distance. A passenger would have to change cars three times to make

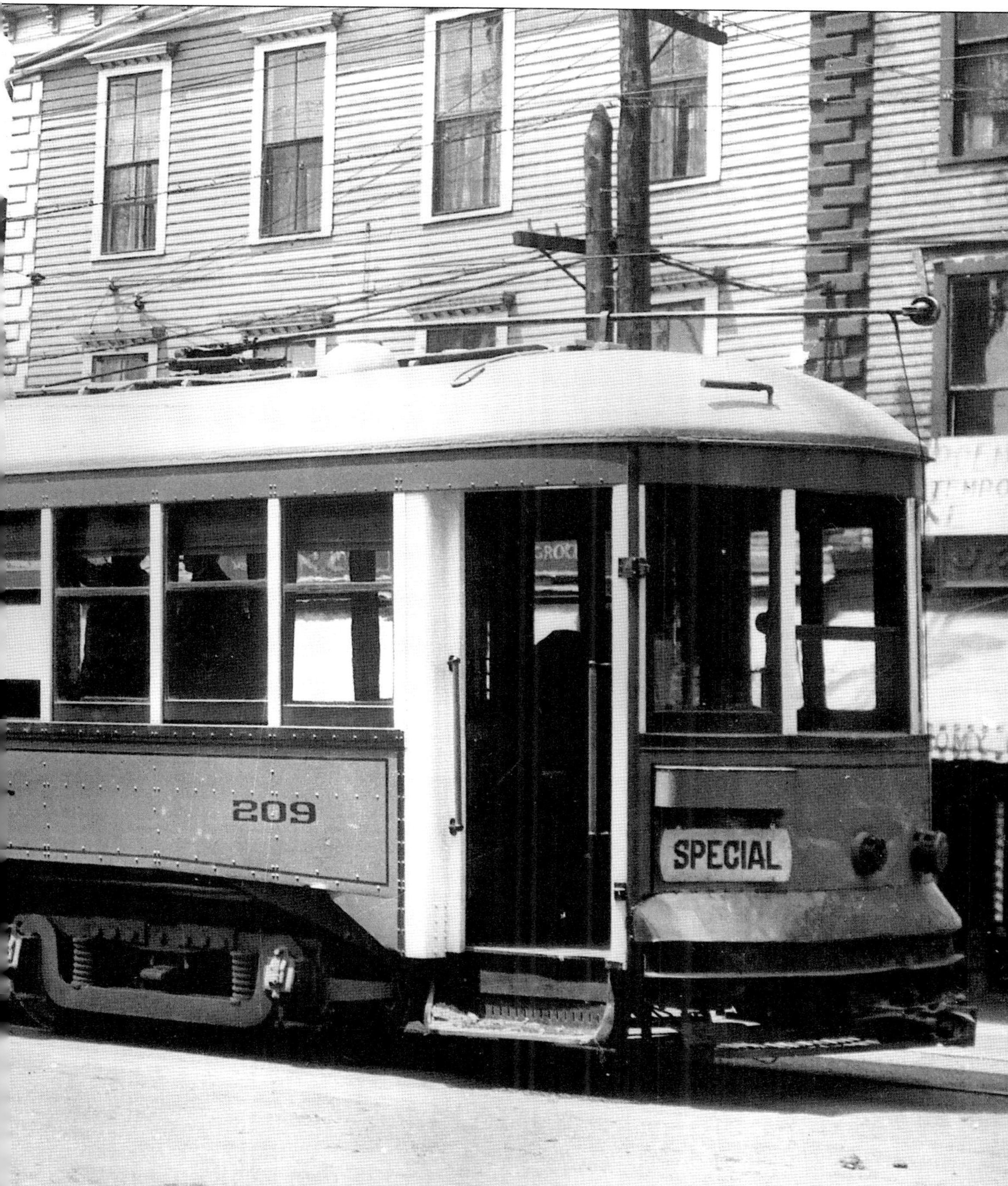

this trip. One of the few exceptions was an occasional inspection trip done by company officials or the public utilities commission.

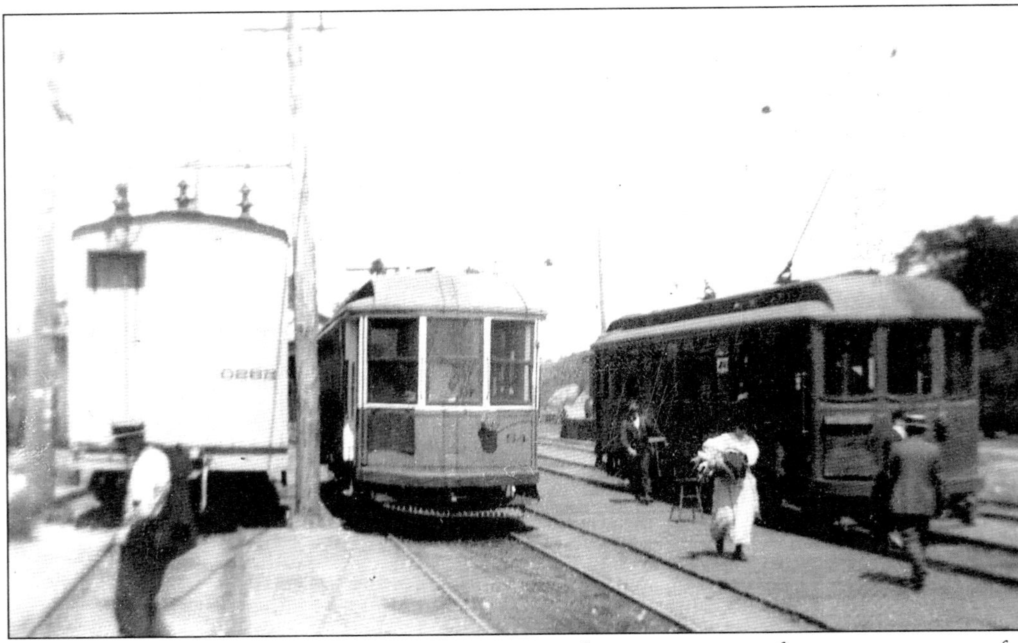

Along the less populated lines, it was not economical to operate a car for passengers, a car for mail, and a car for packages, so the car companies began building combination, or combine, cars. This combination car, shown in Central Village in the 1920s, was built in 1898 by the Wason Manufacturing Company.

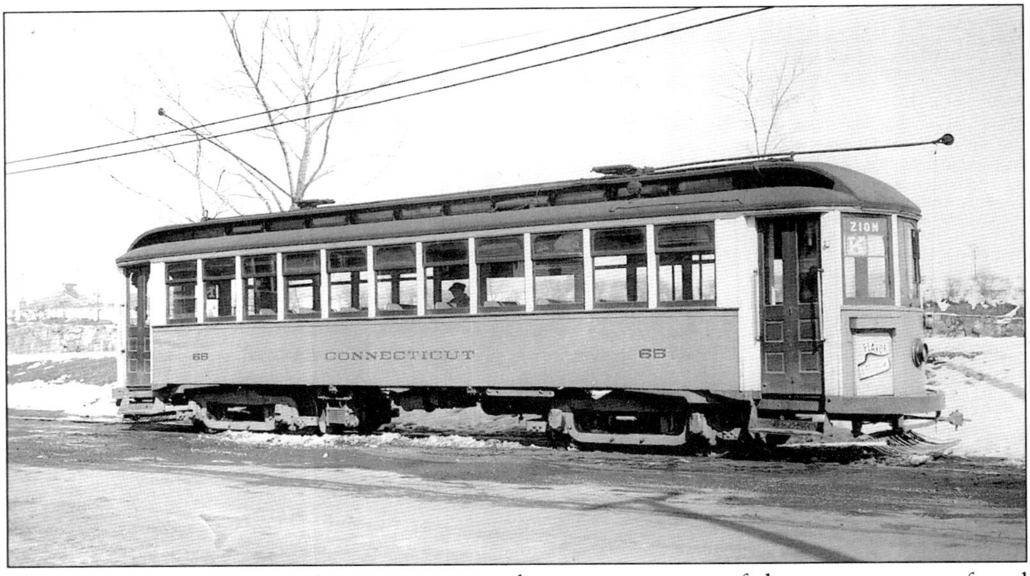

When the lines in eastern Connecticut ceased operations, some of the cars were transferred to other operating lines. In this photograph, car No. 65 is shown operating on Zion Street in Hartford. Prior to its transfer to Hartford, this car ran on the Putnam line. This is also the only car from the eastern Connecticut lines that still survives today. It can be seen at the Connecticut Trolley Museum in East Windsor.

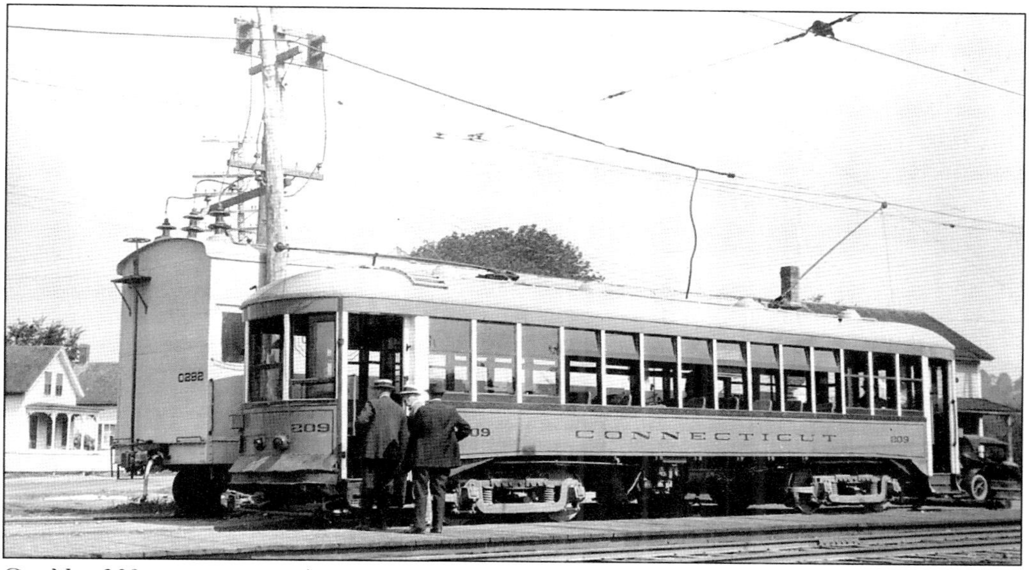

Car No. 209, seen previously in Webster, Massachusetts, is shown here heading southbound through Central Village on an inspection trip. Also shown in this picture is car No. 0292 behind car No. 209. This car is a portable substation used in the conversion of power from AC, which was supplied from the power plant, to DC, which was utilized by the streetcars.

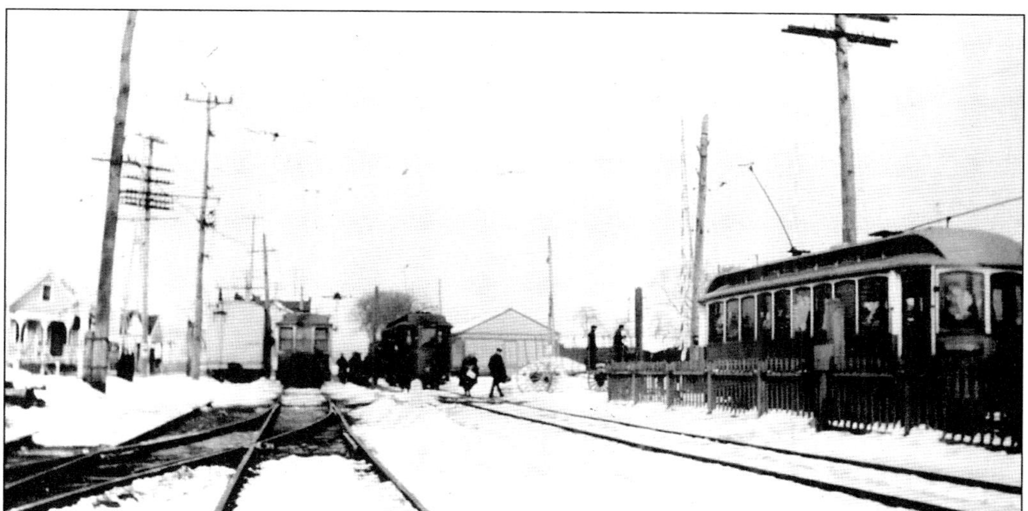

In Central Village, people often transferred from car to car, as only on rare occasions did cars run from Norwich to Putnam. The car on the right is loading passengers bound for Moosup, while the car in the center has just arrived from Norwich over the New Haven Railroad trackage, and the car on the left is loading passengers bound for Putnam.

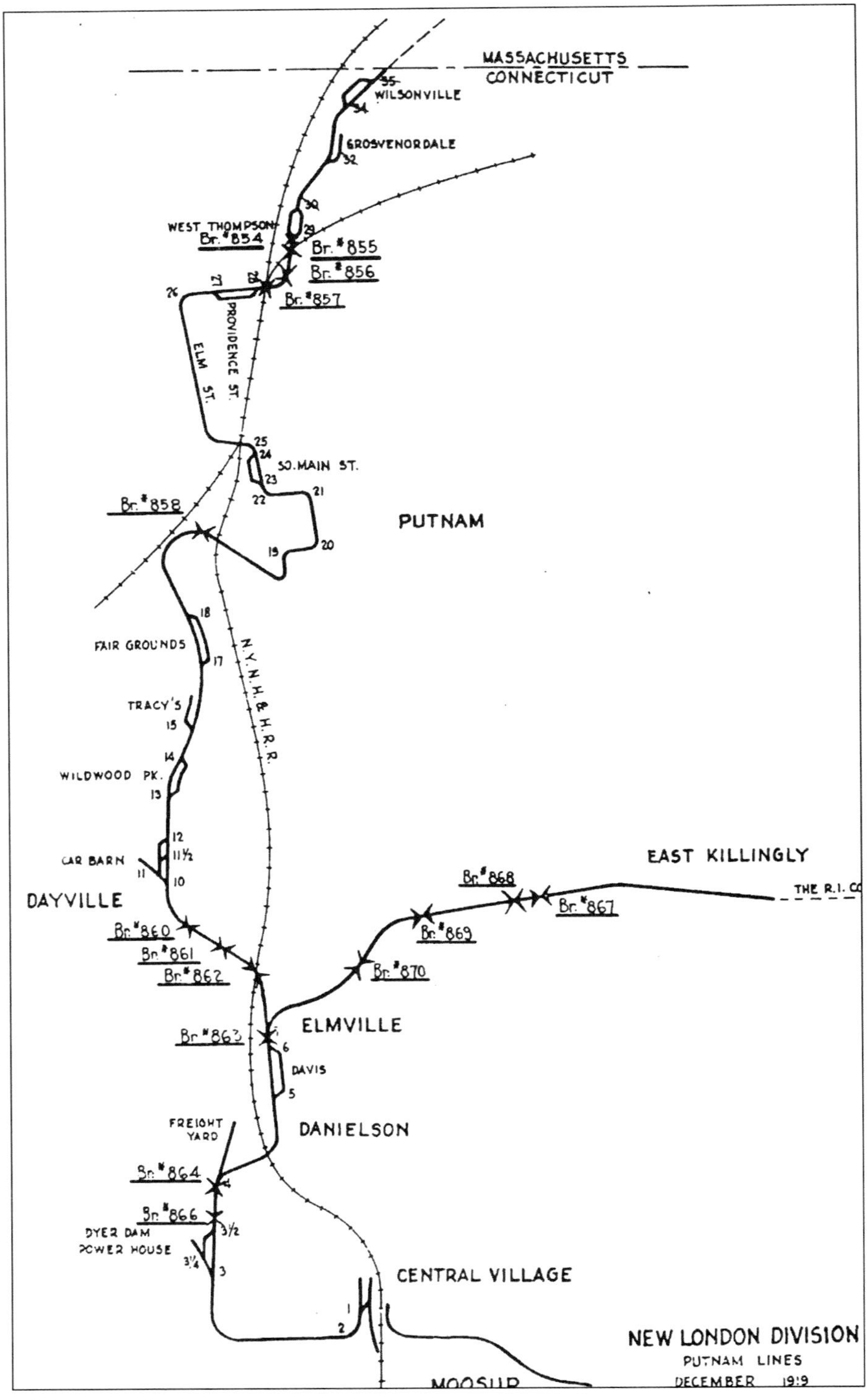

This is a map of the Putnam division in December 1919.

Four

Willimantic Lines

In 1901, the Willimantic Traction Company was chartered to build an electric railway line from Willimantic through the towns of Windham, Lebanon, Franklin, and Sprague to the little village of Baltic. Construction began in July 1902, and the line went into operation by August 1903. Late in 1903, a one-mile extension was built from the New Haven Railroad crossing in Willimantic to Columbia Road. The line did not cross the steam road. Passengers got off the car from Baltic, walked across the tracks, and boarded the car headed to the west end of Willimantic. Four passenger cars were housed in a small barn in Willimantic to service the isolated portion of track. The line was later extended to South Coventry in 1908. This track was never connected with the rest of the state's extensive streetcar system because of the fear that a trolley car would be involved in an accident with a steam locomotive while crossing the New Haven Railroad main line.

An interesting footnote to this line is the Willimantic carbarn mentioned above. This four-car building became the city of Willimantic's highway department garage after the line was abandoned in 1926. It served in this capacity until the 1980s, when it was finally torn down, more than 50 years after trolley service ended on the South Coventry line.

As in Norwich with the horse railroad, the Willimantic Traction Company was far from a financial success. The majority of the people living in Willimantic at that time worked in the vast American Thread complex and lived in company housing nearby. People rarely traveled outside of the town that they lived in during this era, and the most a person could expect to do was go to Norwich once or twice a year. After only a few years, the company fell on hard times and was more than anxious to sell when the Consolidated Railway Company offered $350,000 for the company in 1905. A passenger could then board a streetcar in Willimantic and ride all the way to New London with the same company.

Service from South Coventry to Willimantic ended in November 1926, when it was replaced with a bus operated by another New Haven Railroad subsidiary, the New England Transportation Company. The Norwich to Willimantic line continued to operate until the end of streetcar service in Norwich. The last trip to Willimantic was December 1, 1936.

With the advent of more and more automobiles on the road, even bus service became uneconomical. The Willimantic to Baltic service was discontinued in 1951, leaving this part of Connecticut with no public transportation at all.

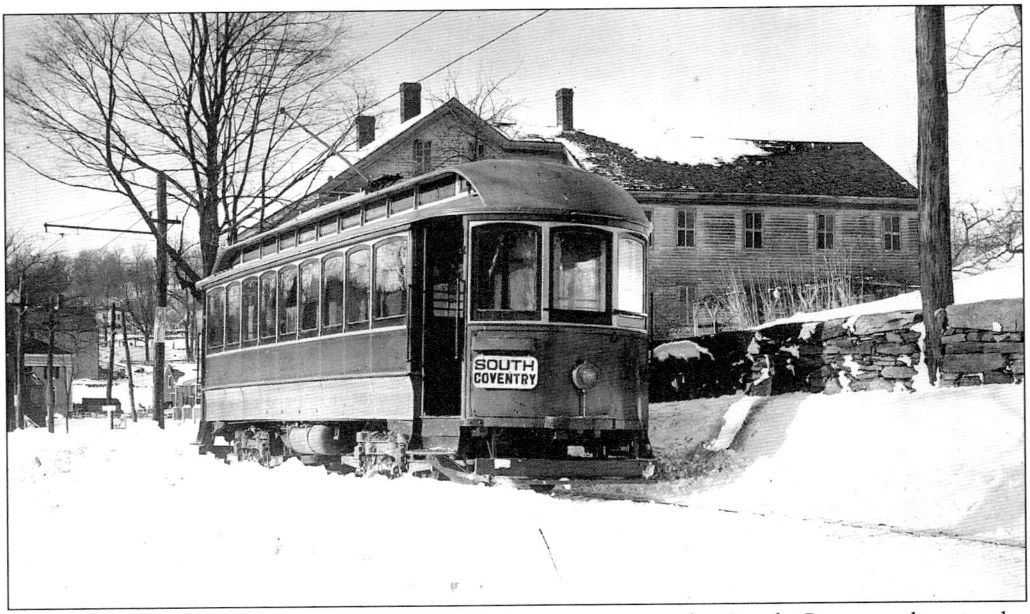

There are no other vehicles to be seen, but this car runs on the South Coventry line in the winter of 1910.

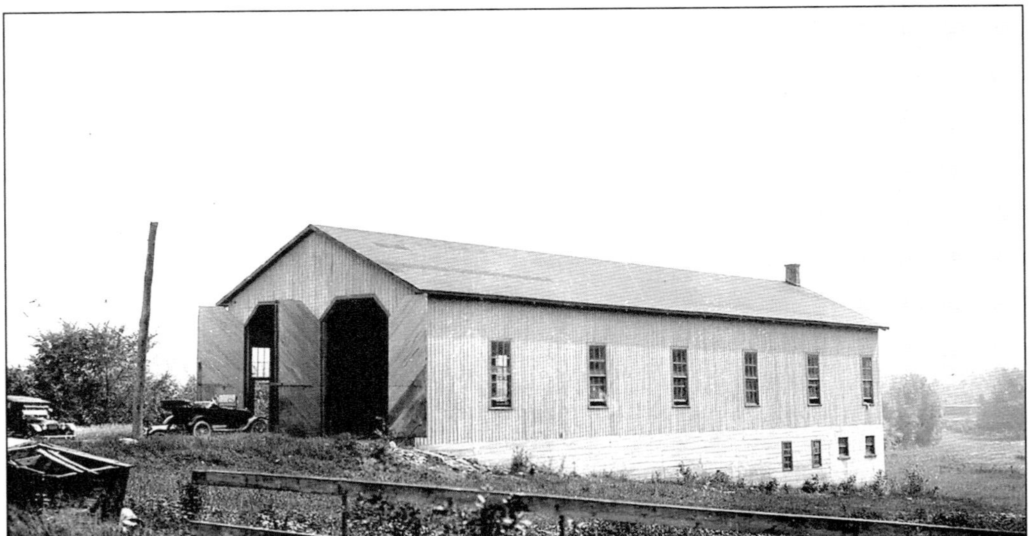

This picture, taken in 1921, shows the carbarn that housed the four cars that served the Willimantic to South Coventry line. Service on this line was discontinued in December 1926. This line was physically isolated from the other Connecticut Company lines in eastern Connecticut because of the lack of track connection over the New Haven Railroad main line in Willimantic. It was feared that the trolley cars and steam trains would try to use the crossing at the same time, thus causing a dangerous situation for the crew and passengers. The carbarn was demolished in the 1980s after having been used by the city of Willimantic to house snowplows.

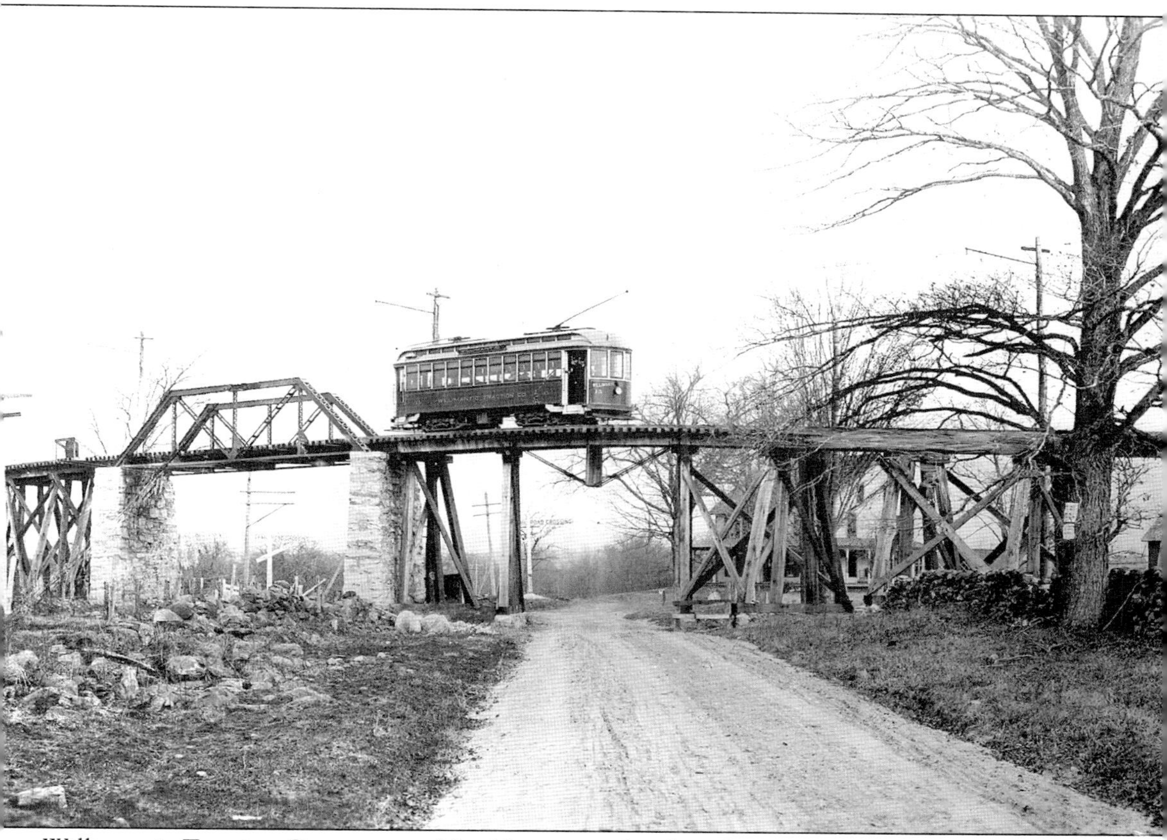

Willimantic Traction Company car No. 15 crosses a local road, now Route 32, and the main line of the Central Vermont Railway, to the left of the road, in this 1904 picture.

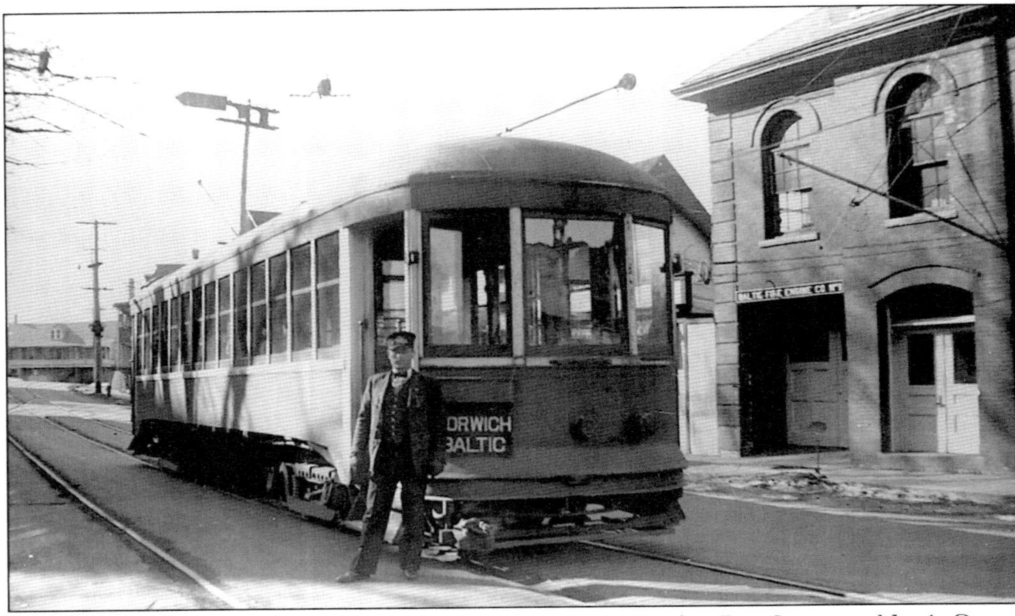

Operator Robert Disco is shown in front of his trolley car at Baltic Fire Company No. 1. Cars to Baltic would only run for a few more years.

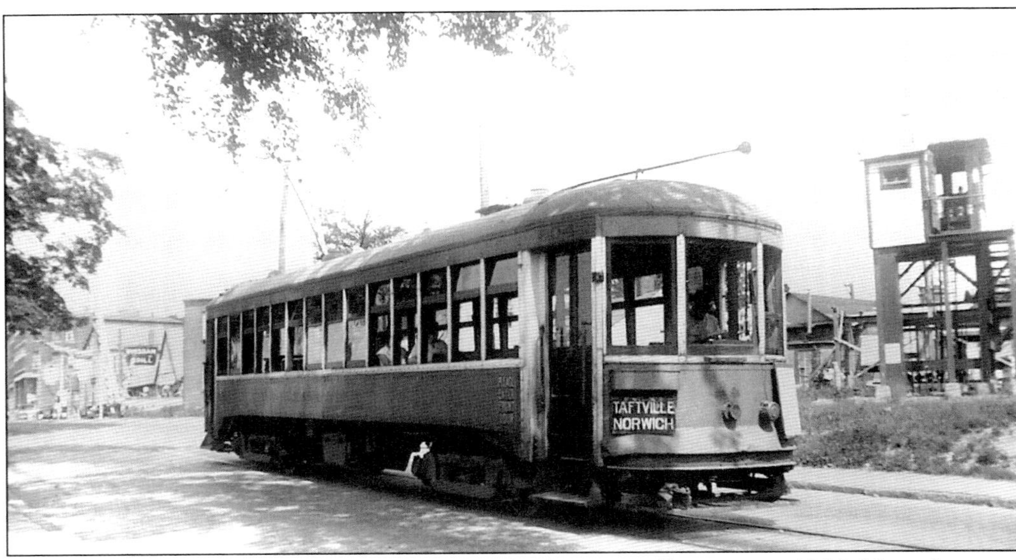

This car is heading to Norwich at the end of the line in Willimantic in 1936. Note the tower that housed the railroad employee who was responsible for lowering the crossing gates on the main line of the New Haven Railroad. Trolley cars did not cross the main line here. Passengers wishing to continue to South Coventry before 1926 had to disembark from one car, walk across the main-line railroad track, and board another car on the other side. South Coventry trolley service was replaced by a bus in 1926.

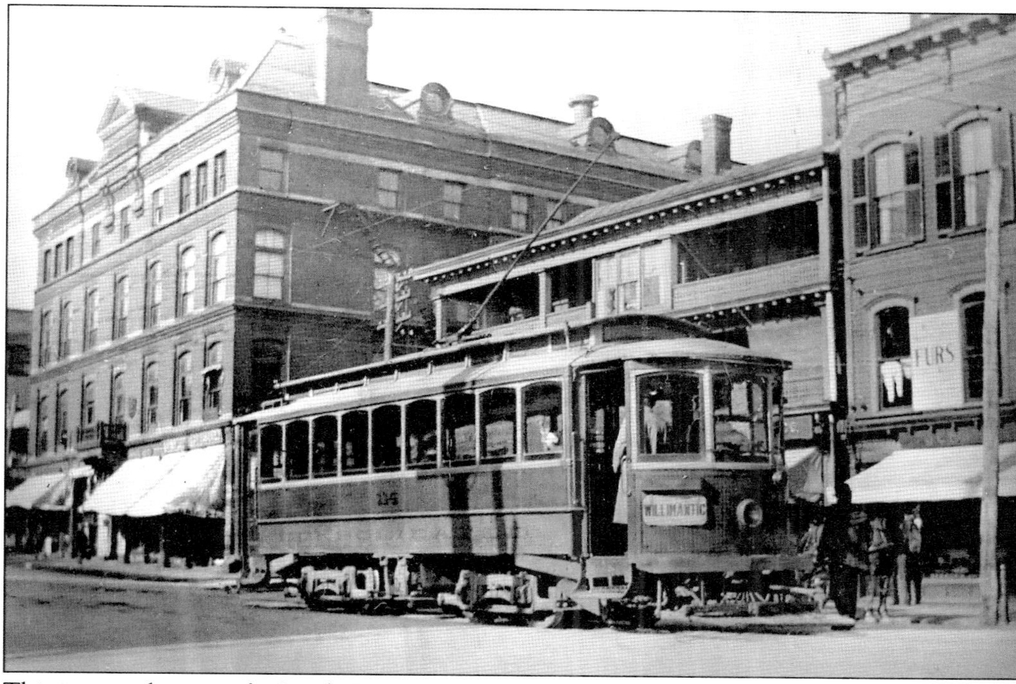

This is an early view of a South Coventry line car in downtown Willimantic in 1910.

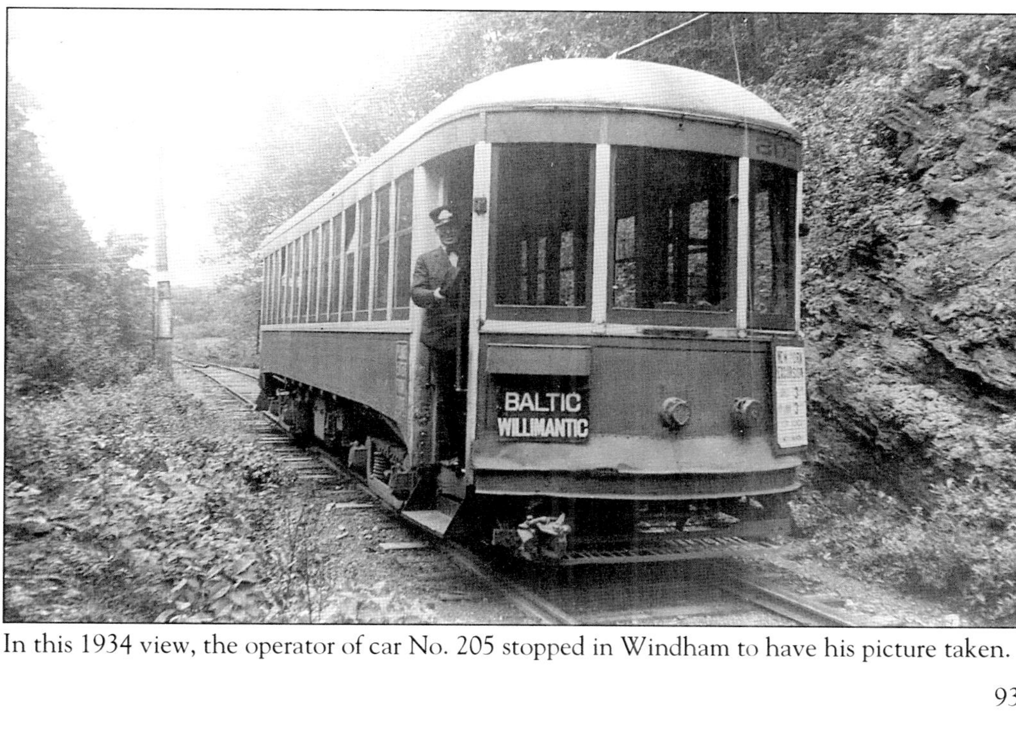

In this 1934 view, the operator of car No. 205 stopped in Windham to have his picture taken.

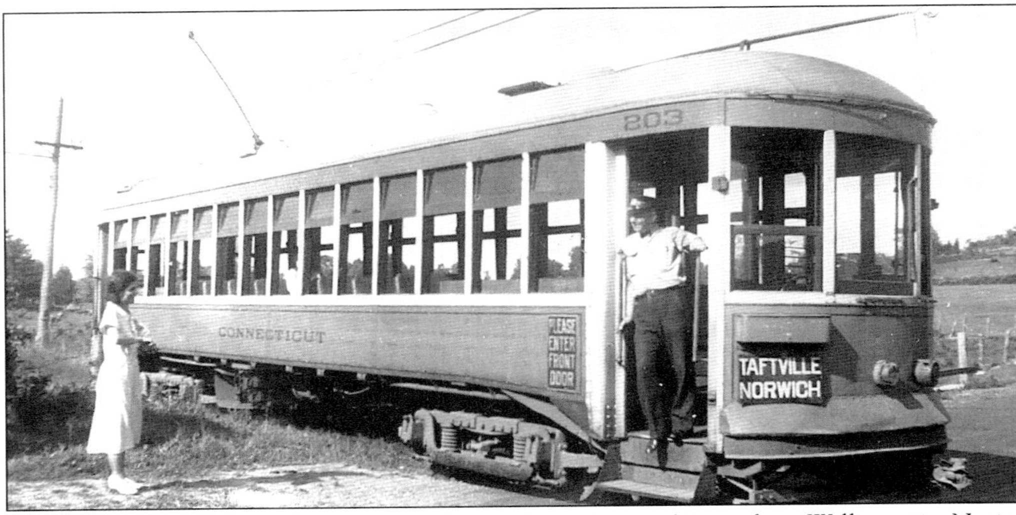

Going shopping in Norwich was convenient with service on this car from Willimantic. Notice the lack of passengers, which, no doubt, prompted the Connecticut Company to discontinue streetcar service in 1936.

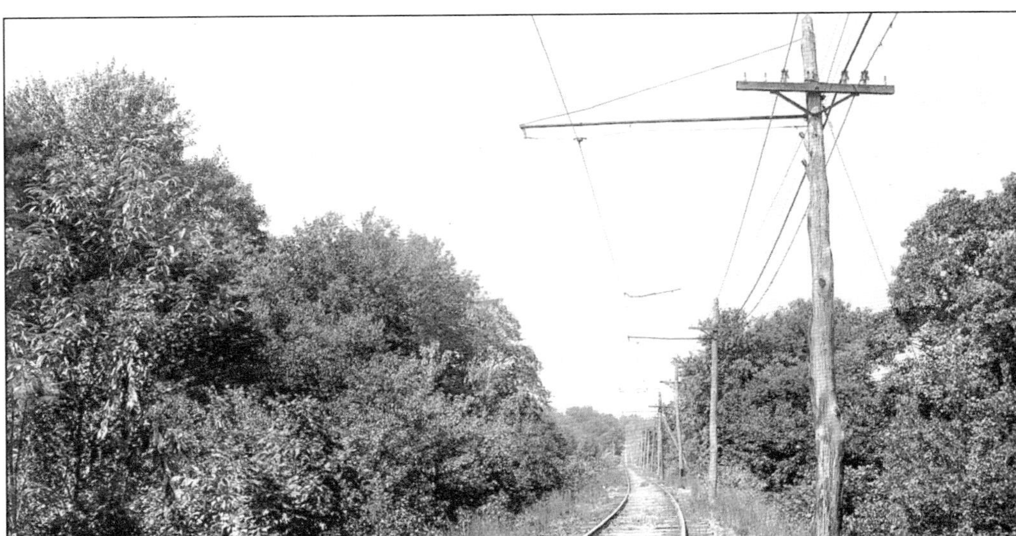

This picture, taken on September 6, 1936, at Dugway crossing in Windham, shows that the line has become weed infested, attesting to the decline of the line.

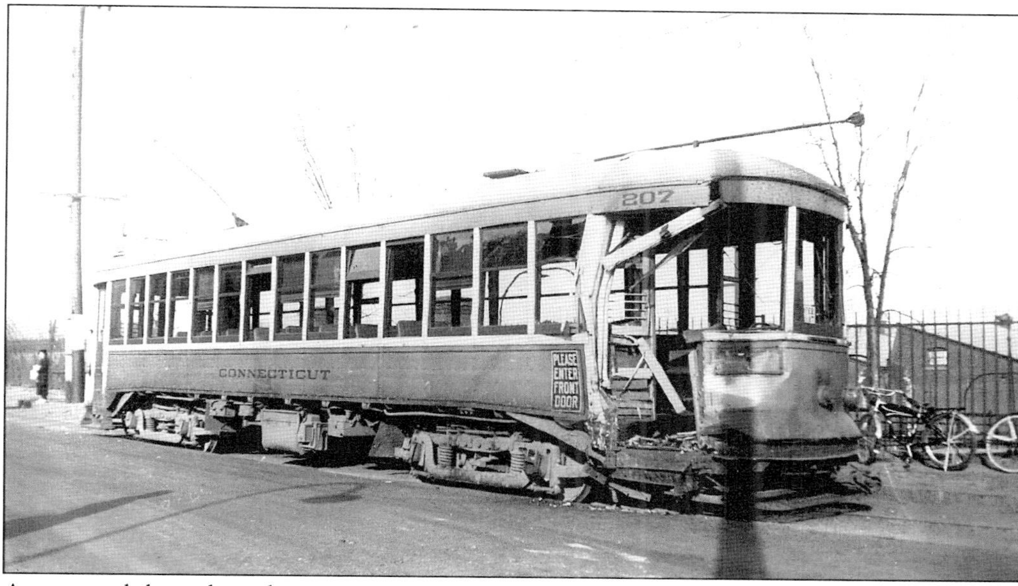

As automobile and truck transportation increased, so did the number of collisions between them. This 1935 picture shows the result of car No. 207 colliding with a Mack "Bulldog" dump truck in Willimantic. Typically, the cars were repaired and back on the road within a few days.

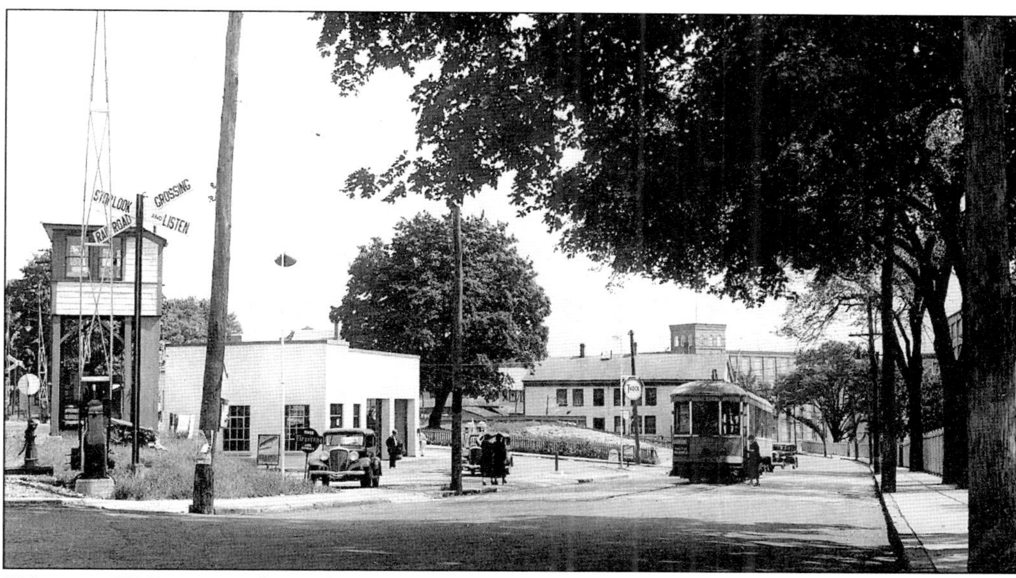

Taken in Willimantic from the New Haven Railroad crossing, this photograph shows a car arriving from Norwich. Note the gate tender's tower on the left side of the picture.

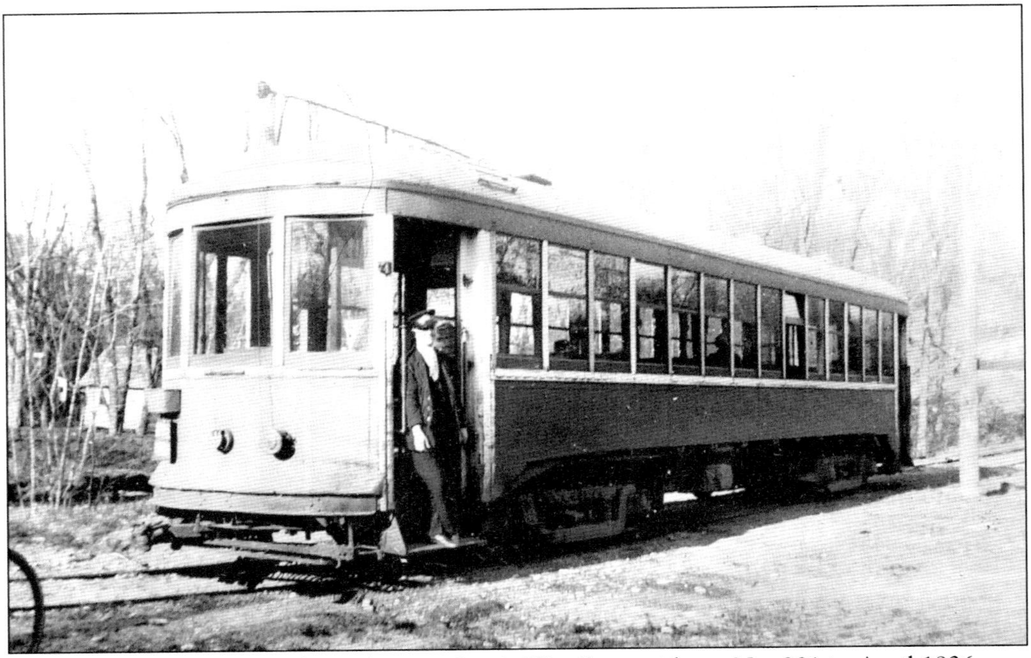

Motorman H. F. Lewan is shown here in South Windham with car No. 201 in April 1936.

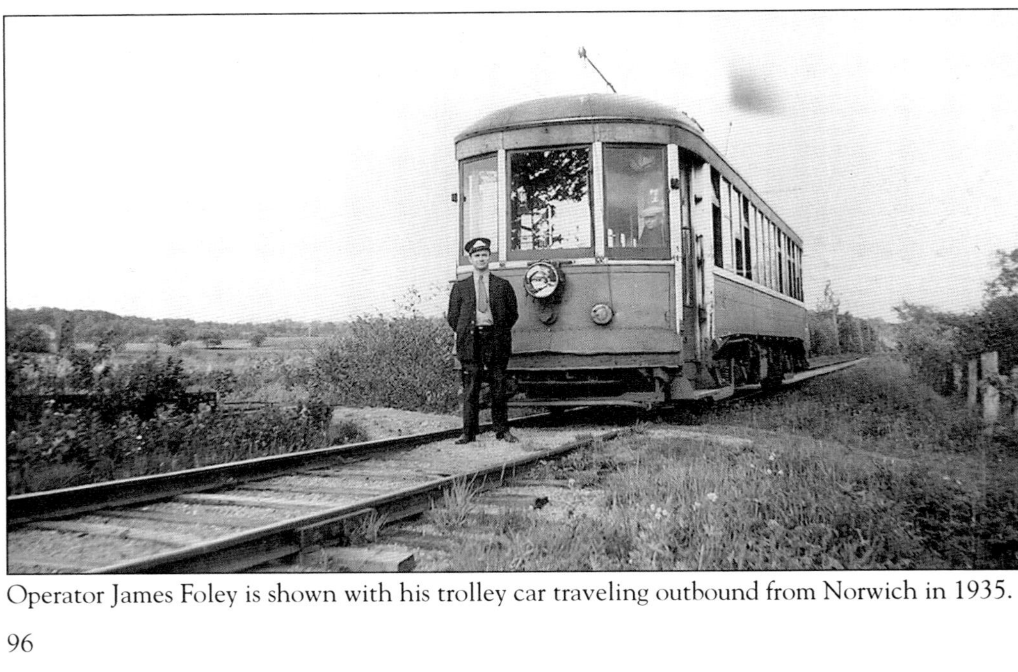

Operator James Foley is shown with his trolley car traveling outbound from Norwich in 1935.

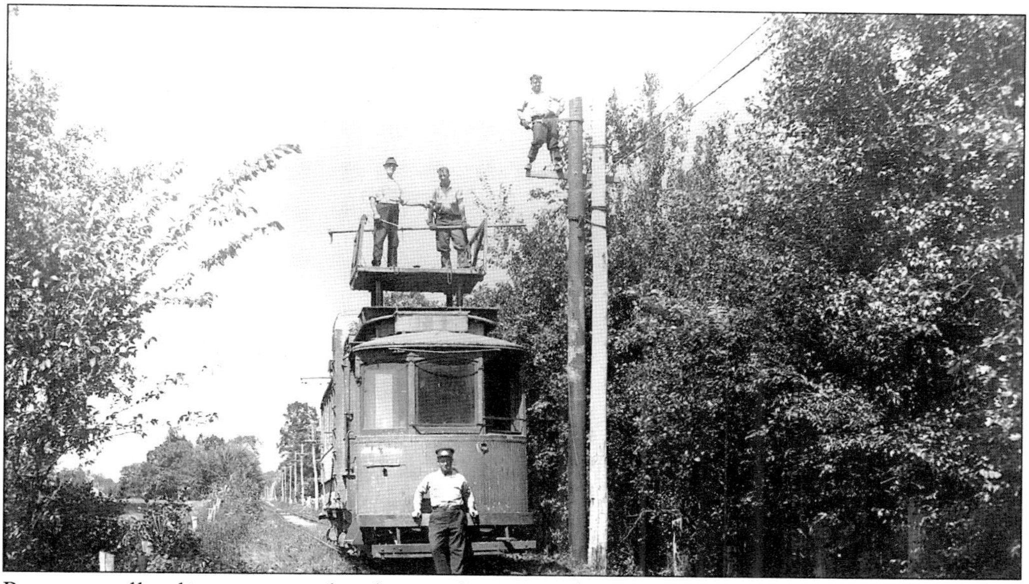

Because trolley lines use overhead wires for power, line crews were needed for both routine and emergency maintenance of the lines. This line crew is working on the Willimantic line in South Windham in October 1936. Operations on this line ceased a few months later.

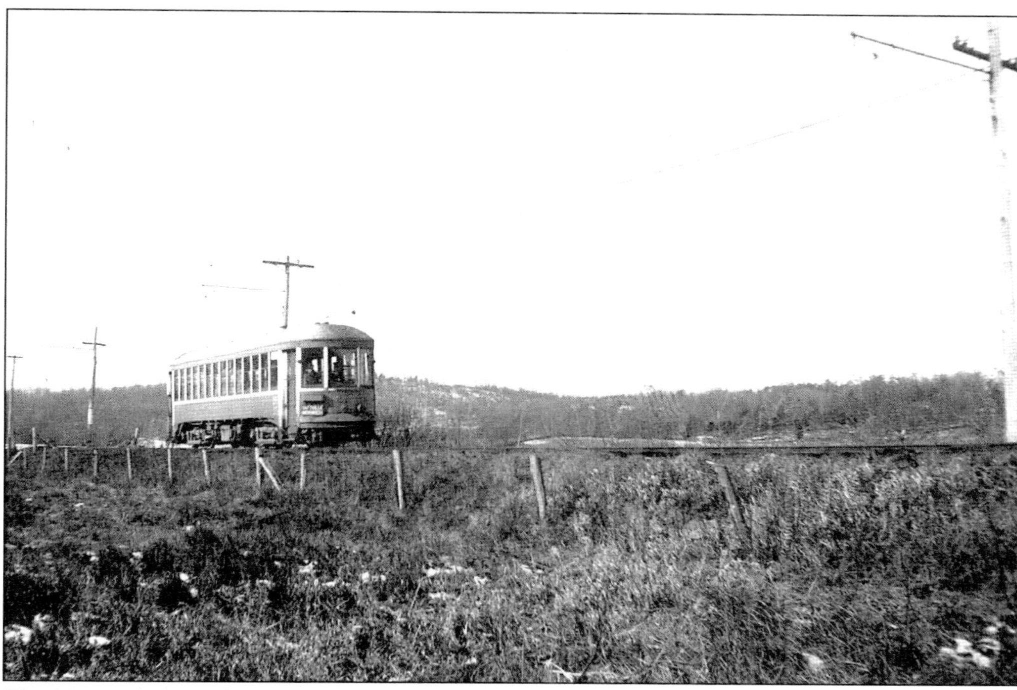

This Norwich-bound car from Willimantic is shown running on a private right-of-way in Baltic. Much of the Willimantic line was on private property. Many sections of this right-of-way are now Route 32.

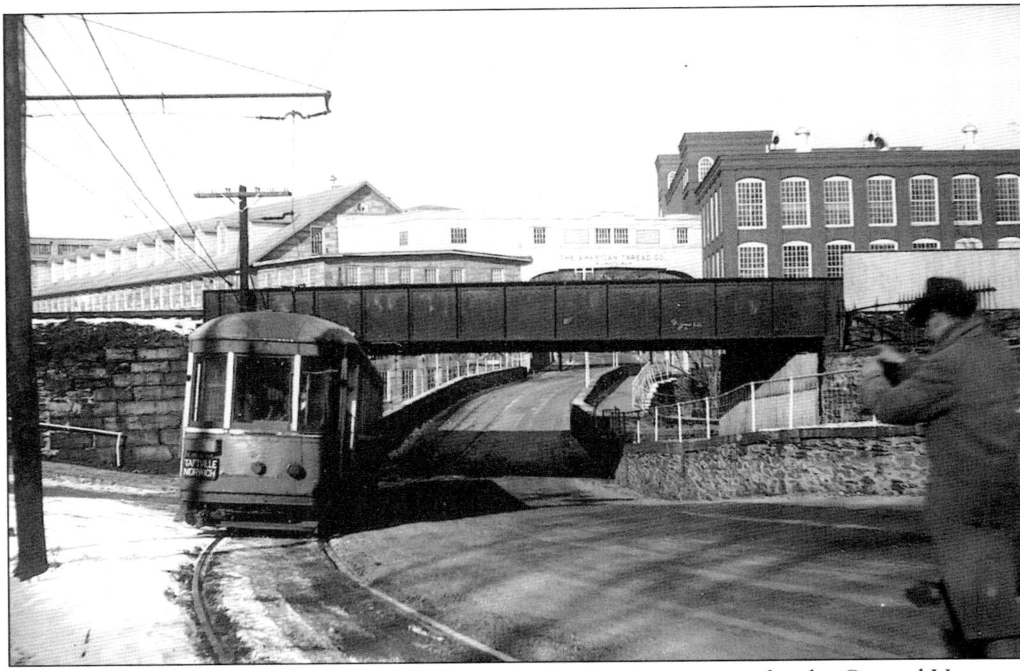

This car is heading to Norwich from Willimantic, having just gone under the Central Vermont Railway bridge. In the background is the American Thread Company, one of the large mills found in the area.

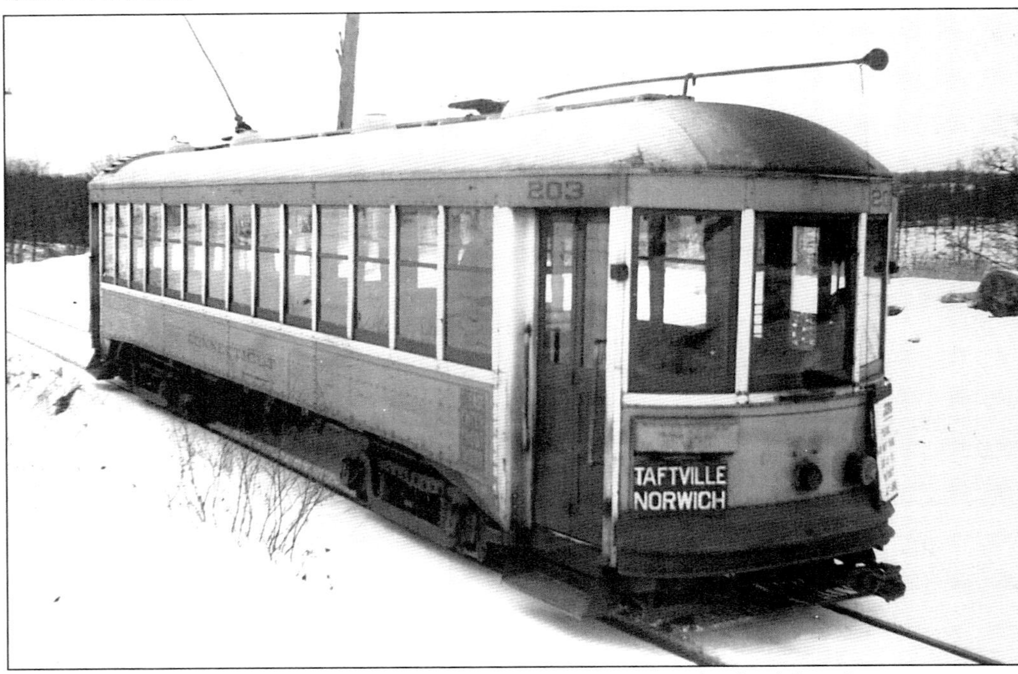

Car No. 203 is shown headed to Norwich on December 1, 1936, the final day of streetcar service on this line. On December 2, bus service started on this line. However, this service ceased in December 1951, ending public transportation in the Baltic to Willimantic area.

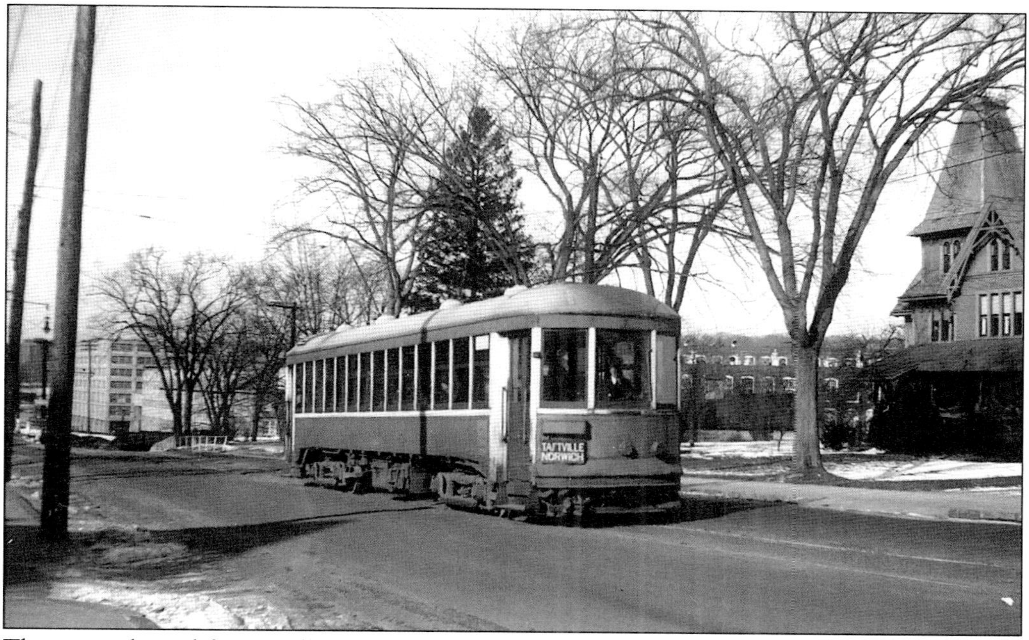

This car, inbound from Willimantic, heads to Norwich on December 1, 1936, the last day of trolley operations in this area.

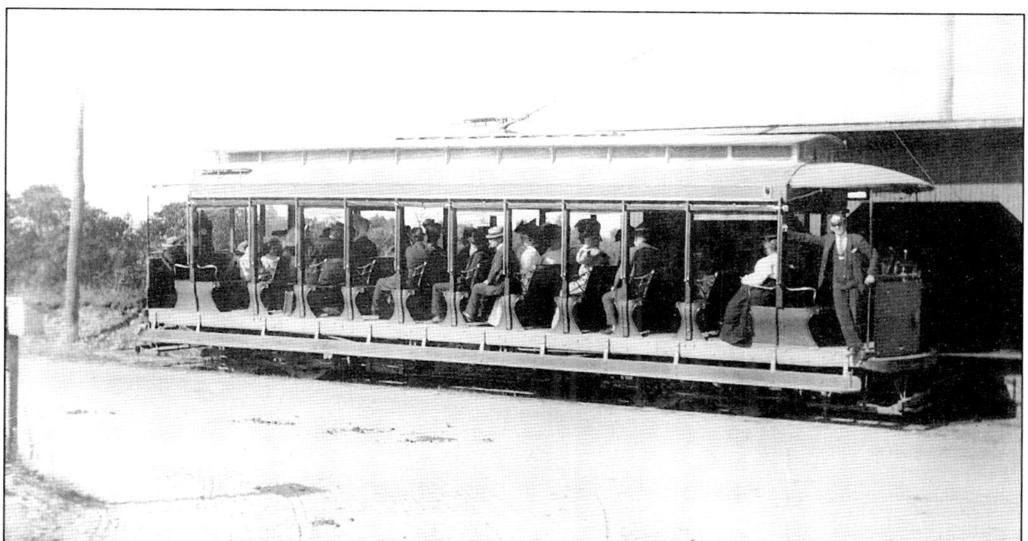

Open cars were very popular in the summer months. This one is pictured in South Windham in 1914.

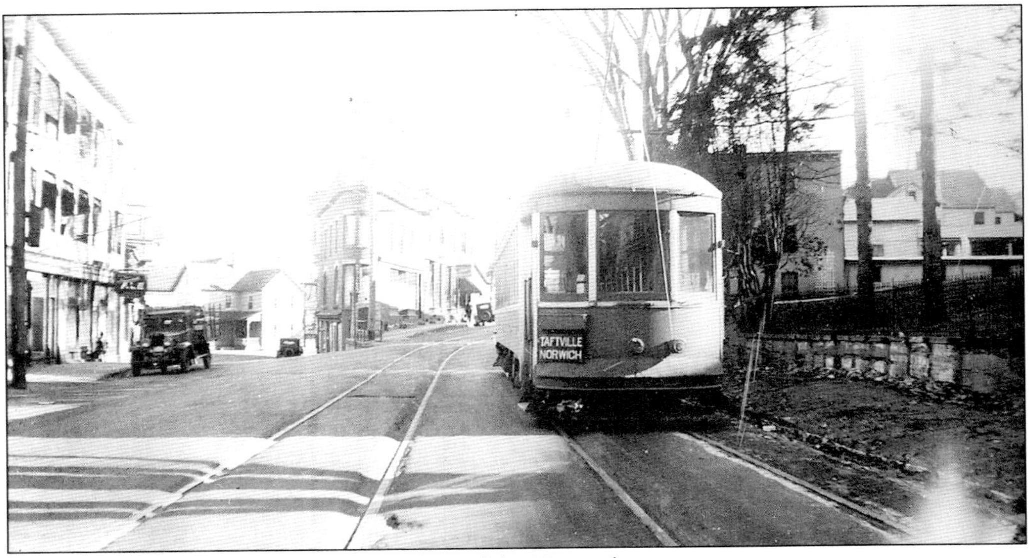

Car No. 201 is shown again, this time bound for Norwich.

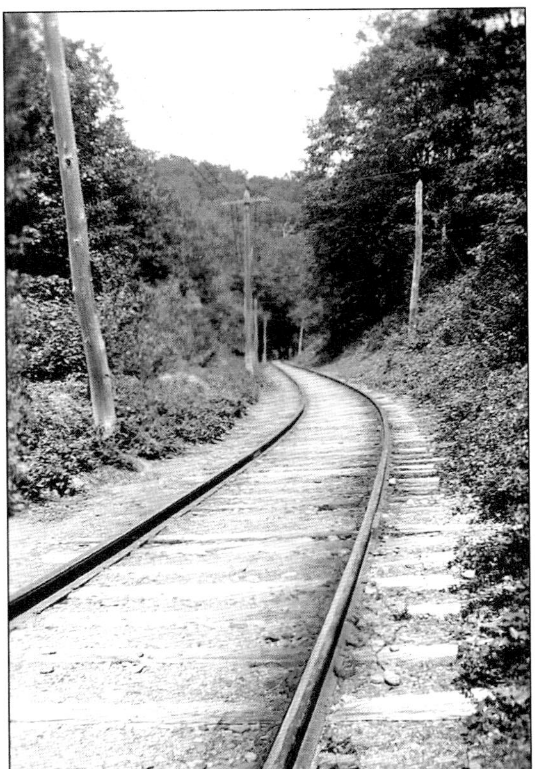

This is the motorman's view from the front of the trolley running south at Bailey's Ravine on September 3, 1936.

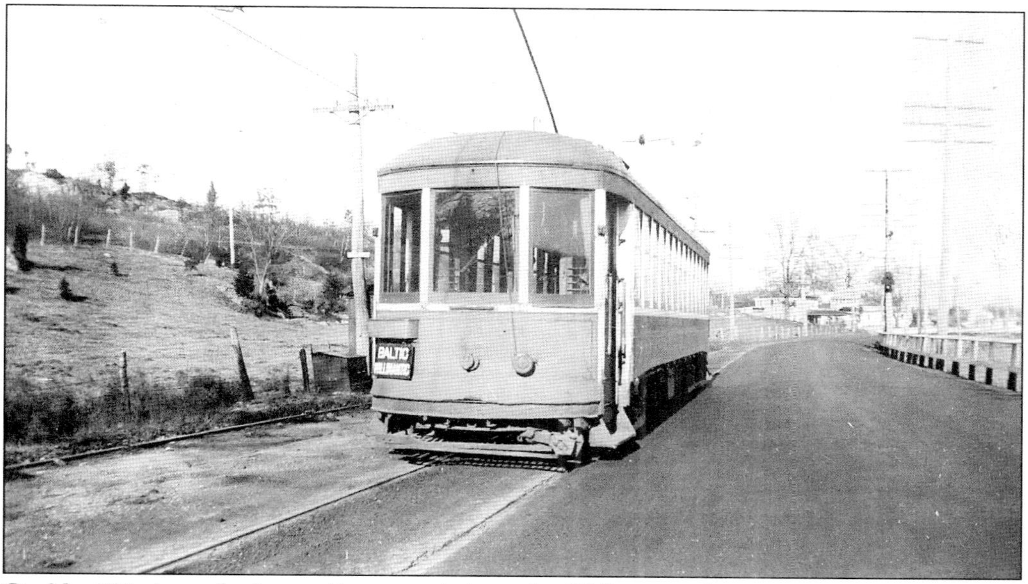

Car No. 201 sits at the Lower Occum switch on the Willimantic line in 1935.

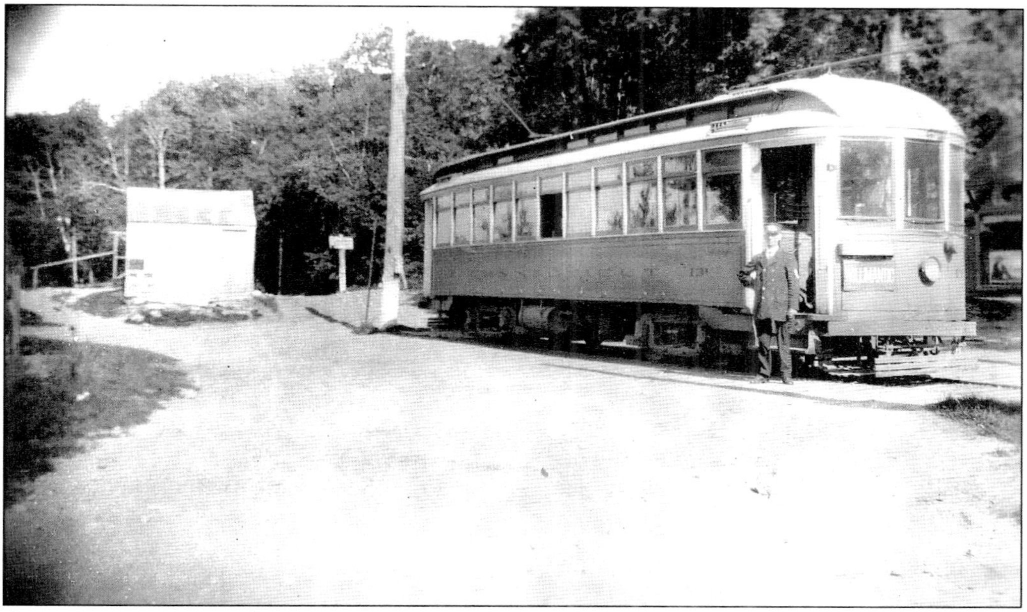
Car No. 131 is pictured at Coventry Lake in 1924.

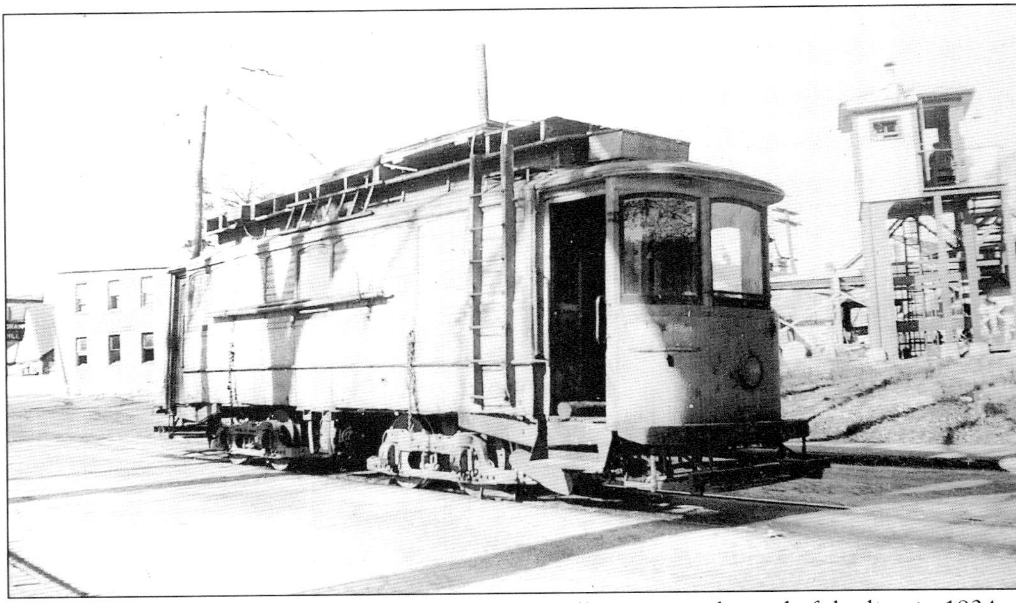

Another example of a work car, this line car is in Willimantic at the end of the line in 1934.

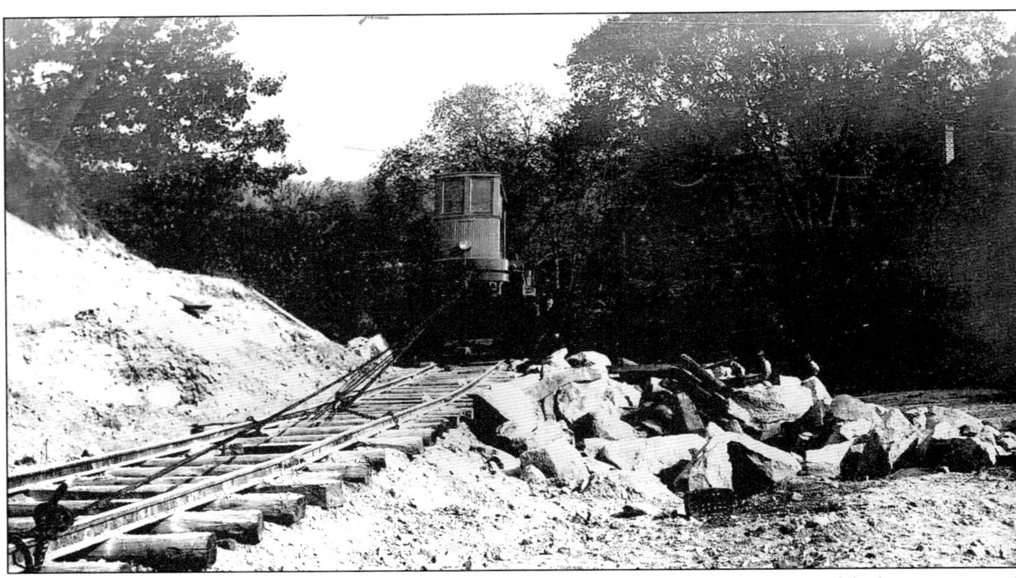

The reason for this 1935 operation has been lost to posterity. It is most likely some track maintenance operation.

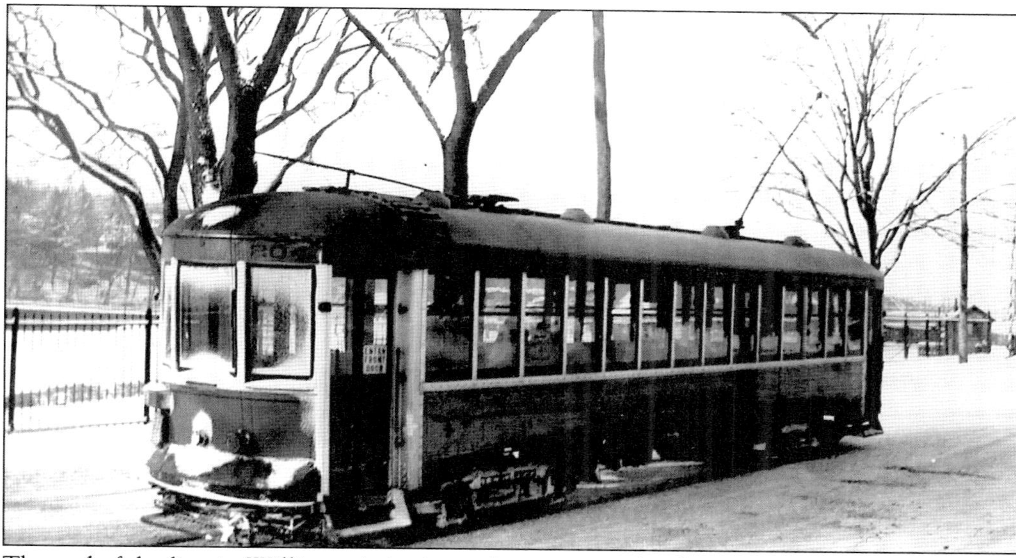

The end of the line in Willimantic is pictured on a snowy day during the winter of 1935.

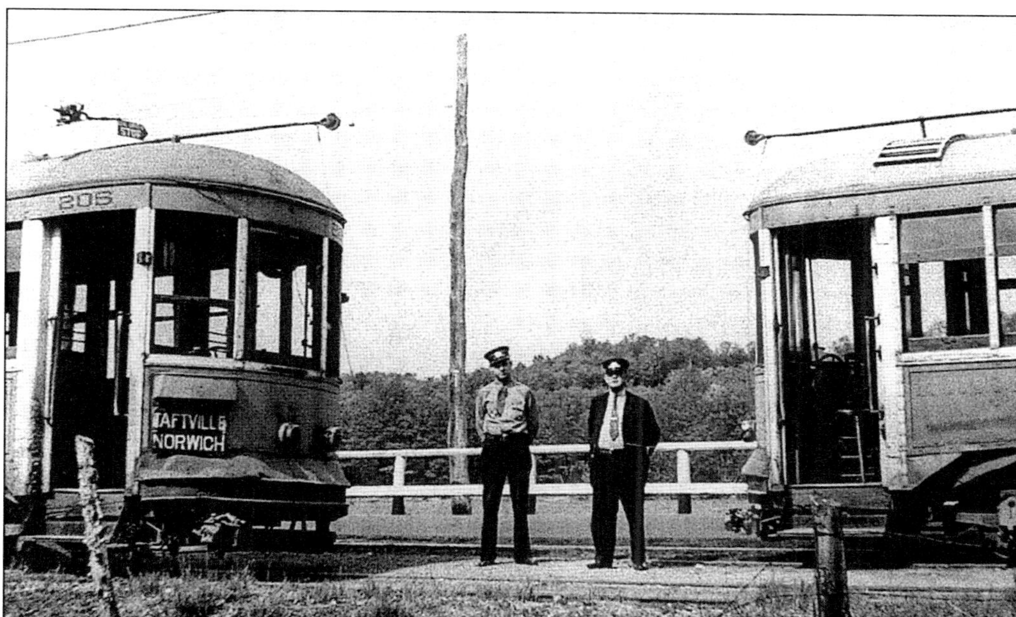

Two cars meet at Lower Occum switch on the Willimantic line in 1936. Notice that the operator on the left is out of uniform.

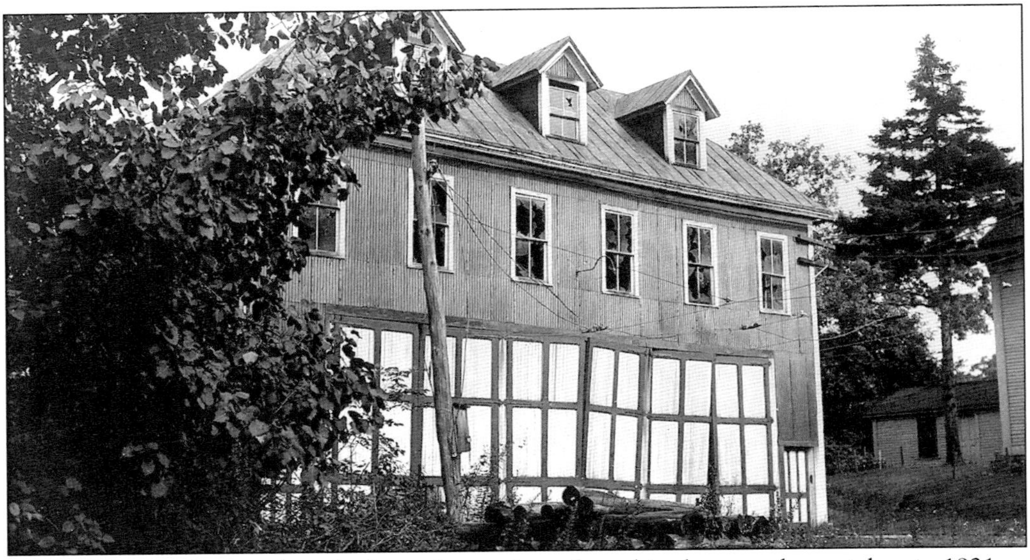

The South Windham carbarn had seen better days when this photograph was taken in 1921.

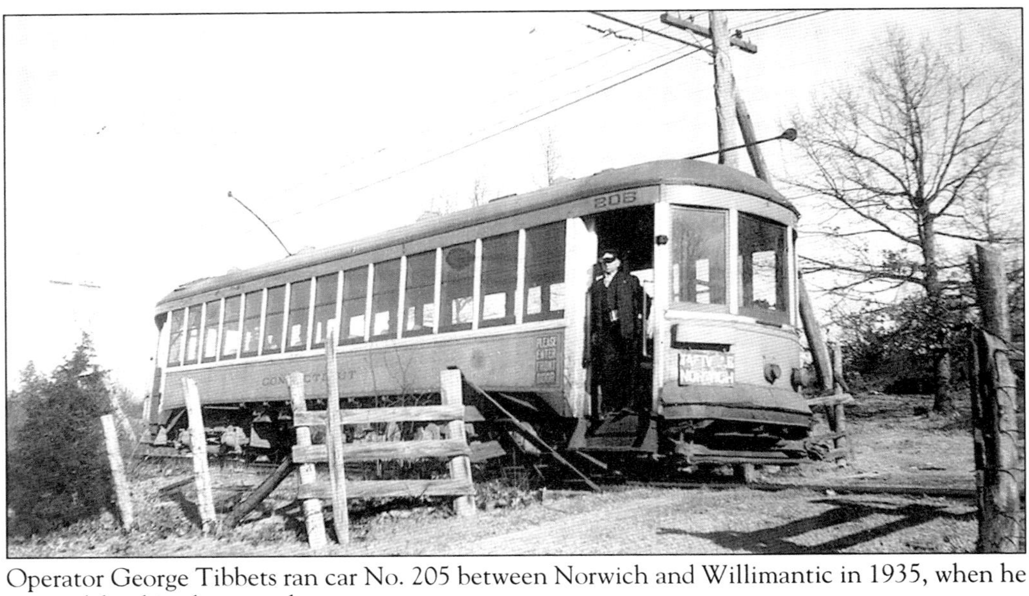

Operator George Tibbets ran car No. 205 between Norwich and Willimantic in 1935, when he stopped for this photograph.

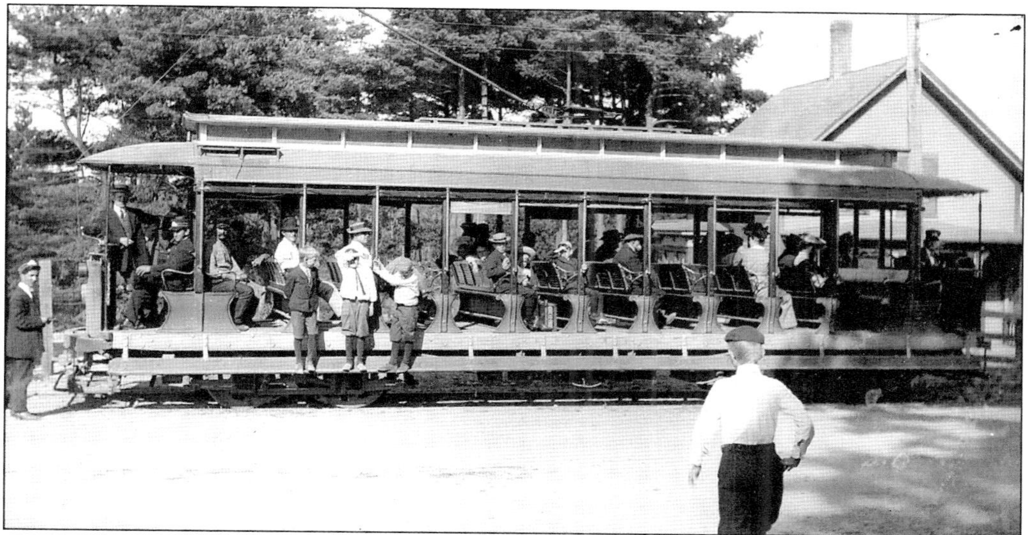

This Consolidated Railway Company open car is pictured at camp meeting grounds in South Windham. This group is most likely on an outing.

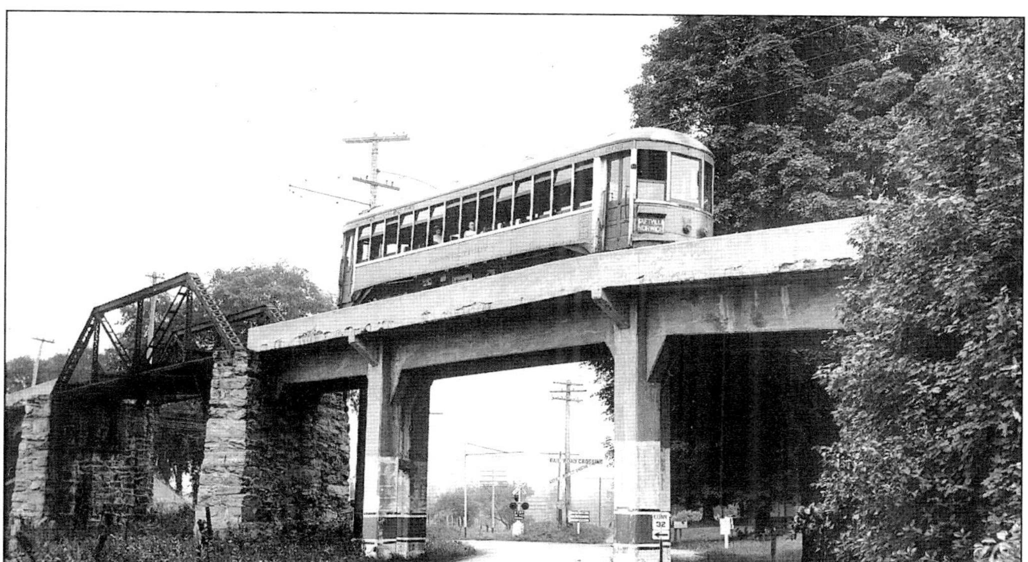

Car No. 205 is shown on the trestle at Williams Crossing in Lebanon in July 1936.

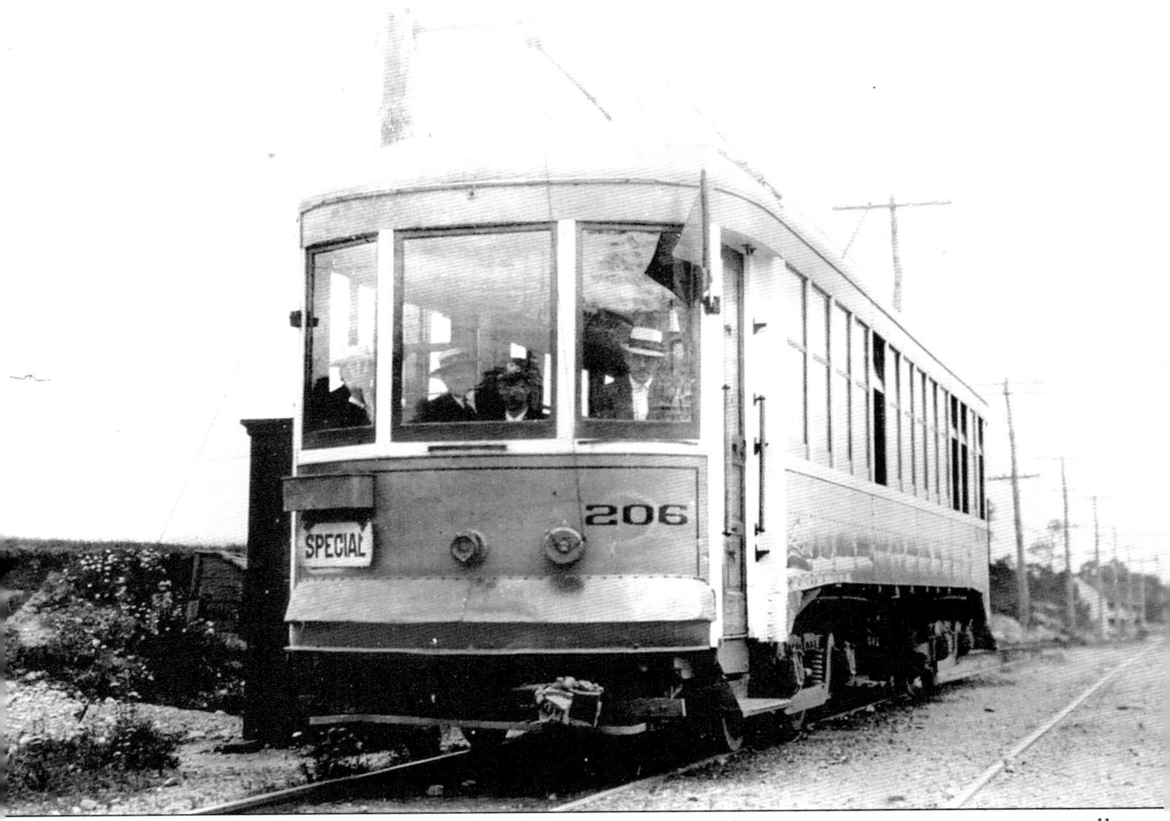

The lines in and around Norwich were inspected routinely; passenger equipment was usually used to do this, as shown in this picture of car No. 206 on an inspection trip on the Willimantic line in 1920.

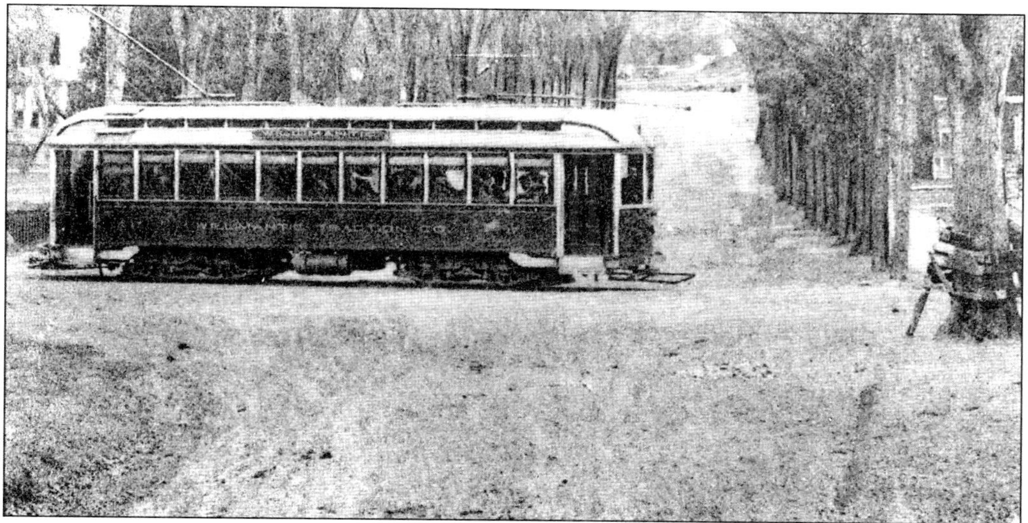

This photograph shows Main Street in South Windham in 1904.

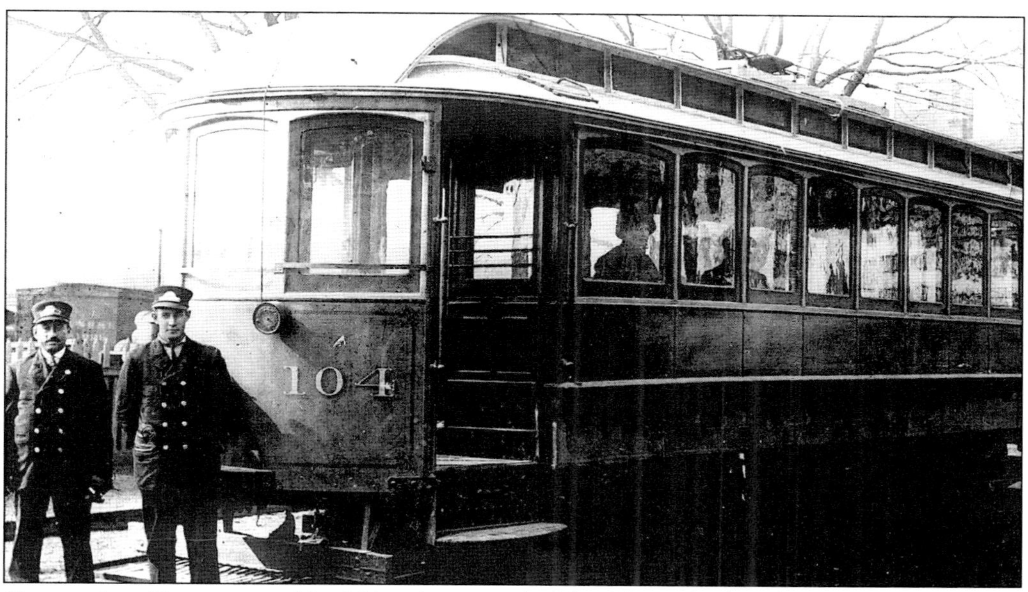

Connecticut Company car No. 104 is shown at the New Haven Railroad crossing in downtown Willimantic. It will soon leave for South Coventry.

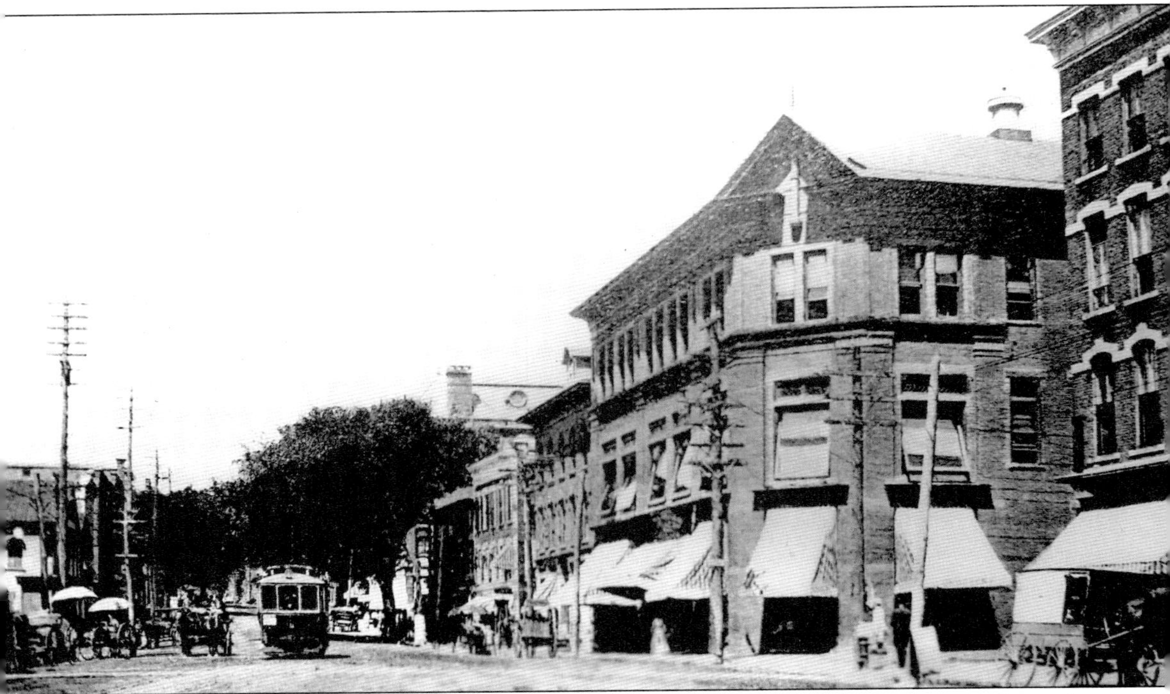

Downtown Willimantic is shown in this 1904 view. Many of these buildings are still standing.

Five

Other Lines

While the Connecticut Company and its predecessors were the largest streetcar operators, other companies also had streetcar lines in eastern Connecticut. The Shoreline Electric Railway, which leased the eastern lines from the Connecticut Company from 1914 to 1920, had its own lines that were never part of the Connecticut Company system.

The Norwich and Westerly Railway (N&W) operated a 60-mile system from Norwich to Westerly, Rhode Island. The line opened in 1906 and was absorbed by the Shoreline Electric Railway in 1916. The N&W was rather unique in that its track was built to very high standards and operated more like a main-line railroad than a rural trolley line. The right of way was designed for high-speed operation, as were the cars. Eight cars, purchased from the Southern Car Company of High Point, North Carolina, were capable of speeds in excess of 65 miles per hour. The line also operated using train orders for each run, like steam railroads. Hourly service was provided for most of the line's operating history. It also had considerable freight business and exchanged freight cars with the New Haven Railroad. Before the line closed in 1924, the cars were housed in a combination carbarn, shop, and power house in the Hallville section of Preston.

The Groton and Stonington Street Railway operated a 20-mile line from Groton to Pawcatuck, on the Rhode Island state line. A car house and power station was located in Mystic. This line was owned by the Norwich and Westerly Railway from 1905 until 1919, after which it became independent. All rail operations were discontinued in 1927.

The New London & East Lyme Street Railway began operation in 1905. It ran from Bank Street in New London to the Niantic railroad station on the New Haven Railroad and later was extended to the Connecticut River in Old Lyme to connect with the Shoreline Electric Railway coming in from New Haven. The line totaled 23 miles. Cars operated on the Connecticut Company line for about one mile, ending at the Parade in New London. Operations were discontinued when the entire Shoreline Electric Railway system closed in 1919.

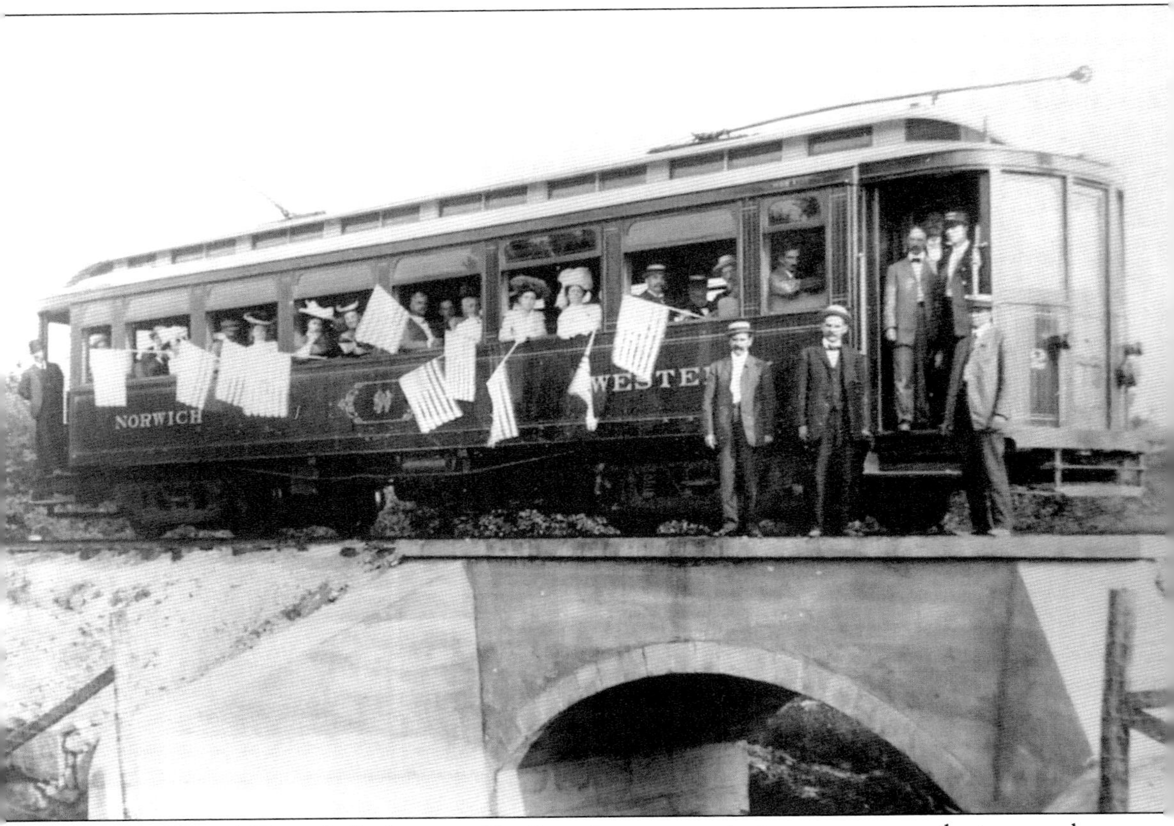

Norwich and Westerly Railway car No. 2 carries some patriotic passengers on the inaugural run over this line in 1906. This car was built by the Southern Car Company of High Point, North Carolina, and was capable of speeds in excess of 65 miles per hour. These were probably the fastest streetcars in Connecticut.

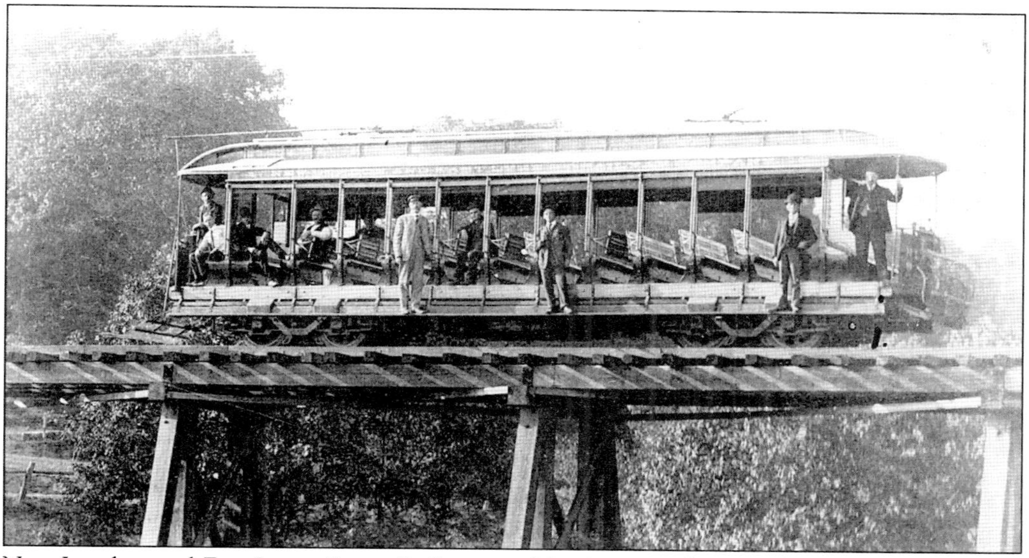

New London and East Lyme Street Railway car No. 9 is seen here in the first trip across the Oswegatchie trestle in 1905. All the passengers on this initial trip were company employees.

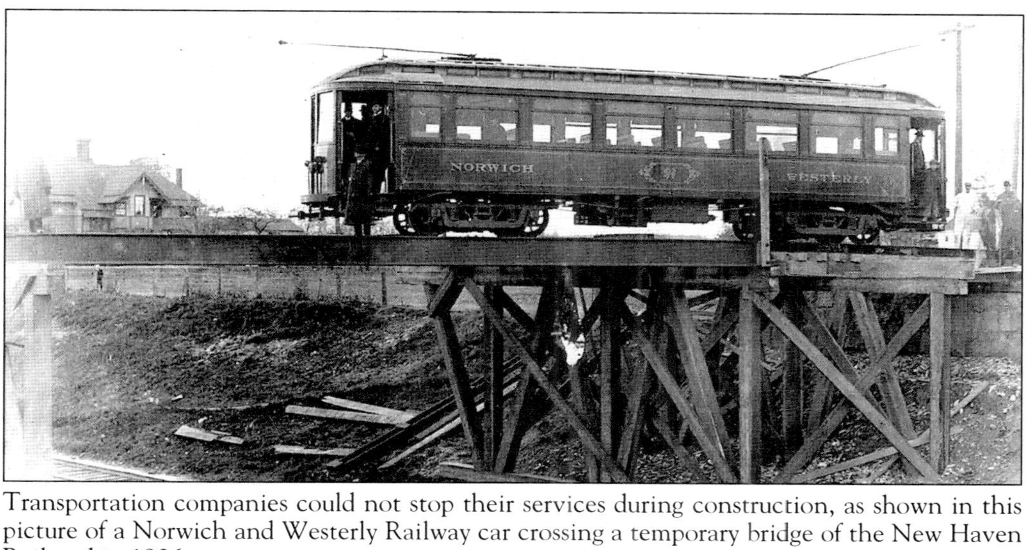

Transportation companies could not stop their services during construction, as shown in this picture of a Norwich and Westerly Railway car crossing a temporary bridge of the New Haven Railroad in 1906.

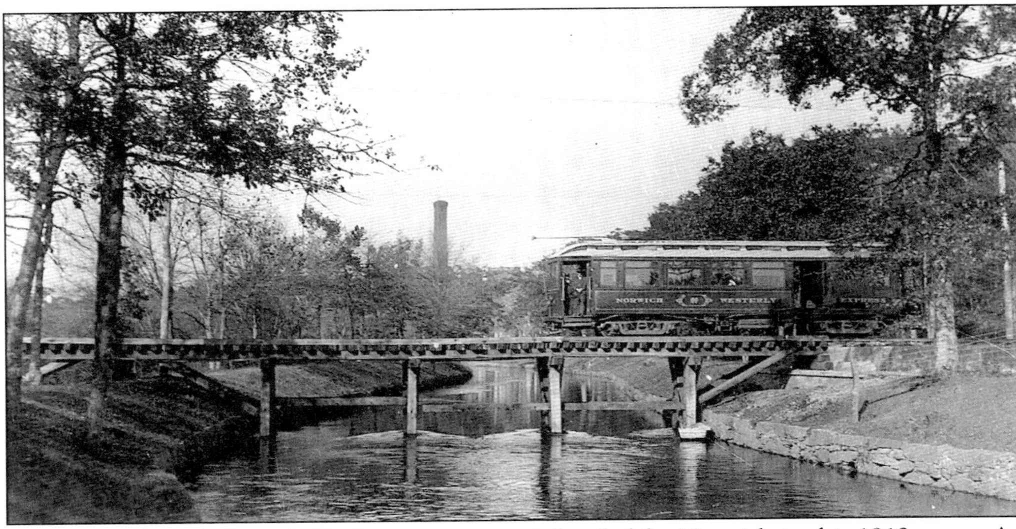

This Norwich and Westerly Railway express car is headed for Norwich in this 1912 scene. An express car carried not only passengers but also small packages and mail.

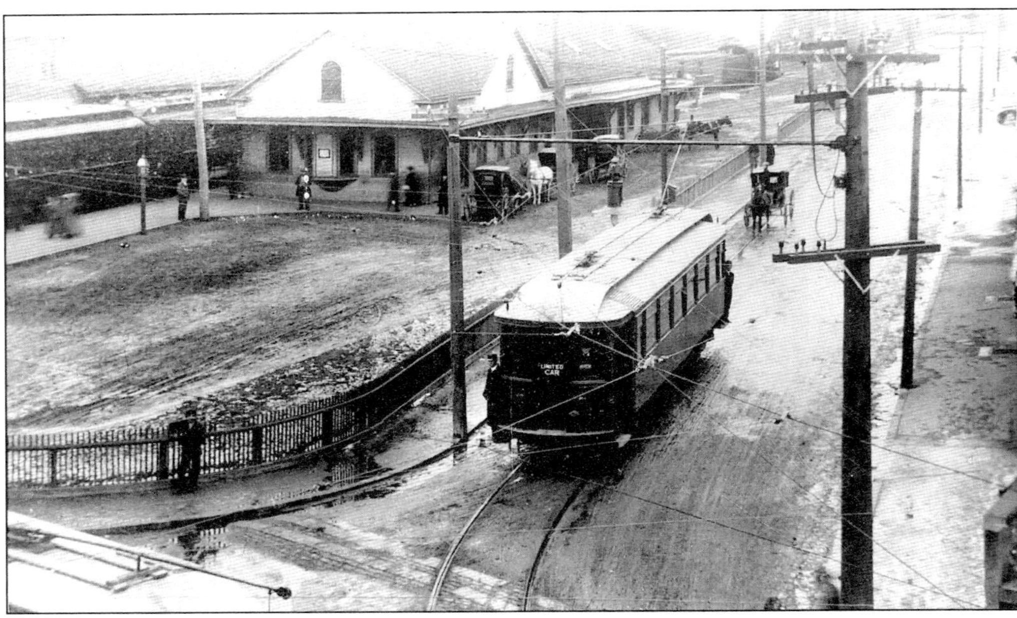

Norwich and Westerly Railway car No. 3 is shown at the Westerly, Rhode Island, railroad station sometime before World War I.

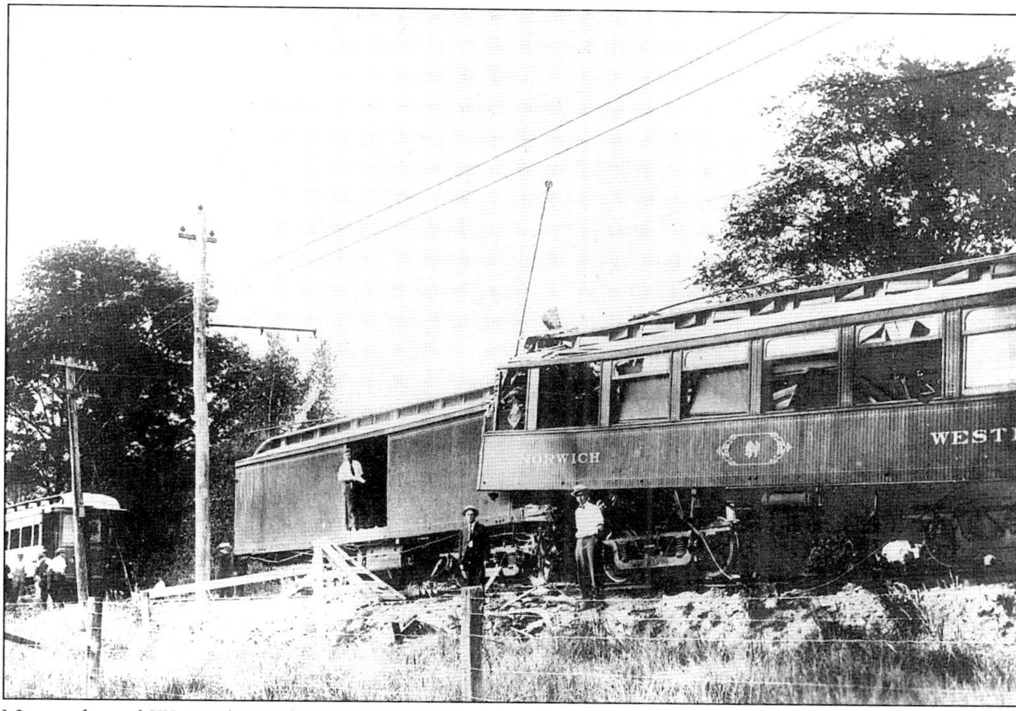

Norwich and Westerly Railway car No. 2 was demolished in a wreck with a freight motor car in August 1907. The motorman and two passengers were killed. The car was subsequently rebuilt and returned to regular passenger service.

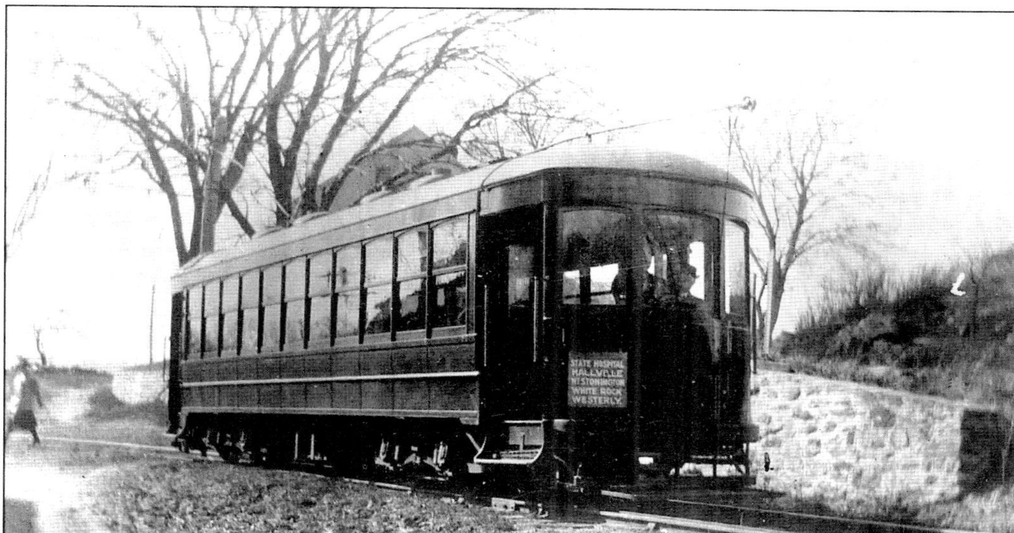

Norwich and Westerly Railway car No. 28, built in 1910 by the Wason Manufacturing Company of Springfield, Massachusetts, is shown here in Poquetanuck.

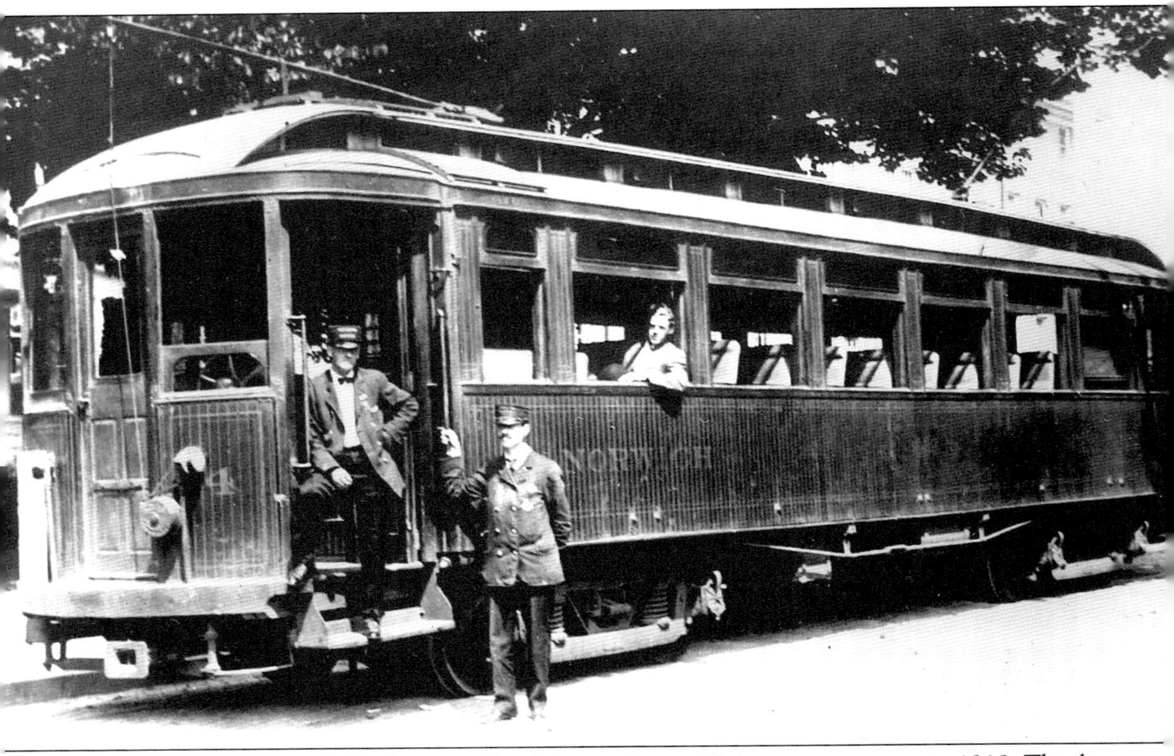

Norwich and Westerly Railway car No. 4 is seen here with its two-man crew in 1918. This line maintained two-man crews until it closed in 1924. This car was built to be run in units of two or more cars and, therefore, had a door in the back and front to allow passage between the cars.

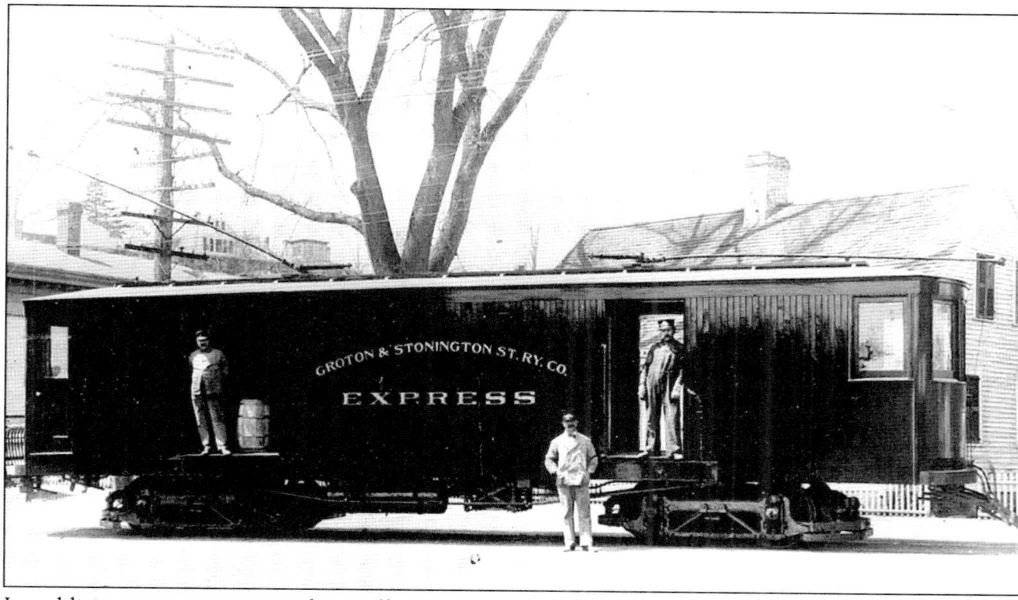

In addition to passengers, the trolleys carried packages in express cars, such as the Groton and Stonington Street Railway car in this photograph. These cars operated throughout the northeast, frequently visiting towns and villages not serviced by the railroad. This was the precursor to services such as UPS and FedEx.

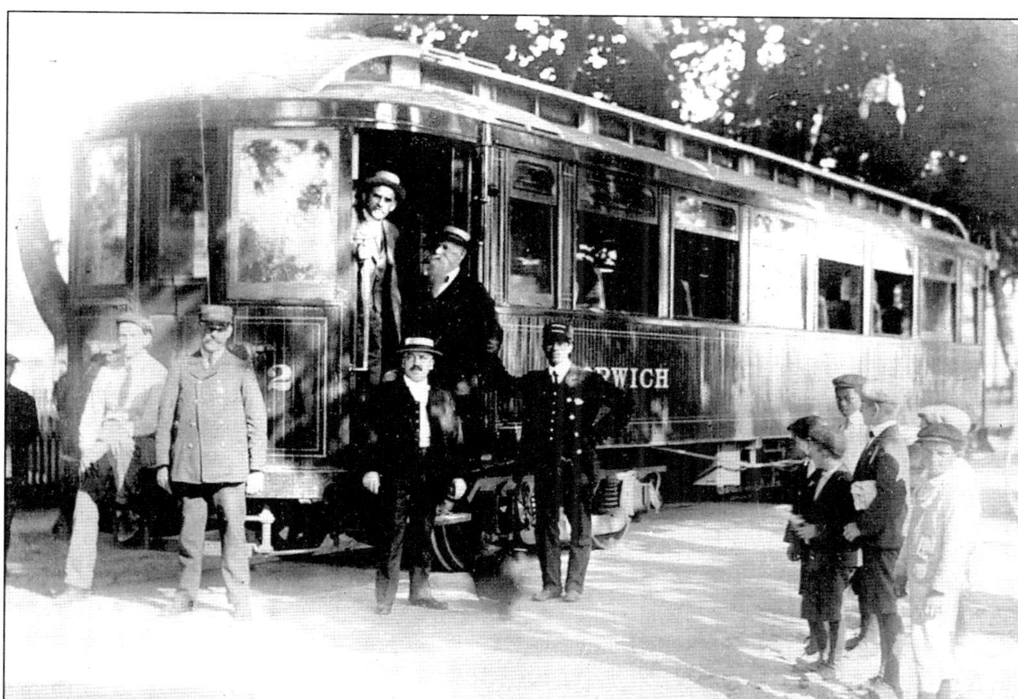

In many areas, streetcars were used for school transportation as well as to transport people to and from work, as this photograph attests.

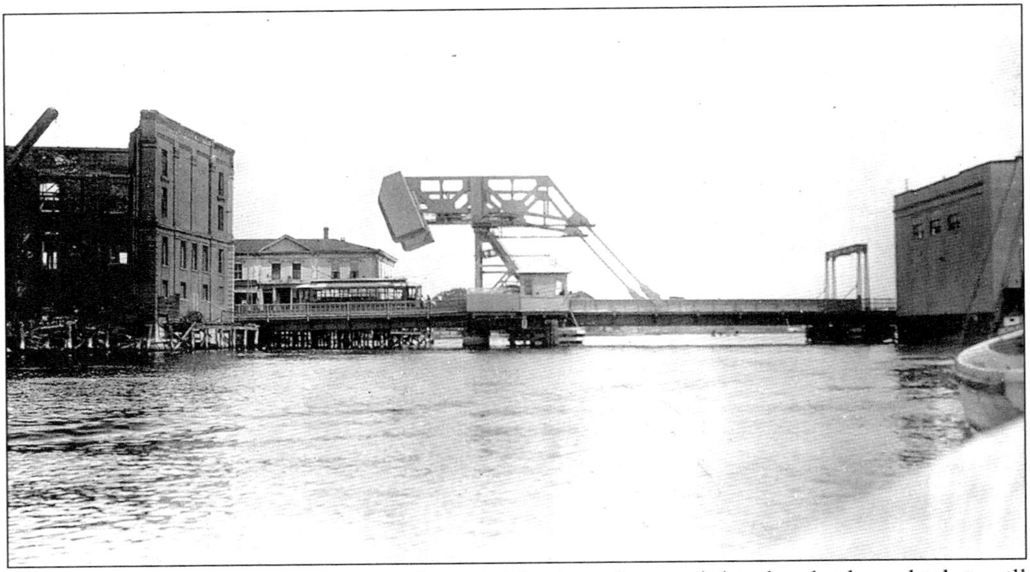

The Groton and Stonington line ran through Mystic and crossed this drawbridge, which is still used for automobile traffic today.

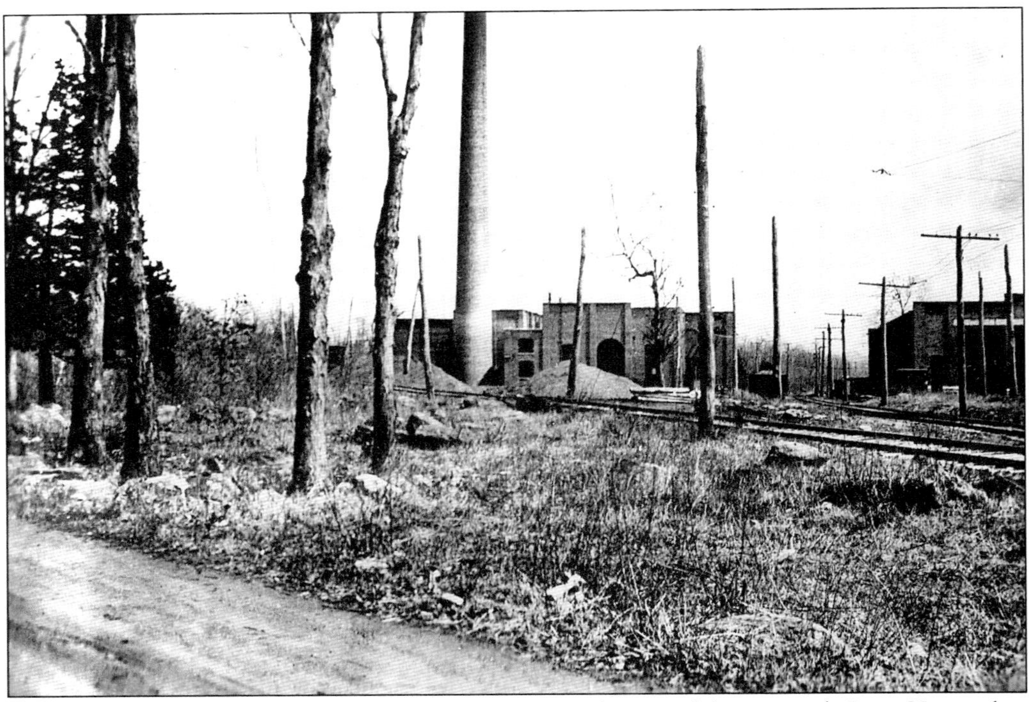

The Hallville carbarn and power station, located near the site of the Norwich State Hospital in Preston, belonged to the Norwich and Westerly Railway *c.* 1914.

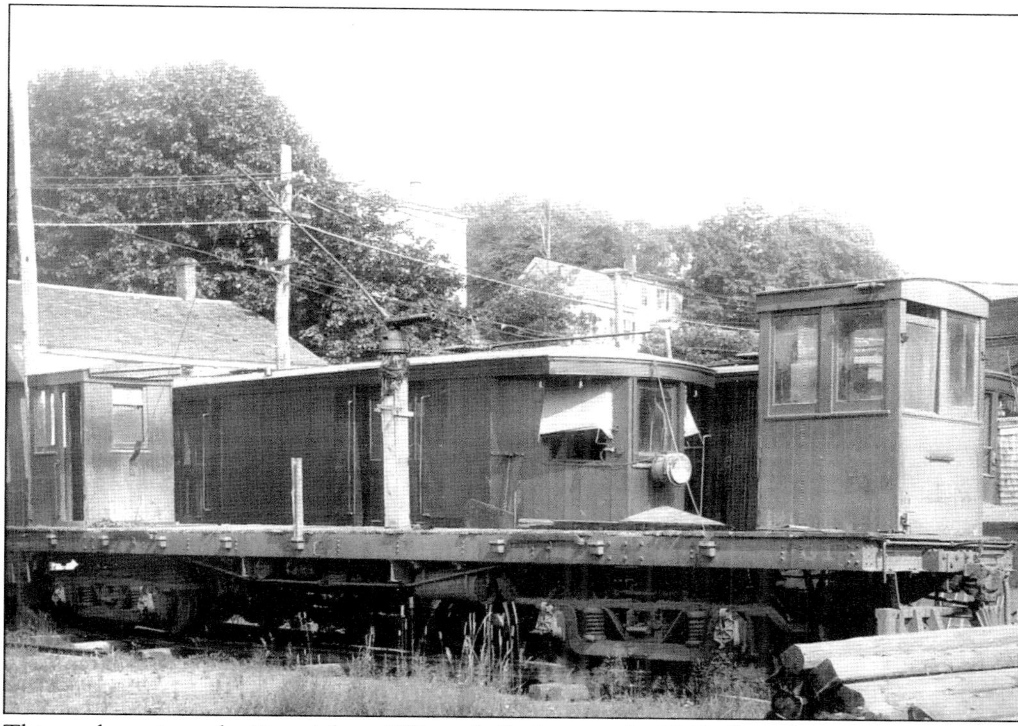

This work car is on the Norwich and Westerly Railway at the Hallville carbarn in 1914. Various styles of work cars were used throughout the area.

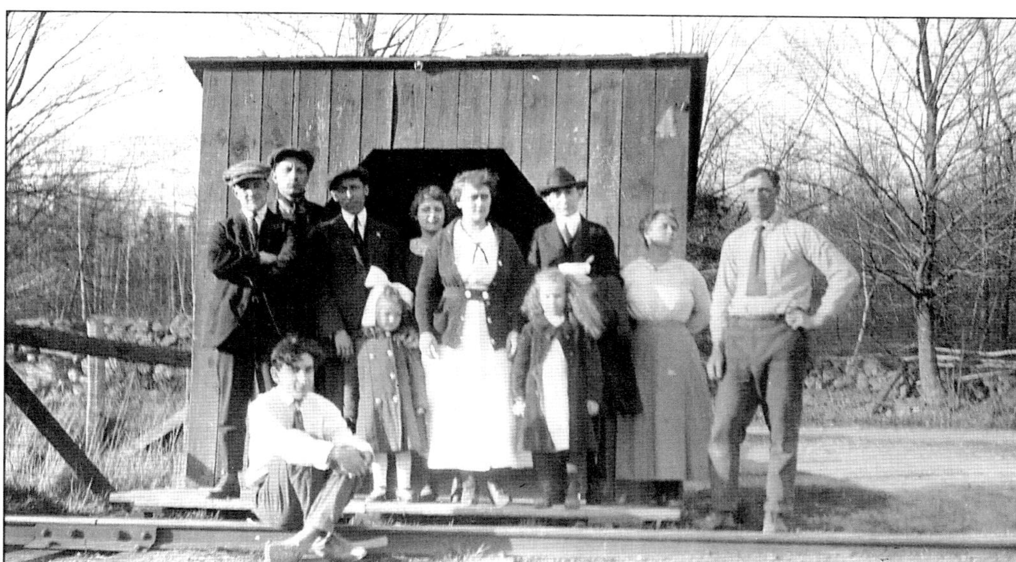

These people are waiting for the next trolley in the Lantern Hill waiting station on the Norwich and Westerly Railway.

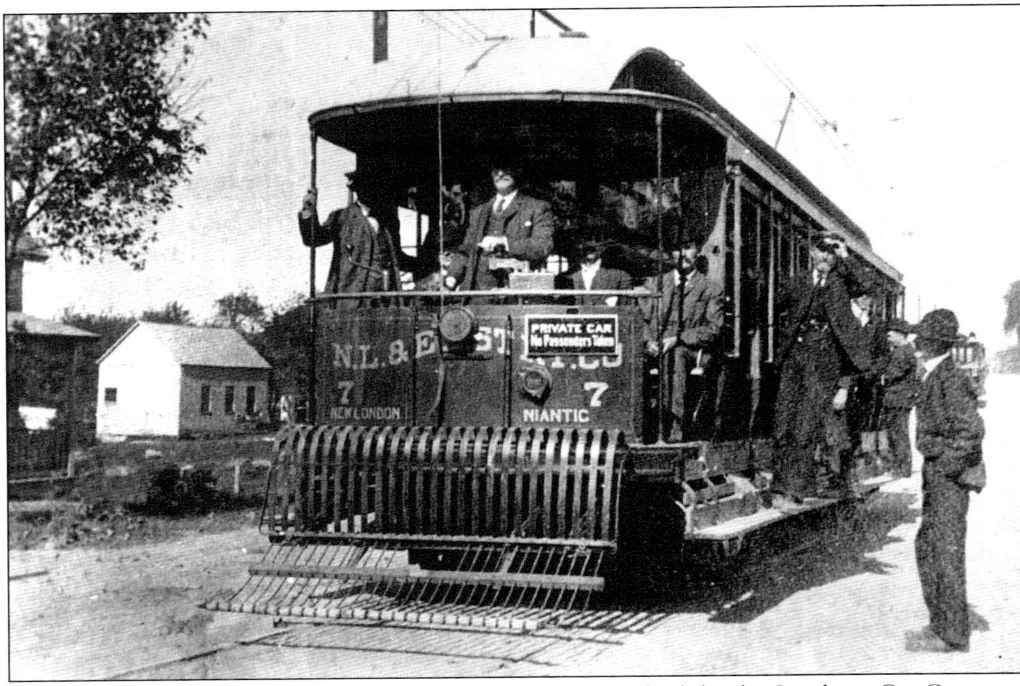

New London and East Lyme Street Railway open car No. 7, built by the Southern Car Company of High Point, South Carolina, is shown on Bank Street in New London. This inspection run on October 5, 1905, was the first trip over the line. Regular service began two days later.

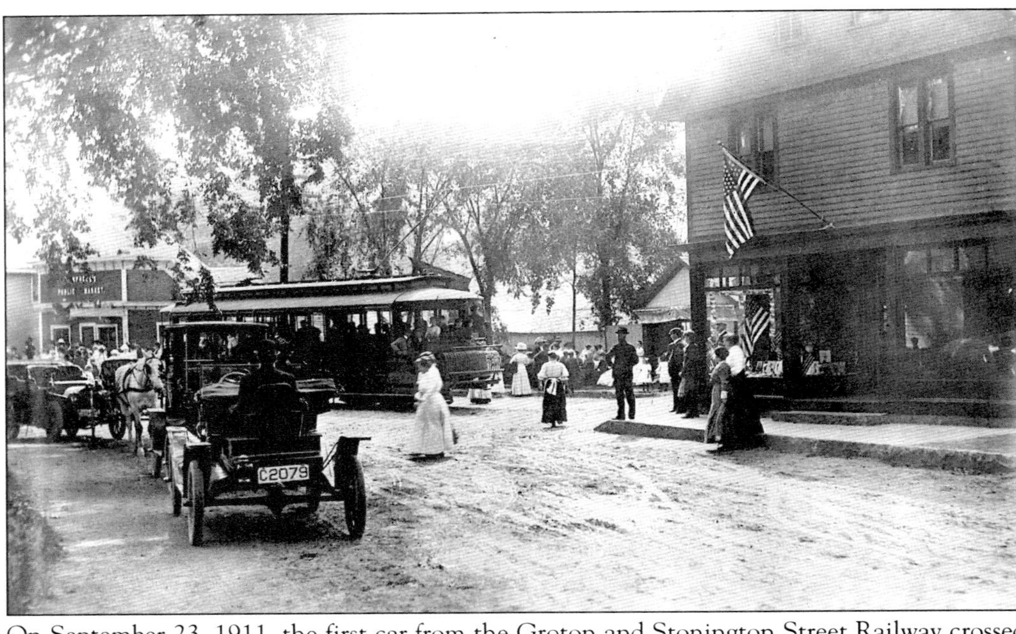

On September 23, 1911, the first car from the Groton and Stonington Street Railway crossed into Old Mystic.

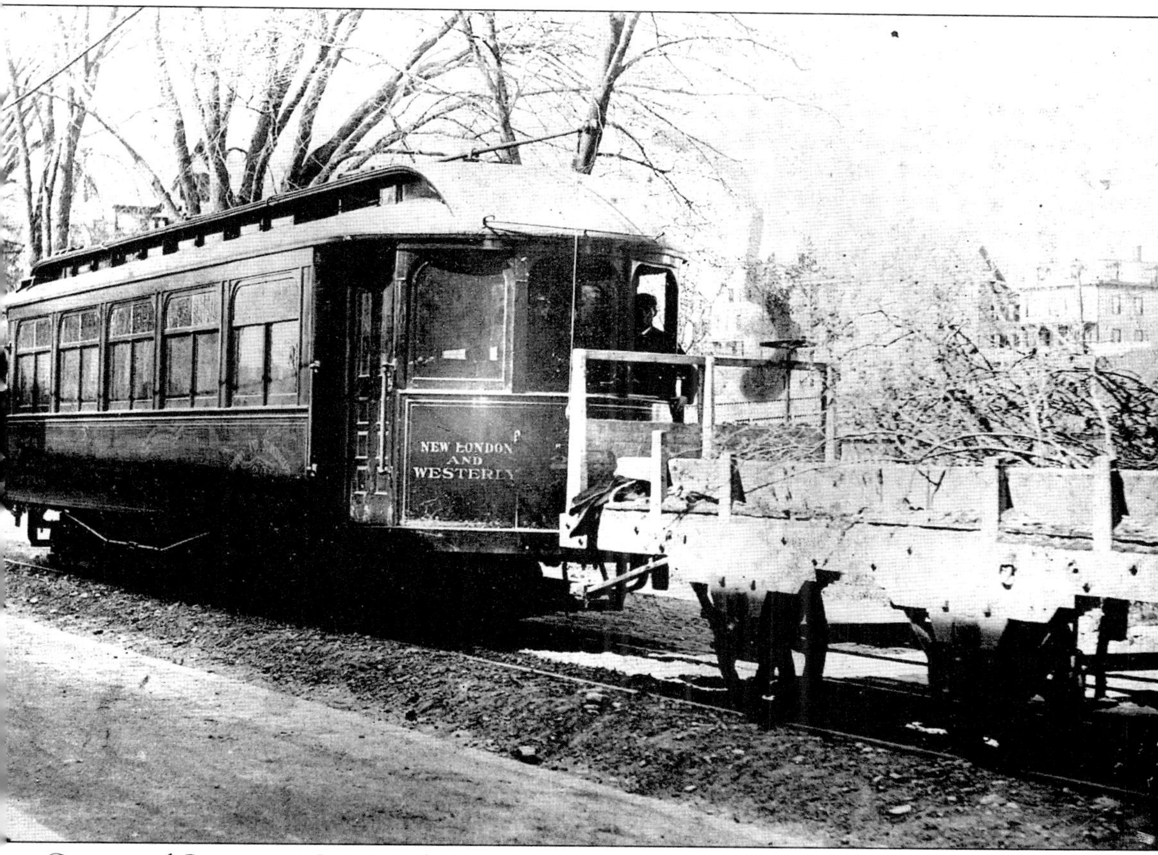

Groton and Stonington Street Railway car No. 20 is used in this 1914 scene as a work car to clean up fallen tree limbs after a storm.

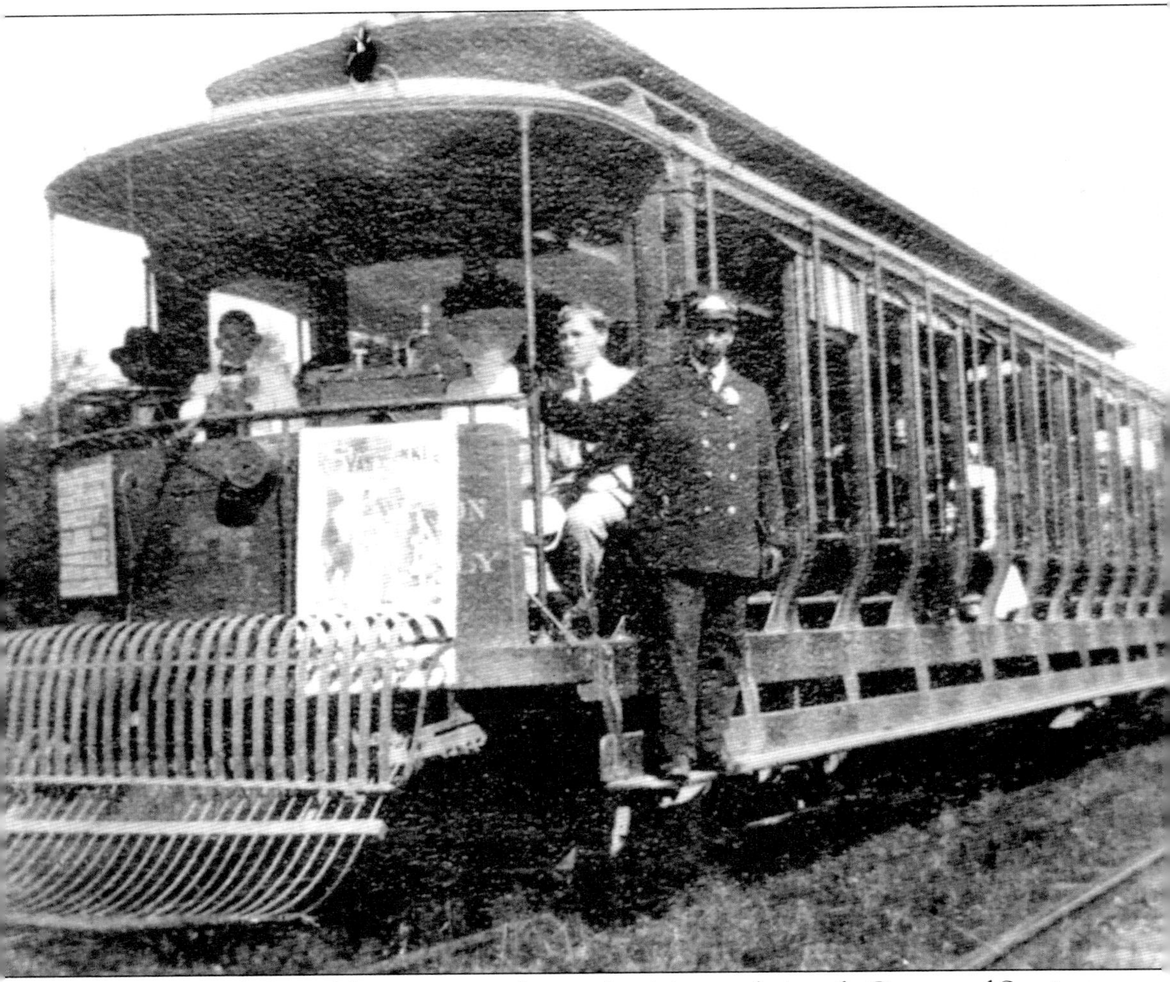

The time and place of this picture is unknown, but it is a good view of a Groton and Stonington Street Railway open car. The safety fender in the front of the car was dropped by the motormen to prevent the car from running over a person or small animal that was laying on the tracks.

Six

THE END

Except for the few cars shipped to New Haven and the sweeper sold to a railroad in New Jersey, all the cars on the property after the last Norwich lines closed in December 1936 were unceremoniously burned and used as salvage scrap metal in early 1937. Open cars that had been recently repainted in the Greenville shops, which were intended to be sold to another operator, were burned along with the rest of the cars when no buyer came forward. The era of the open car had passed, and the Connecticut Company was the last major operator to use this type of equipment.

If the Norwich lines had lasted until December 7, 1941, they most undoubtedly would have continued to operate until at least 1945, as the conversion of streetcar lines to buses was not permitted because of the need to conserve fuel and rubber. This of course did not happen, and only the lines in New Haven survived to December 1941. As a result, New Haven saw streetcar service until September 1948.

If one drives through Norwich today, many of the scenes in this book will look familiar; the Greenville barn and the vast Ponemah Mills complex still stand and look like they did when photographed in the 1930s.

Streetcars still operate today in Connecticut at museums in East Windsor and East Haven. The Connecticut Trolley Museum in East Windsor is the home to car No. 65, which ran on the Putnam division, and the two Ponemah Mills locomotives. The museum staff converted Ponemah Mills locomotive "C" into a line car that is used almost weekly to maintain their two-mile line.

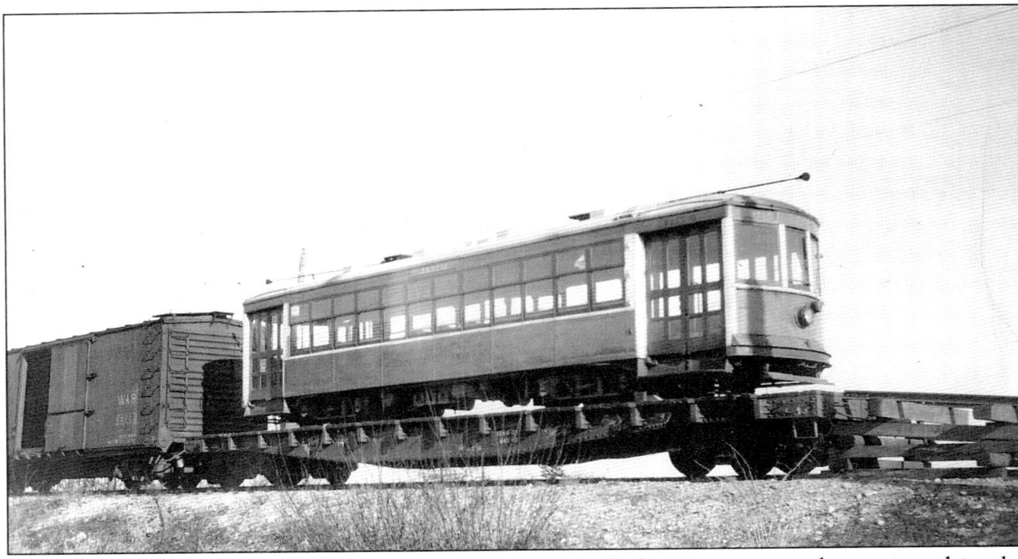

Not all the cars from the Norwich lines were scrapped after service was discontinued in the end of 1936. Some of the newer steel cars were transferred to the New Haven division of the Connecticut Company, like No. 3124 shown in this scene.

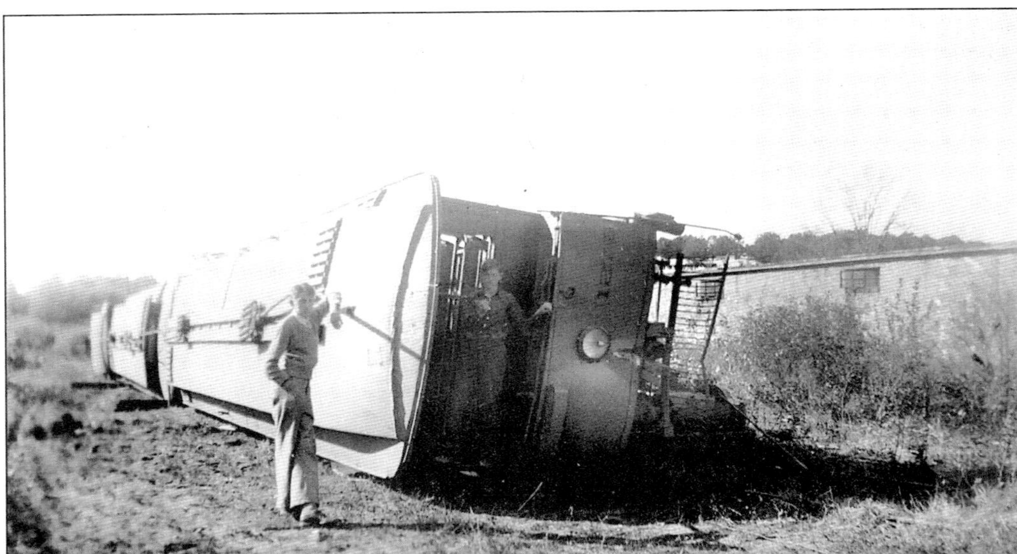

Most of the cars were pushed over and burned for the scrap metal, like in this scene.

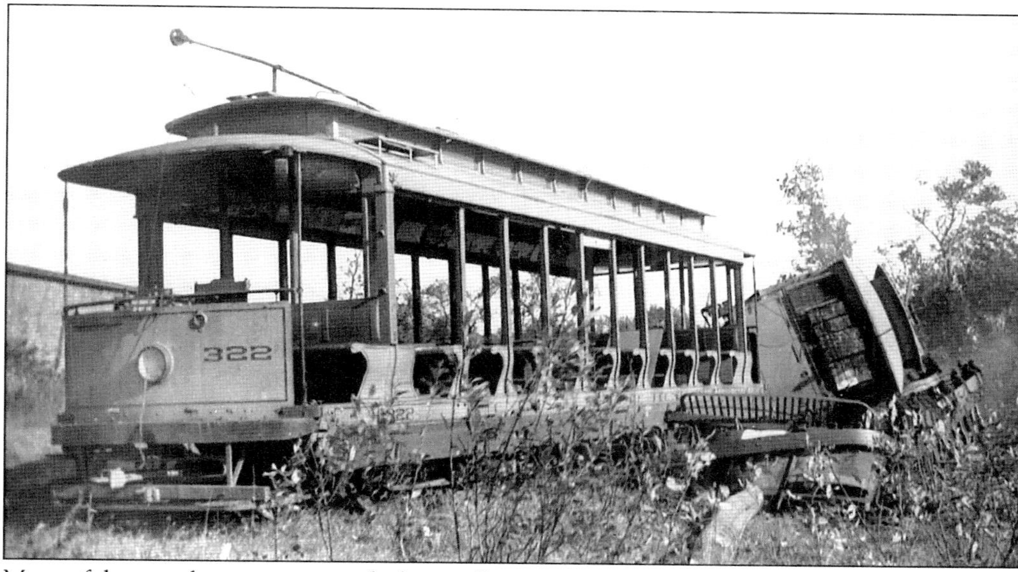

Many of the cars that were scrapped when trolley service was discontinued were in good condition and would have been serviceable for many years to come, as is shown in this 1936 photograph.

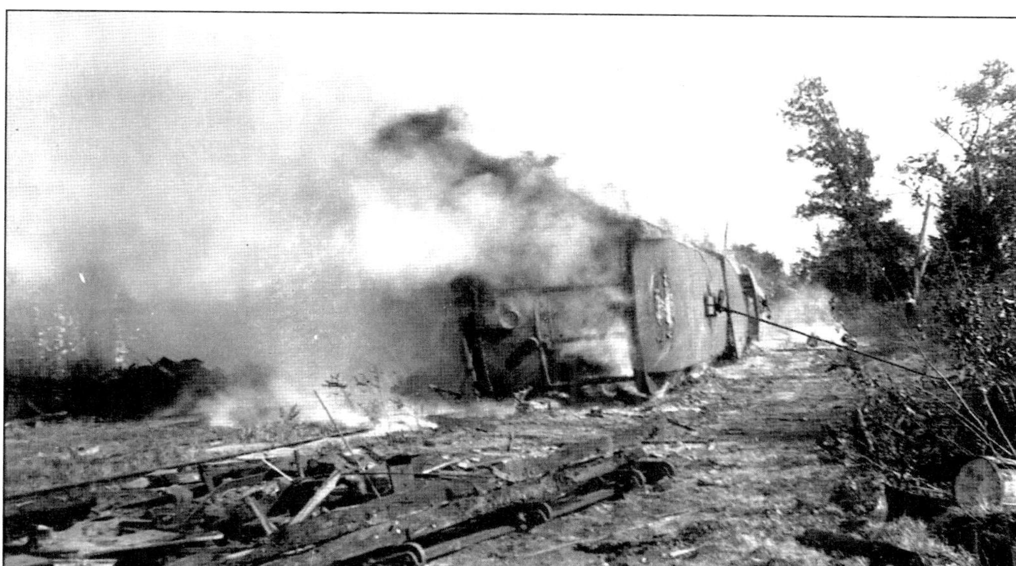

When cars were scrapped, the wood portion was burned so that the metal could be retrieved and sold.

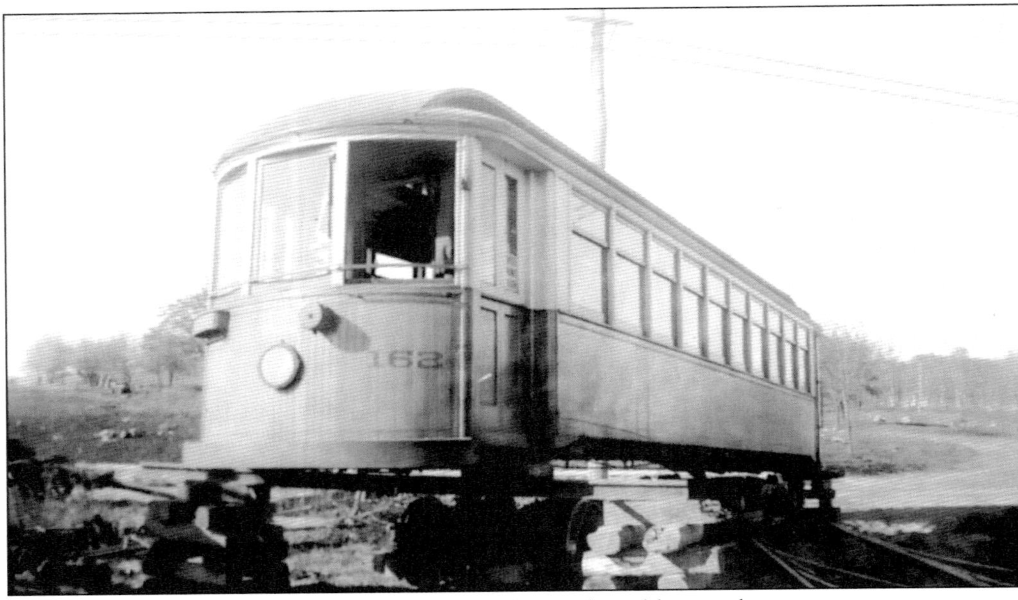

Car No. 162, without its trucks and motors, will soon be sold as a cabin.

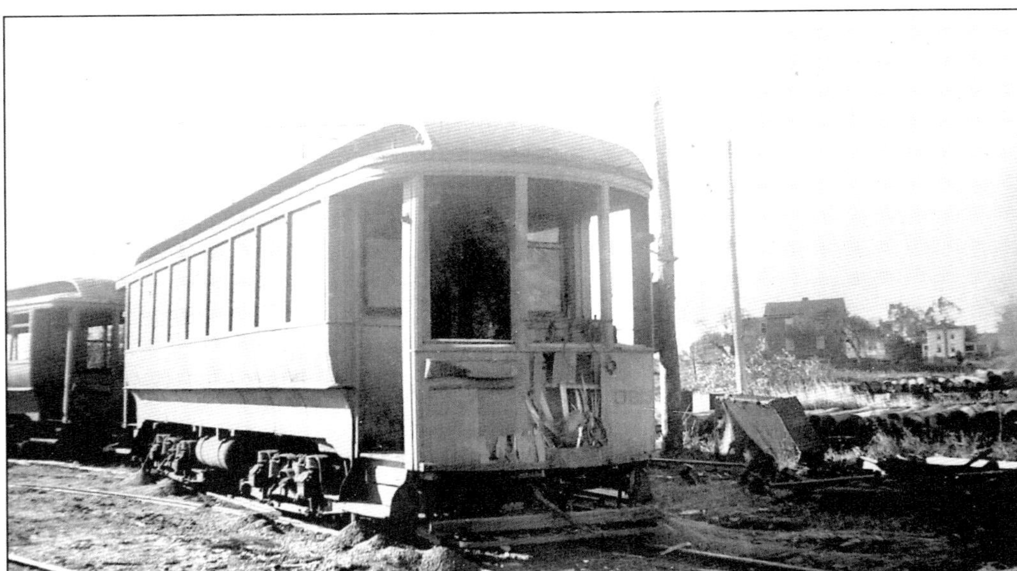

This car represented an earlier, simpler time when the operator would wait for someone running to get on and remember everyone's name. This car was destroyed in 1937.

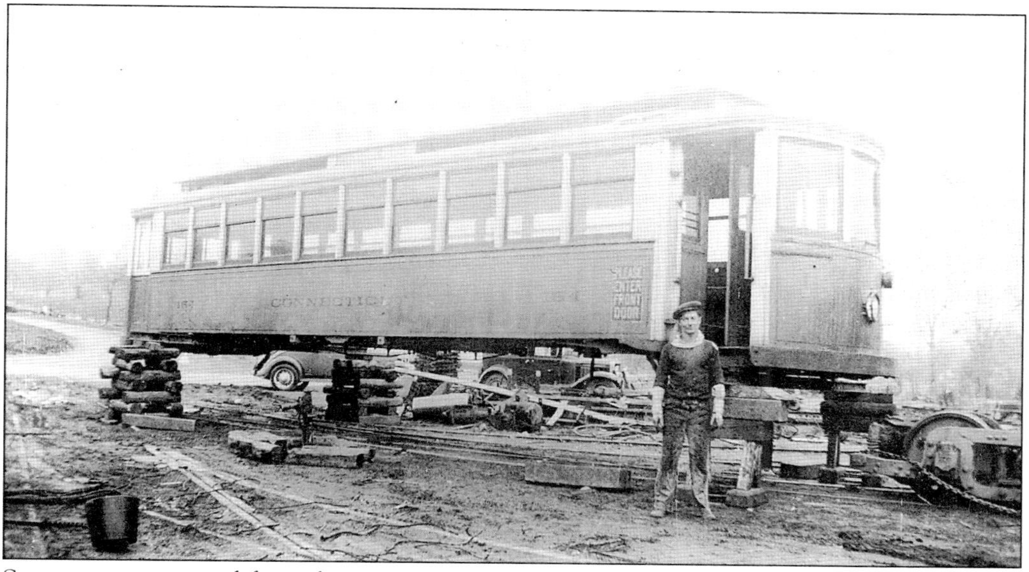

Some cars were saved from the scrapper when local residents purchased the bodies for use as summer cottages, like No. 154 shown here.

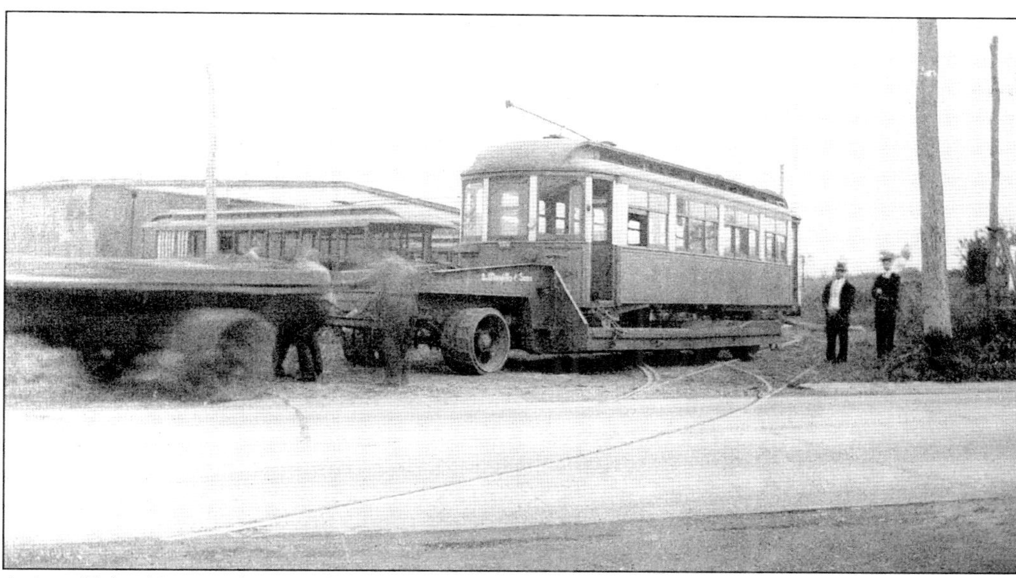

A handful of Norwich cars that were removed from their wheels were sold as cabins after streetcar operations came to an end. This scene shows car No. 158 en route to someone's campground in 1937.

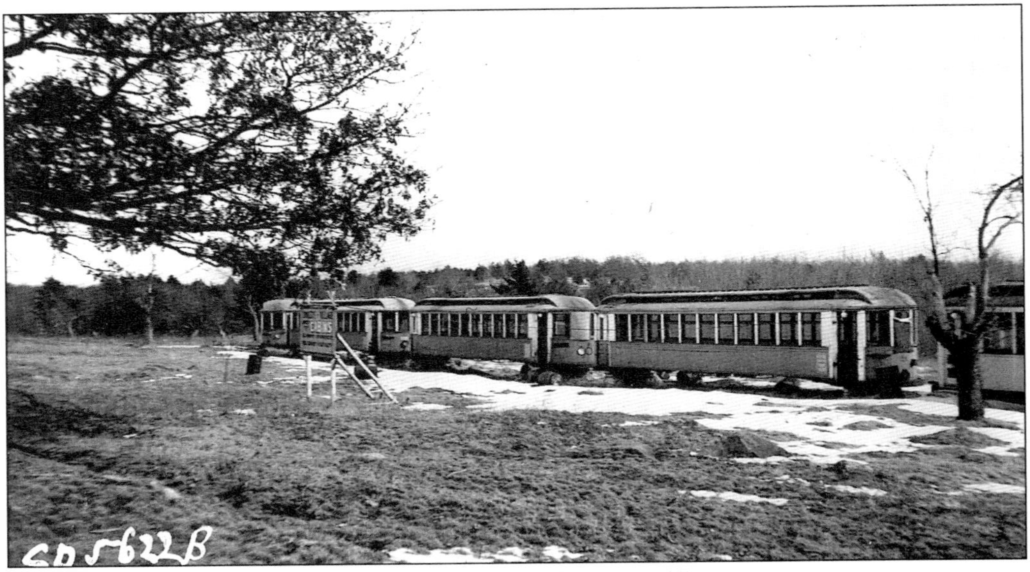

This view shows former Norwich cars made into cabins in 1937.

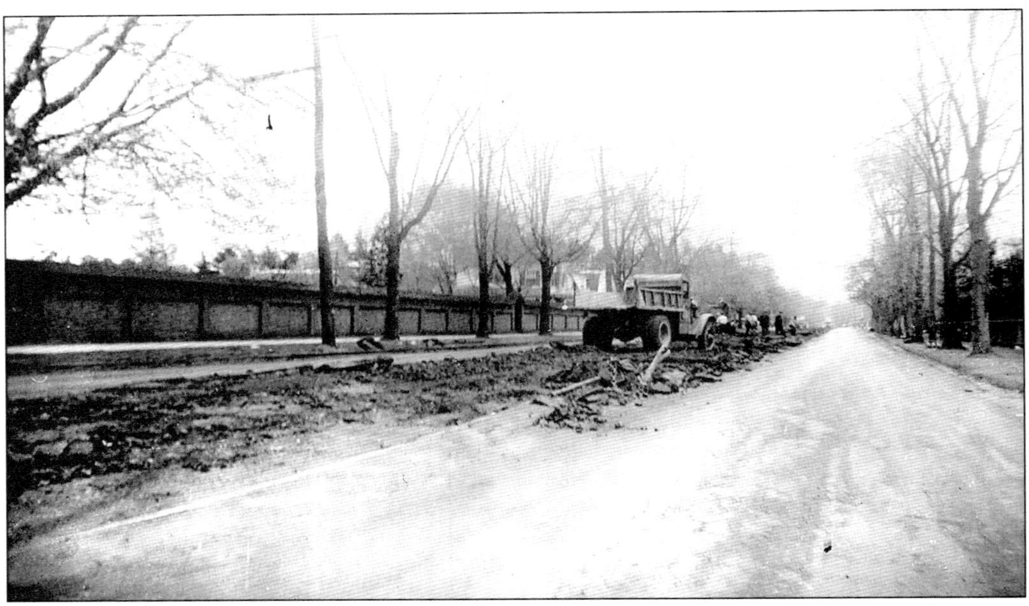

In the summer of 1937, the tracks were pulled up in Norwich, and streetcars were gone forever.

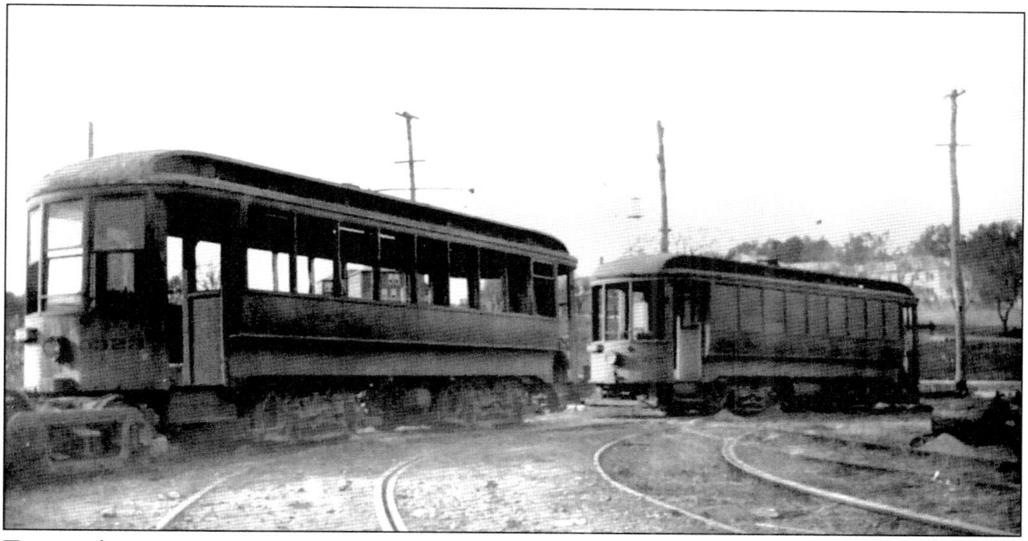

Two work cars are prepared for burning in early 1937. Any useful parts that might not survive the fire were removed beforehand.

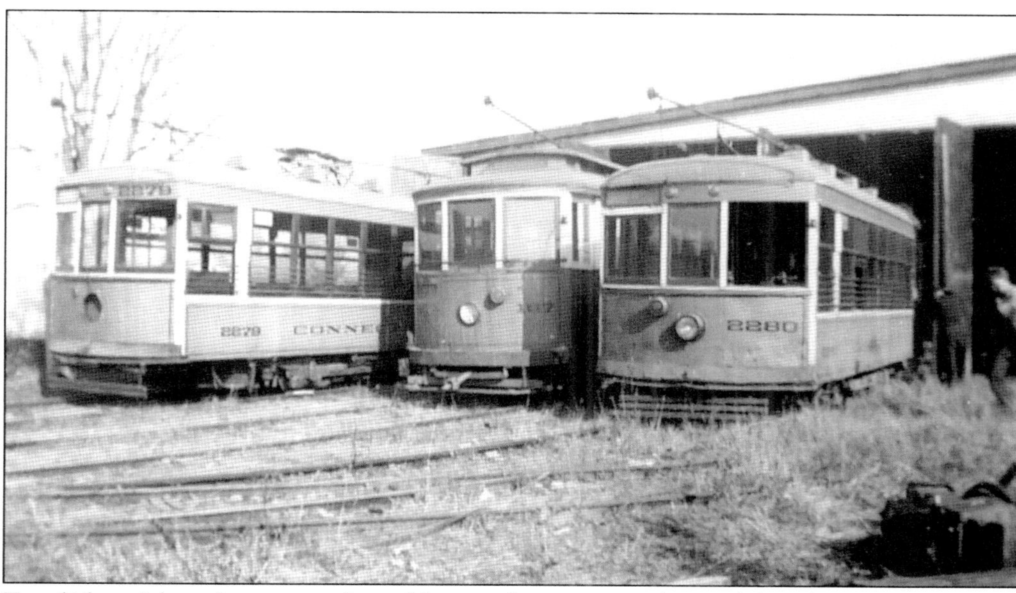

Two lightweight safety cars and an older wooden car sit in front of the Thamesville carbarn, waiting their turn at destruction.

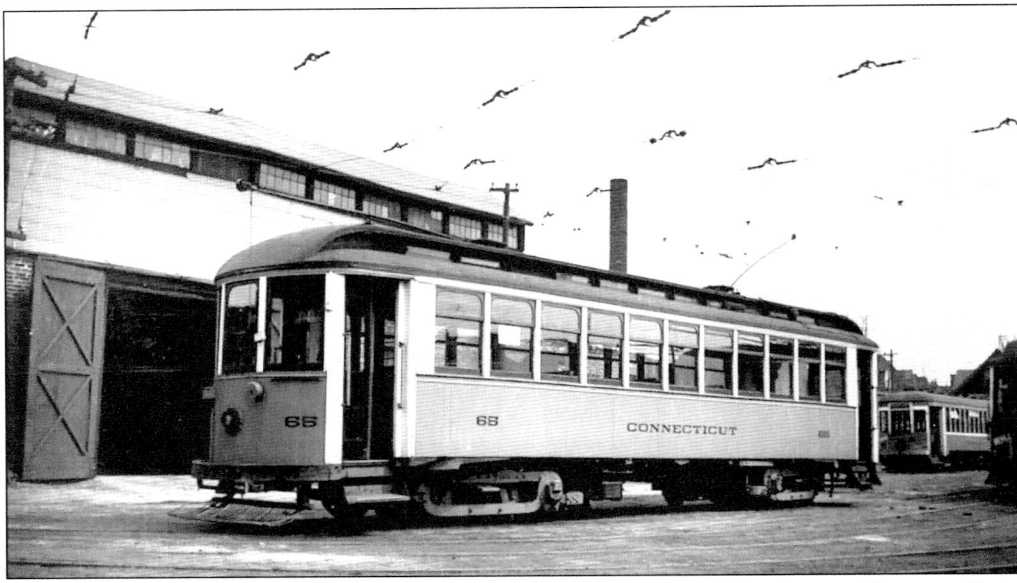

Car No. 65 was safely in Hartford and escaped the carnage that took place in Thamesville in 1937. It ran in Hartford until 1941, when it was purchased by the then-infant Connecticut Trolley Museum. This photograph was taken in 1937 at the Wethersfield Avenue carbarn.

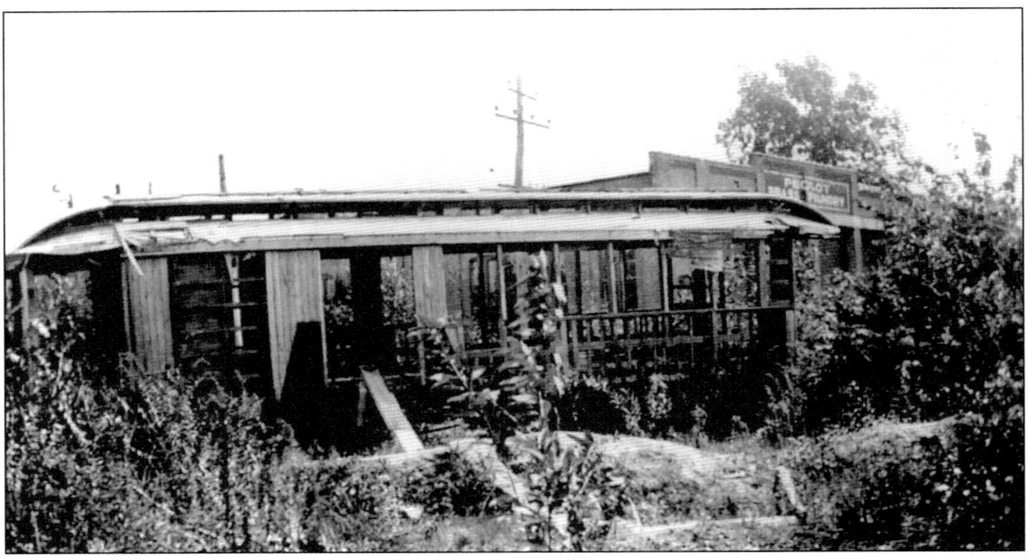

This car has not been identified, but it was most likely one of the all-wooden cars in the 150 to 169 series. The years have not been kind to it. This picture was taken in the 1950s in Norwich.